e224 1st enr: Whole-body Trai
New owner moves in, old o
would have to be young.
e224:3 Red—Incubis under the
e228:3 The being is ... magic
e250? Christie... Teueraneton
interpretation by the ...

HAVE YOU LIVED
BEFORE THIS
LIFE?

L. RON HUBBARD

HAVE YOU LIVED BEFORE THIS LIFE?

Publications International ApS

A **HUBBARD**® PUBLICATION

Published by
NEW ERA® Publications International ApS
Store Kongensgade 55
1264 Copenhagen K, Denmark

ISBN 87-7336-644-7

Published in the U.S.A. by
Bridge Publications, Inc.
4751 Fountain Avenue
Los Angeles, California 90029

ISBN 0-88404-447-5

Printed in Denmark by
NEW ERA Publiactions International ApS

Important Note

In reading this book, be very certain you never go past a word you do not fully understand.

The only reason a person gives up a study or becomes confused or unable to learn is because he or she has gone past a word that was not understood.

The confusion or inability to grasp or learn comes AFTER a word that the person did not have defined and understood.

Have you ever had the experience of coming to the end of a page and realizing you didn't know what you had read? Well, somewhere earlier on that page you went past a word that you had no definition for or an incorrect definition for.

Here's an example. "It was found that when the crepuscule arrived the children were quieter and when it was not present, they were much livelier." You see what happens. You think you don't understand the whole idea, but the inability to understand came entirely from the one word you could not define, *crepuscule*, which means twilight or darkness.

It may not only be the new and unusual words that you will

have to look up. Some commonly used words can often be misdefined and so cause confusion.

This datum about not going past an undefined word is the most important fact in the whole subject of study. Every subject you have taken up and abandoned had its words which you failed to get defined.

Therefore, in studying this book be very, very certain you never go past a word you do not fully understand. If the material becomes confusing or you can't seem to grasp it, there will be a word just earlier that you have not understood. Don't go any further, but go back to BEFORE you got into trouble, find the misunderstood word and get it defined.

Definitions

As an aid to the reader, words most likely to be misunderstood have been defined in footnotes the first time they occur in the text. Words sometimes have several meanings. The footnote definitions in this book only give the meaning that the word has as it is used in the text. Other definitions for the word can be found in a dictionary.

A glossary including all the footnote definitions is at the back of this book.

Introduction

Where did you come from? Have you lived before?

There is evidence that you *have*.

The belief in past lives has been suppressed at times, especially by those who had a vested interest in forgetting what they had done or been. However, despite any skepticism, the conviction that a man doesn't really die but is reincarnated and lives again in another body is one of the oldest and most constant religious beliefs in man's history.

Reincarnation means occupation by the soul of a new body after the death of the former body. The word comes from Latin, meaning literally "taking on flesh again." This definition has been distorted and complicated over time, but the original and *correct* meaning of the word is simply "to take on a new body."

From the ancient Egyptian to the present-day Buddhist,[1] from

---

1. **Buddhist:** one who follows the doctrines of Buddhism. *See also* **Buddhism** in the glossary.

the classic Greek philosopher to the modern religious scholar, the belief in the immortality of the soul has endured.[2]

Reincarnation was a fundamental belief in the Roman Catholic Church until 553 A.D. when a company of Catholic church officials decided the belief could not exist. They held a meeting, without the Pope[3] present, and issued orders which resulted in all references to reincarnation being removed from the Bible. Since that time, though many Christian scholars and teachers have still held the conviction that the soul lives on in a new body after death, the belief in past lives has been officially denied in the Christian religion.

The strange idea that man lives but once has also been propagated by the basic theories of psychiatry, which teach that "man is nothing but an animal." But despite any opposition, the fundamental knowledge that man has lived before and shall live again has persisted through the ages.

In 1950, L. Ron Hubbard, renowned author and philosopher, made an incredible breakthrough which opened the door to being able to actually recall past lives. In researching the mind and human spirit, he found that many of the problems and illnesses that people suffer from in the present stem from painful experiences in the past, and he developed precise techniques by which one could effectively recall such experiences and handle them. Many people applied these techniques to improve conditions in their own lives, and in doing so, past lives soon presented themselves.

Continuing his research, Mr. Hubbard found that if past life

2. For more information on man's belief in reincarnation throughout history, see the historical sketch on reincarnation and past lives in the appendix of this book.

3. **Pope:** head of the Roman Catholic Church.

experiences were not handled or acknowledged just as the experiences from the person's present life, the person would not recover. And, when people *were* permitted to recall their past lives, full knowledge of them brought about not only miraculous recovery but also marked improvement in the person's spiritual well-being.

As a result of L. Ron Hubbard's breakthroughs on the subject of past life recall, it is now accepted and popular to have awareness of one's past. More and more is being discovered about man's existence through recall of experiences in former lives.

This book contains forty-one fascinating case histories from a 1958 experiment in which the actuality of past lives was scientifically explored.

It also includes examples of the ease with which a person can contact past existences using modern techniques, and an essay on the true phenomena of death.

You are invited to read these accounts and decide for yourself: Have *you* lived before this life?

The Editors, 1989

Contents

1

The Conditions
of the Experiment

1

The Conditions of the Experiment

In the fall of 1958 in London, a group of Scientologists convened to acquire the latest and most advanced Scientology techniques yet developed.

These people were all trained practitioners, well-versed in the technologies of Dianetics and Scientology.

Dianetics technology (and its spectacular discoveries) is today a broadly known and used subject. Millions of persons have read Dianetics books. *Dianetics: The Modern Science of Mental Health* has been a bestseller since it was published in 1950. The word *Dianetics* comes from the Greek *dia*, through, and *nous*, soul. Dianetics is defined as what the soul is doing to the body.

Scientology philosophy is the broad unified study of the phenomena of the physical universe, the body, the human mind and human life source. Scientology means *scio*, knowing in the fullest sense of the word and *logos*, study. In itself the word means literally *knowing how to know*.

The main interest of the Scientologists involved in this

experiment was in *clearing*,[1] the newest and highest state that had been reached by man. The action of *clearing* brings about a condition of greatly increased intelligence and increased effectiveness in personal relations, a freedom from spiritually caused physical illness, and other goals of interest.

The Persons of the Study

The group undertaking this study consisted of forty-one practitioners of Scientology.

The intelligence of the group as a whole was well above that of the average professional person and, being Scientology practitioners, none had more than normal aberrations.[2] They, like any professional people in their own fields, were inclined to be critical of advances and even skeptical.

The activities of the group were conducted by myself and three American experts in Scientological theory and techniques.

Character of Scientology

Scientology, which has been remarkably effective in handling

---

1. **clearing:** the actions involved with bringing a person to the state of Clear. The word Clear can be used to describe the state itself or an individual who has achieved this state. A Clear is a being who no longer has his own *reactive mind*—that portion of a person's mind which works on a totally stimulus-response basis, which is not under his volitional control and which exerts force and the power of command over his awareness, purposes, thoughts, body and actions. *See also* **Clear** in the glossary.

2. **aberrations:** departures from rational thought or behavior. It means basically to err, to make mistakes, or more specifically to have fixed ideas which are not true. The word is also used in its scientific sense. It means departure from a straight line. If a line should go from A to B, then if it is *aberrated* it would go from A to some other point, to some other point, to some other point, to some other point, to some other point, and finally arrive at B. Taken in its scientific sense, it would also mean the lack of straightness or to see crookedly as, for example, a man sees a horse but thinks he sees an elephant. Aberrated conduct would be wrong conduct, or conduct not supported by reason. Aberration is opposed to sanity, which would be its opposite. From the Latin, *aberrare*, to wander from; Latin, *ab*, away, *errare*, to wander.

conditions and various mental states, uses no hypnotism[3] or drugs or shock.

The application of Scientology (or Dianetics) procedures to another is called *auditing:* the action of asking a person a question (which he can understand and answer), getting an answer to that question and acknowledging him for that answer. A trained practitioner in Dianetics or Scientology techniques is called an *auditor,* "one who listens."

Attitude of the Group

Before the group was convened few of its members could have answered affirmatively the question "Have you lived before?" Their individual replies would have ranged from the emphatic negative to the ridiculing skeptical.

The E-Meter

The E-Meter is an electronic device used to detect areas of spiritual charge[4] and stress. It is *not* a lie detector. It does not diagnose or cure anything. It is useful to the auditor as it denotes that something is troubling a person and then makes it possible to locate it in time and character. Some people with guilty consciences are justifiably afraid of the E-Meter since it reveals anything and everything they have done and been when used by an expert auditor.

---

3. **hypnotism:** the act of putting a person into a trance for the purpose of planting suggestions. Hypnotism reduces self-determinism by entering the commands of another below the awareness level of an individual's mind.

4. **charge:** harmful energy or force accumulated and stored within the reactive mind, resulting from the conflicts and unpleasant experiences that a person has had. Auditing discharges this charge so that it is no longer there to affect the individual. *See also* **reactive mind** in the glossary.

The E-Meter was used in this experiment to help locate incidents which were heavily charged.

Scientology and Dianetics Techniques

Scientology and Dianetics techniques differ greatly from hypnotism. In hypnotism the aim is to put the patient to sleep and make him as irresponsible as possible for his answers. In Scientology and Dianetics, the reverse is true—the person is made more and more alert, more and more responsible and truthful.

A "past life," for instance, brought out of a patient by hypnotism has little value since it is taken from an irresponsible subject. A "past life" recovered by Scientology or Dianetics techniques is detailed by a fully alert, responsible person who, by heightened powers of awareness, has direct and full knowledge of anything that has occurred to him. Therefore, if this were simply a recounting of forty-one experiences taken from hypnotized people, it would have little value. But forty-one experiences recovered from fully alert people with *no* hypnotism, suggestion or persuasion is of new scientific value and casts a different light on the subject of "past lives."

In the first place, none of these people were told to recover a past life. They were asked only to "enter" the engram[5]

5. **engram:** a mental image picture which is a recording of an experience containing pain, unconsciousness and a real or fancied threat to survival. It is a recording in the reactive mind of something which actually happened to an individual in the past and which contained pain and unconsciousness, both of which are recorded in the mental image picture called an engram. It must, by definition, have impact or injury as part of its content. These engrams are a complete recording, down to the last accurate detail, of every perception present in a moment of partial or full unconsciousness.

"necessary to resolve the case.[6]"[7]

Past lives and deaths are evidently painful experiences, and without the techniques of Dianetics and Scientology they can be recalled in full only with great difficulty and with much determination. That a person does not remember them, if they exist, is then no matter of mystery. If he remembered them in full before they were addressed with auditing, he would be in agony. Thus we see why there is a considerable reluctance to recall them unaided. And if they *are* recalled, only the presence of an expert auditor can make the person discharge the violent emotions contained in such engrams. Record of this is found throughout these actual case reports.

In this experiment, forty-one conservative Scientologists were put through and put other people through engrams which give evidence of past lives.

Their experience and conclusions are therefore of interest to the scientific world.

6. **case:** a general term for a person being treated or helped. It also refers to his condition, which is monitored by the content of his reactive mind. A person's case is the way he responds to the world around him by reason of his aberration.

7. **"necessary to resolve the case":** a phrase used in Dianetics techniques. If an auditor asks a person for the *engram necessary to resolve the case,* he will always get the engram that is next available to be *reduced* or *erased.* To *reduce* an engram means to take all the charge or pain out of it and render it free of aberrative material as far as possible to make the case progress. To *erase* an engram means to cause it to "vanish" entirely by recountings, at which time it is filed as memory and experience.

2

A Note
on Past Lives

2

A Note on Past Lives

$\mathbf{P}$ast lives, or times we have lived before, are suppressed by the painfulness of the memory of those former existences.

The memory is contained in mental image pictures[1] which, on close viewing, are capable of developing a reality[2] "more real" than present time.[3]

Where a person has been tortured or killed without adequate reason, the injustice of it causes him or her to protest by holding in suspension in time the picture.

---

1. **mental image picture:** a copy of the physical universe as it goes by; we call a *mental image picture* a facsimile when it is a "photograph" of the physical universe sometime in the past. We call a *mental image picture* a mock-up when it is created by the thetan or for the thetan and does not consist of photographs of the physical universe. We call a *mental image picture* a hallucination, or more properly an automaticity (something uncontrolled), when it is created by another and seen by self. *See also* **facsimile** in the glossary.

2. **reality:** the agreed-upon apparency of existence. A reality is any data that agrees with the person's perceptions, computations and education. Reality is one of the components of understanding.

3. **present time:** the time which is now and which becomes the past almost as rapidly as it is observed. It is a term loosely applied to the environment existing in now, as in "The preclear came up to present time," meaning the preclear became aware of the present environment.

To restore the memory of one's whole existence, it is necessary to bring one up to being able to confront such experiences.

A person with amnesia is looked upon as ill. What of a person who can remember only this life? Is this then not a case of amnesia on a grand scale?

Psychosomatic illnesses such as arthritis, asthma, rheumatism,[4] heart trouble, and on and on for a total of 70 percent of man's ills—and women's too—are the reaction of the body against a painful mental image picture or *engram*. When this picture is cleared away—if it is the right picture—the illness usually abates.

Actual fevers and pain, etc., can turn on just by restimulation[5] of mental pictures in a person.

The recovery of whole memory could be said to be a goal of processing.[6]

Past lives are "incredible" only to those who dare not confront[7] them. In others, the fact of former existence can be quickly established subjectively.[8]

---

4. **rheumatism:** a popular term for any of the various painful conditions of the joints and muscles, characterized by inflammation, stiffness, etc.

5. **restimulation:** reactivation of a past memory due to similar circumstances in the present approximating circumstances of the past.

6. **processing:** the application of Dianetics or Scientology processes to someone by a trained auditor. The exact definition of *processing* is: The action of asking a preclear a question (which he can understand and answer), getting an answer to that question and acknowledging him for that answer. Also called **auditing.**

7. **confront:** to face without flinching or avoiding. Confront is actually the ability to be there comfortably and perceive.

8. **subjectively:** in a manner which proceeds from or takes place in an individual's mind.

There are many interesting cases on record since Dianetics gave impetus to Bridey Murphy.[9] One was a case of a young girl, about five, who, hanging back at church, confided to her clergyman that she was worried about her "husband and children." It seems she had not forgotten them after "dying out of" another life five years before.

The clergyman did not at once send for the chaps in white coats. Instead, he questioned the truly worried child closely.

She told him she had lived in a nearby village, and what her name had been. She said where her former body was buried, gave him the address of her husband and children and what all their names were, and asked him to drive over and find out if they were all right.

The clergyman made the trip. Much to his astonishment, he discovered the grave, the husband, the children and all the current news.

The following Sunday he told the little five-year-old girl that the children were all well, that the husband had remarried pleasantly and that the grave was well kept.

She was very satisfied and thanked the clergyman very much—and the following Sunday could not recall a thing about it!

Past lives are not the same as the theory which has been called "reincarnation" in Hinduism. That is a complex theory

---

9. **Murphy, Bridey:** a widely published account of a woman who was regressed back to the 1800s through the use of hypnosis during which a full and detailed life in Ireland was contacted. Her name in that life was Bridey Murphy. Dianetics discoveries inspired and were the impetus behind this 1952 episode.

compared to simply living time after time, getting a new body, eventually losing it and getting a new one.

The facts of past lives, if you care to pursue them, are best seen from a preclear's viewpoint in the hands of a competent auditor. The hypnotic handling of such is not advised. Only by higher levels of awareness does one learn, not deeper levels of unconsciousness.

An amusing sidelight on past lives is the "famous person" fixation. This more than anything else has discredited having lived before. There is always some madman "who was Napoleon,"[10] always some girl "who was Catherine the Great."[11] This evidently means that the person, living a contemporary life to a famous figure, was so unsuccessful that he or she "dubbed in"[12] the great personage. An auditor who runs into "Beethoven,"[13] after the preclear has run[14] it for a while, finds the preclear was really the handler of a street piano[15] in that life—not Beethoven!

But all rules have exceptions, and an auditor once found a

---

10. **Napoleon:** Napoleon Bonaparte (1769–1821); French military leader and emperor of France (1804–15).

11. **Catherine the Great:** (1729–96) Catherine II, Empress of Russia (1762–96); married to Peter III (Russian Emperor) whom she deposed in order to take over the throne.

12. **dubbed in:** created unknowingly a mental picture that appears to have been a record of the physical universe but is in fact only an altered copy of the past. (It is a phrase taken from the motion picture industry, meaning to record dialogue and various sounds and then integrate them into the film after it has been shot. This is done for scenes where the original recording is faulty, for scenes where it is simply more convenient to add dialogue and other sound later, and for films playing abroad which require new dialogue in the native language of the host country.)

13. **Beethoven:** Ludwig Van Beethoven (1770–1827); famous German composer of symphonies.

14. **run:** to undergo processing on.

15. **street piano:** a large music box that is made to play tunes by turning a crank.

preclear who claimed to have been Jim Bowie, the famous frontiersman who died at the doubly famous Alamo[16] in Texas. And after much work and great skepticism found he really did have Jim Bowie!

People have also been animals and perhaps some animals have been people. There evidently is no gradient scale of advance, as in the theories of reincarnation, but there are cases on record of preclears who got well after a life as a dog or other animal was run out[17] by an auditor.

One case, a psychotic girl, recovered when a life as a lion who ate his keeper was fully run out!

And we have also known horses and dogs of "human intelligence." Perhaps they had just been generals or ministers of state and were taking it easy for a life or two to cure their ulcers!

Viewing children in the light of knowledge of past lives causes us to revise our estimations of causes of child behavior.

Evidently the newborn child has just died as an adult. Therefore he or she, for some years, is prone to fantasy and terror and needs a great deal of love and security to recover a perspective of life with which he or she can live.

Life is never dull in the researches and practice of Dianetics and Scientology. The motto is — *What is, is,* not what we wished it were.

---

16. **Alamo:** a fortified mission in San Antonio, Texas. In 1836, during the Texas rebellion (against Mexico — as Texas was originally Spanish territory), a force of Texans was besieged at the Alamo by a much larger Mexican army. After 13 days of fighting, the Mexicans were able to break into the Alamo and every remaining defender was killed in hand-to-hand combat.

17. **run out:** erased. *See also* **erase** in the glossary.

3

The Incidents

3

The Incidents

The following are the incidents in the past of people indicating that they have lived before. Some are the reports of the auditors who did the processing; some are the reports of the people themselves.

Here we find various phenomena well known to the experienced auditor but not so well known to the public.

The fact that a person is not his body but can be detached from his body is too well known for much discussion. Anyone can be detached from his body, and the conclusion is that one is not his body. Auditors had known this for a very long while, but had never drawn the final conclusion that one has had other bodies and therefore "past lives."

People forget these on the assumption of a new identity. But the startling fact that is new is that the consequences of having lived before can be reflected in a present life.

Here we find persons who have been troubled with ideas and illnesses in their present lives which they could not explain. The practitioner, using Scientology methods, located the mental image pictures of the former experience and made the person confront them repeatedly. In the process of confronting these, full memory of the incident returned. And with the memory came the shock and pain of the loss, and this had to be confronted as well.

This is the story of what happened to many people to whom this occurred.

Remember in reading these that this is the data that was given during processing. It is a scientific assessment of what the subjects said. It contains no evaluation of the truth or falsity of data.

The data, however, seems to indicate that man has been "on the way" a very long time, has lived on other planets and in other places. He has engaged, evidently, in space travel, in barbarous jungle warfare, has lived as kings and commoners, citizens and commissars for a very, very long time.

These people have greater or lesser evidence now that they have lived before. These are their stories.

Reports
On Cases
1 to 41

Case 1

Preclear's Report

Former Condition

Not certain that I was able to audit, not willing to state my opinion, although I knew I was right. Letting a counter-intention[1] overwhelm me, and take me off being cause point.[2]

Mental Outlook

I am now more confident and sticking to my own decisions.

Physical Improvement

Need less sleep, body less tired.

What You Attribute Improvement To

Auditing a preclear, being audited, confronting the postulates[3] made in the engram.

---

1. **counter-intention:** an intention that is in opposition to one's own intention. For example, Joe wants to join the army (intention); his wife does not want him to join the army (counter-intention).

2. **cause point:** the originator of something; the point from which something was begun or dreamed up.

3. **postulates:** conclusions, decisions or resolutions made by the individual himself; to conclude, decide or resolve a problem or set a pattern for the future or to nullify a pattern of the past.

Auditor's Report

While exercising the preclear in facing up to things, a process on confronting, I noticed that she became very upset and uncooperative when questioned. She remarked that it was like being questioned by the police and she didn't like it.

Later in the course we were locating with the aid of an E-Meter the details of various painful experiences; whilst doing this I asked the preclear for the date of an incident which involved questioning. This was revealed by questioning and interpretation of the meter[4] reactions, as having occurred 651 years ago, and there were indications of other painful experiences at intervals over the previous twenty years.

Eventually this was the incident selected as responsible for this preclear's difficulties in this current life and we proceeded to work on it.

Little by little, pictures came to mind of stone walls, straw, a flagstone and grass around it. A monk, a naked body of a handsome white-haired man stretched on the rack.[5] The preclear recognized that she was that man at that time and went through a period of grief. As she confronted the things that had been done to that person, his ability and high station in life, she realized that her present unwillingness to accept responsibility and make good use of her abilities were due to the sufferings of that previous life when she had been highly intelligent and capable. Although she could not see the rack, she could hear the creak of the wheel turning as the body was stretched.

4. **meter:** short for **E-Meter**. *See* **E-Meter** in the glossary.

5. **rack:** an instrument of torture having a frame on which the victim is bound and stretched until his limbs are pulled out of place.

As the process was continued, by me asking the preclear "What part of that incident can you confront?" she got more and more details of her surroundings at different periods of time. When something unpleasant came up she would get angry and doubtful of the incident before confronting it. A scene gradually unfolded of a part of the incident prior to stretching on the rack, where the man was subjected to torture by means of the thumbscrew.[6] At this the preclear was waving her hands about, but became very angry when I told her to hold the E-Meter cans[7] still, and when I repeated this she said, "I'll kill you if you make me hold them still." I asked her, "Who made you keep your hands still?" And she answered, "The monk," and then broke down and cried. After this the preclear could see a heavily built soldier standing outside administering the thumbscrew under the direction of the monk who was sitting opposite the man (the preclear) across a large table in the large hall, as I was sitting opposite her during the auditing session.[8] She was seeing me as the monk directing the torture.

Pictures came up of a scene on the beach, a ship at sea, a date or time mark in the sand, and a man's figure standing on the sand and then driving a camel across the sandy waste. Eventually it was discovered that the man was waiting for the ship. Later it came that the man was captured by four steel-helmeted soldiers, one of whom first read out a proclamation from a scroll. What happened next was quite unreal for a number of hours of processing and different parts of the whole incident came into view. A night spent in a small cell, a man

---

6. **thumbscrew:** an old instrument of torture by which one or both thumbs were compressed.

7. **cans:** electrodes used with the E-Meter. They resemble ordinary cans and are tin plated. Electrical leads from the E-Meter are connected to the cans with clips, and the cans are held in the preclear's hands.

8. **session:** a precise period of time during which an auditor audits a preclear.

sitting at a desk near a shop window within view of the wharf and ship, the man talking to a bearded wise man with a long gray robe tied with a cord. The man handcuffed and mounted on a gray horse, in front of a drawbridge over a moat, stone steps, a soldier leading the man up curved steps to a cell and carrying a candle to light the way, the man sitting eating a bowl of soup, the man on the rack face downwards, whilst the soldier takes a whip off the wall, and prepares to whip him (at this time the actual whipping could not be confronted), soldiers dragging the body across the roof of the castle and throwing it into the sea. A scene came up of eyes being put out with red-hot tongs, and this was found to belong to another life altogether. It only came up once.

The preclear was becoming rather confused, and particularly when the thumbscrew period was confronted; with some difficulty it was discovered that the man was drugged and hypnotized at this time. The hypnosis was started in a cell by a candle flame being held in front of the man's eyes, then the man was carried into the hall and given a glass of wine in which was a drug. Then he was further hypnotized when the thumbscrew was applied and a suggestion instilled. The actual words that were spoken had not been confronted by the end of the course, but the preclear knew that these were such as to leave the man thoroughly confused and subject to other people's will.

Whilst confronting this period the preclear's eyelids were fluttering continuously and she was swaying about in her chair as though in a trance. However, as she confronted it better and better these manifestations wore off. After this the preclear could reexperience and confront more easily the pain and sound in the incident and scenes, rather than just still pictures. She also felt much brighter. The next part to come up was when the man was still free; there was a pretty, fair-haired girl whom he wanted to marry, but for some reason, which couldn't here be decided, "It was no use trying." Preclear recognized that this was often the way she acted in her present life when things got difficult. When this part which included the girl came up, we checked if it included the torture incident, as the scenery had not been encountered before. However it was, there seemed to be some confusion as to the date of the incident and it was discovered that the preclear was setting the time of the incident according to the time of two different calendars; by one the date was 1700 B.C. and by the other, the lunar calendar, it was 651 years ago. Scenes had been on a hill with a girl, and in a bedroom with her, and of a king upon a throne, being given the king's black ring, and rows of soldiers coming up. Then a banquet at which the girl's engagement to the king was announced and the man was tricked into and later defeated in a duel, after which he was taken to a tent to rest.

All this part was rather sketchy and the emotion was not confrontable at that time, although pain was felt in the elbow which was run through by a sword in the duel.

By confronting thoroughly the girl, the king, and the girl's father one at a time, this part became much clearer. An earlier part where the man, the girl and her father were in a ship came up and the preclear experienced some of the seasick feeling that the man had on board ship. This all became rather unreal and the sequence of events confused.

The preclear was showing embarrassment at being questioned, when it was found that the period in the incident was when the man was embarrassed when the torture on the rack was taking place. It was decided that this part of the incident needed more attention. The preclear was then gotten to confront the body of the man, little by little; and this was quite difficult, as the picture would fade out and become unreal.

Each time this happened she was brought to confront a few hairs on the right leg and from this she got the body more and more real. After each period of unreality some more pain or unconsciousness would be confronted, reexperienced and run off; after which the whole body was fairly confrontable and the preclear could confront it without consequence. A window, a door, a wall, and then another wall, and then another wall were confronted many times each.

Much the same phenomena were observed when confronting these except on the last wall which was the one the man was facing as he lay on the rack. While confronting this the preclear reexperienced and confronted the actual death and exteriorization[9] from the body, going up into space, coming down again and staying near the body until after it went to the bottom of the sea, then going away into space again. The next picture was of a baby's body (the next life).

Continuing and confronting the same wall she went through quite a lot of pain and unconsciousness, emotion, etc., and got three postulates, "I've got to get out of here, I can't bear it any longer," "It's too late now, I'm dying" and "I'm free at last." A discussion on these brought to her awareness that these decisions had been having a considerable effect on her present life. She would feel compelled to "get out" when things got difficult, put on an act of pretending she was dying when she felt embarrassed or silly, and did not like to be tied down or in any way have her freedom restricted.

Continuing on confronting that wall, it completely faded out and I got her to confront the door in the cell for a while until she could see the wall again. After confronting the wall again a number of times she reexperienced the effort and pain

9. **exteriorization:** the act of moving out of the body with or without full perception.

of having her right arm stretched; when this wore off she was less nervous and her hands had ceased perspiring.

Later she realized that her embarrassment had been due to the monk and one or more soldiers affronting[10] her right to die alone by watching her die on the rack. It was only at the last that she failed to put on a good front, and this left her ashamed and embarrassed. Her discovering that this was the underlying reason for her unwillingness to be watched or questioned left her feeling much more composed and secure than she had ever been previously.

The details of the incident were not complete by course end but it was known that the preclear was a man of high station, education and intelligence, had lived an adventurous life which included life at court, soldiering and politics. (There were indications that this man was the king's brother, but was not particularly favored by the king, whom he called a tyrannical fool.) The man was tricked into challenging the king to a duel in honor of the king's engagement, at the banquet, to the former's mistress. Another swordsman took the king's place and defeated the man by wounding him in the elbow of his sword arm. After this the king arranged for his exile to another land. However, the man was arrested on the beach and taken to the castle where he was drugged, hypnotized and cruelly tortured with a thumbscrew and by whipping and stretching on the rack. Although there was still quite a lot more work to be done to completely dispel the effects of this incident the preclear was, by end of the process, observedly calmer, more self-assured, more cooperative, prettier, her skin much clearer, and her body movements were more graceful.

---

10. **affronting:** insulting openly or purposefully.

Case 2

Preclear's Report

Former Condition

My former condition was fairly good. Certain defects, pertinent here, are concerned with the fact that I was difficult to rouse in the morning; and that, when tired after long work, I would have muscle fatigue, especially in the neck, shoulder and back muscles, and some ache in the head and upper left arm. My olfactory[1] sense was slight.

Mental Outlook

Since the running of this engram I am much more cheerful much earlier in the morning, rousing myself with comparative ease. I communicate more easily, have become more sensitive to slight odors, and am no more offended by strong ones.

Physical Improvement

I have experienced no more muscle fatigue, as mentioned in *Former Condition*, nor ache in head or arm when tired after long work. As a matter of fact I am not tired after long work, though I do get a bit bored.

---

1. **olfactory:** of or relating to the sense of smell.

What You Attribute Improvement To

The whole engram was based upon oversleeping in a very bad mood on that particular day. I ran very heavy neck, shoulder and back efforts[2] (muscular) at decapitation, with left arm ache and headache. The incident was full of strong odors, notably me.

The Engram

Life was hard for almost everybody in nineteenth century China, but the coolie[3] had the worst of it. Half enough to eat, and a wall to sleep by, was our idea of prosperity. The incident which I am about to tell, though of no consequence save to its narrator, is remarkable for the complete apathy which pervades it. For apathy knows a thin little emotional life of its own. Apathy can feel a semblance of terror, though it cannot flee; anger, though it cannot fight; love, though it cannot reach; grief, though it cannot weep. These actions were quite beyond me at the time, but I yet could whimper, complain, need and endure. This all happened at a time when there was not much work for people of my sort, and I was not one of the best of my calling. The year was 1874, and at forty-two, I was getting on. I had to roll out[4] at dawn and scrounge around the town begging odd manual jobs. Sometimes there would be a boat loading or a piece of porter's[5] work for the day; usually just a couple of brief tasks, paid by table scraps.

The woman woke me timidly that May morning, and then again a bit later to tell me the sun was up. I struck out at her, caught her a good clout, then sulkily went back to sleep. I

---

2. **efforts:** motions with definite direction and purpose. *Effort* is different from motion. Motion could be anything, but *effort* has to be specific: it is at a known point in time, it has a known direction and it is known whether it is inhibited or compelled.

3. **coolie:** an unskilled native laborer, especially formerly in India and China.

4. **roll out:** arise from bed; get up.

5. **porter:** a person who carries things.

didn't mean to hit her really, but when I rolled myself out later I was sulking because I had done it. I did not look at her directly where she sat in the stern of our boat, picking over some rags, and making something from them. Leaving her, I walked over the neighboring boats, pausing to relieve myself between them, and clambered up on to the quay.[6]

The sun was well up. Obviously I was too late to find subsistence that day. I went up the steep ramproad[7] from the quay, and through the square with its big tree, its stalls and children. After a few turnings I came to the bottom of the street, a crowded fare of business and noise. Soon I came to my first call, a great house by the tea shop. Humbly I waited by the little door until it was opened. The servant there was a relative of mine, and not a bad fellow if one abased[8] oneself sufficiently. He had no jobs for me this day, but he did give me a handful of rice scraped from the bowls. This was better than new rice, because the scrapings had the flavor of sauce, and this also had three acorns in it, rather tough, but nice. Having eaten, I started on my way, which led up into the main part of the town.

Before I had reached the bottom of the street there was a sudden commotion. The crowd was in panic, and soldiers pressed upon us. Mounted archers came down from the top, pushing all the people before them, and at the bottom, a troop of mace-men[9] on foot channeled us across the broad avenue and into the gate. The gate, as I knew well, led into the grand

6. **quay:** a wharf, usually of concrete or stone, for use in loading and unloading ships.

7. **ramproad:** a sloping, sometimes curved, road joining different levels.

8. **abased:** reduced or lowered, as in rank, office, reputation or estimation; humbled, degraded.

9. **mace-men:** soldiers carrying a mace, a heavy medieval war club, often with a spiked, metal head.

cour[10] of the palace which lay all along the avenue. This palace
was no royal residence, but a sort of customs house where the
Imperial Agent, his Provincial Council, the Guard and the local
Bureau of State were all located. I knew the cour well, for I had
often seen soldiers there at practice, and quite a few executions, and had even been whipped there once, when suspected
of complicity[11] with some thieves who were put to death. In
recall this was the most terrible moment of the incident; being
swept along toward that awful gate. After that my fear was of
some event ever more nearly known; but the first moment of
terror was entirely animal, unreasoned, unspeculated, unquestioning; I must not approach that gate. The alternative, however, was resistance, an idea unknown to me; so I jostled along
with the crowd. Near me was an old man in black, and I heard
him tell some neighbor what was going on. It seems that a
gang of bandits or outlaw men had been detected incognito[12] in
the town. When chased, they had ducked into the street, and
had lost themselves. The troops were taking everybody from
the street into the cour so that the felons could be sorted out.
I never found out whether or not this was the true story of why
we were pushed along; the old man may just have surmised it.

Inside the gate a squad of soldiers weeded us out. Women,
children, old men, a begging monk, a cangued[13] convict, they
roughly pitched into the cour behind them. We nondescript
were hustled past to the right, along the wall inside, down to
the corner by the palace, where we waited. Some officers and
known men of the town came to inspect us. Many were thrown

---

10. **cour:** (*French*) courtyard.

11. **complicity:** partnership in wrongdoing; the fact or state of being an accomplice.

12. **incognito:** with true identity unrevealed or disguised; under an assumed name,
rank, etc.

13. **cangued:** placed in a *cangue* (in China, a large, wooden yoke formerly fastened
around the neck as a punishment for petty crime).

out, including one proper priest in a big hat. Soldiers bound those of us who remained. Across the cour the other group was also vetted,[14] and a few of them were sent over to us.

As the soldiers bound my hands behind me and hobbled[15] my ankles with cords, I kept telling them over and over that they had the wrong party; that I was someone else—in fact, that I was nobody at all. They were entirely noncommittal. They almost did not even hear me. They bound us all, thirty-five to forty of us, in this way, and stood back on guard while we sat waiting in the shadow of the wall for perhaps half an hour. The rejected group was herded out of the cour. We who remained were all poor types, mostly coolies and boatmen, together with a few low travelers. We were obviously people of no importance; that was sufficient qualification for us to be elected honorary bandits. So we sat in the dry clay-sand and waited. Soldiers, officers, came and went. We did not speak. We waited.

After a while we were led out into the center, about half of us, eighteen to be precise. We were placed in a long line across the cour, four to five feet apart, and we were made to kneel, facing the great steps down from the palace. It was then that I really knew what was to happen; I refused to know, yet I knew. We all knew for we had seen this many times. Kneeling, we waited while the headsman came slowly from his little door beside the palace, slowly down the steps, diagonally across to the right-hand end of our line. It seemed to me that he should have started from the left, and I snatched a momentary hope from this; but I was confused at the time, and when he made his address I saw that he was left-handed.

---

14. **vetted:** appraised, verified or checked for accuracy, authenticity, validity, etc.

15. **hobbled:** tied the feet together to hamper the movement of (a person, horse, etc.).

The first two victims were expostulating[16] vigorously by this time. The headsman took the great black-handled sword from his boy, kicked the first man lightly on the shoulder, and gestured. The victim shouted, then bowed his head for the address. We groaned with one voice as the head rolled in the sand. The No. 2 man protested, and, although he bowed, he reared up again at the wrong moment. The blade sliced into his skull. Old Frozen-Face chopped the dead head from its shoulders, and wiped the bright steel clean with a towel carried by his boy. He wiped it almost every time as he progressed along the line. He met no more resistance. I watched, horrified, as the heads rolled this way and that, the blood spurted and flowed from the bodies, and the grimaces of death spun in midair. I remember especially No. 6, a plump, composed fellow, the only one of us, I think, who realized what was happening and bore his part calmly. One of the bandits? Perhaps.

As the headsman approached the No. 10 man, just before me, I was going quietly mad. Rigid and limp by turns, with an apathetic kind of terror, I could hear someone screaming inside my skull, and I could feel the flesh of my face a wooden mask. The No. 9 head spun into his path where he walked around the pool of blood; he kicked it out of his way, and it struck No. 10 on the knee. As the man bowed his head, I saw a little vomit on his lips. I did not want to look, but I saw the glittering blow, and I saw the body hop twice like a frog, and I remembered that we used to think that very funny to watch. Then I saw blood on the lower trousers of the headsman, and the bloody sand caked wet on his feet and sandals. I saw him rear the glaive[17] for his address. I stuck my little neck out as far

---

16. **expostulating:** earnestly reasoning with a person, objecting to his actions or intentions.

17. **glaive:** a broadsword.

---

as I could, I shut my eyes and squinched up my face, and I got almost ready. But not quite. I needed just another few seconds to get really ready. . . .

It is interesting what happens when you take a head off. All the shoulder muscles pull in violently, and the neck and back muscles too, partly by their own elasticity, and partly in a stupid frantic effort to recover their lost burden. There is pain in the neck, of course; but for that instant I also had a rather bad headache (the result, I assume, of poor cranial circulation), a feeling of bruised eyeballs, pain from my twisted left shoulder and elbow, and a wrenched hip when the body fell over into a most uncomfortable position. I also bit my tongue, not badly; and got sand in my eye where my head, that delicate black box I had lived in so long, lay on its right cheek and temple, just at the high-tide mark,[18] so to speak, of my thin red blood. I did not really notice the other seven victims, though they were not uninteresting when my auditor finally dug them out. The No. 17 man tried to get away, and had his arm chopped off, his shoulder butchered and his backbone split before the boie[19] got him. All I noticed was my own small head lying there a feast for flies.

I did not exactly leave it, but rather drifted away, far up into the sky. From there I saw the whole scene: the line of bodies, the low sun, the next batch awaiting their turn, the meat wagon,[20] the crowd at the gate. . . .

Soon I came back to my boat, not reasonably, but in such an agony of grief and loneliness that this seems the only place

---

18. **high-tide mark:** literally, the mark left after high water has receded. Used figuratively in this sense.

19. **boie:** an executioner.

20. **meat wagon:** a wagon used to carry the dead.

to go. The woman is there, eating half a fish, sucking the bones. Our daughter, aged four, stands by her; she has the tail. Her mother has told her to be careful of tails and fins, and she has a morsel of spiney membrane on her back teeth, crunching and grinding very slowly, watching her mother with a kind of faraway concentration; she is being a good little girl.

I tried to communicate with the woman but could not. Then I wondered what she would think when I never came back; would she find out what had happened, or think I had simply left home? I had gone away that morning without speaking, after swatting her one; I was sorry for that then. I came back in the night while she slept on the boat with the children; I got into her head; I tried to move her limbs; I haunted her, but she would not move, even in sleep. Desperate, I tried again next day. By then she was worried about me, and although she had heard about the executions, she had had no definite word of me. I screamed, I hooted, and beat with my little fists upon the inside of her skull, but she did not hear. At last I could not stay. The harder I tried to reach to the boat, the faster the planet drew beneath me, until at last I drifted, powerless, in the upper air.

So much for that story. But the auditor was not quite satisfied with it as it stood. "Why was he there in the first place?" is always the crucial question; and he had to turn over an almost complete life story to answer it. We need not dwell upon the somewhat discreditable incident which started this business in train.[21] I was a servant, aged fourteen. My first love, my true love, was a maid in the same house. I stole some fine silks, and fenced[22] them off through my connections among the local

---

21. **in train:** in proper order, arrangement or sequence; in process.

22. **fenced:** sold something which was stolen to a person or place which deals in buying and selling stolen goods.

teddy-boys.[23] Months later she was accused. Eventually she confessed, under the bamboo,[24] our intimacy, which had given me access to the storeroom. I denied it. Forced to confront her, I managed to clear myself. She died as a result, by execution. This early misdeed, at the time a heavy blow to my adolescent amour-propre,[25] was really the end of my unpromising career. I spiraled steadily downward after that, and ended up with my head in the sand, unable even to haunt my own family. It was her screams I heard there in the cour. I wondered at the time why I would be screaming my own name. My name was Han by the way. More than that; but they called me Han for short.

---

23. **teddy-boys:** uncouth, rough, idle, usually low-class young toughs (about fifteen to twenty-five years old), often violent; juvenile delinquents.

24. **under the bamboo:** beaten or caned with bamboo.

25. **amour-propre:** (*French*) self-esteem; self-respect. Literally, self-love.

Case 3

Preclear's Report

Former Condition

I was in grief—easily invalidated[1] and unsure of my own potential.

Mental Outlook

Now more sure of my own potential for probably the first time.

Physical Improvement

Body feels clearer (more relaxed) and lighter.

What You Attribute Improvement To

Confronting engram which has resolved my case as follows: I did not know I had lived before.

Auditor's Report

I located a moment of loss in the preclear's past and she

---

1. **invalidated:** made to feel worthless as a result of someone refuting, degrading, discrediting or denying something one considers to be fact.

gave me the number 56. By using the E-Meter, the time of this moment of loss was 56 B.C., the date being March 19th. On questioning the preclear, she told me that she had lost a body at this time by suicide. The body was that of a Roman soldier on garrison duty in Greece.

The preclear went quickly into the incident and there was a great amount of grief over what she thought had been the slaughter of family and friends. Later on, the preclear found this to be a hallucination due to poison he had been given, and it was not more than four hours before I had a good outline of the incident. The incident ran thus:

On the morning of March 19th the soldier (preclear) took his wife to a grove a few miles away from the city for a picnic, accompanied by many friends all riding in chariots. He then returned to the city to see his mistress, knowing that he shouldn't see her. He was rebuffed[2] at her house and, because of the jealousy of his mistress, she gave him a poisonous drink. The drink dulled his senses to a marked degree and caused a lot of misemotion.[3] He made his way back to the grove by chariot. On the way back the chariot broke down, the wheel coming off after being jolted by a boulder.

The soldier walked and ran the rest of the way suffering agony from the poisonous drink and being delirious. On arrival the soldier went through hallucinations of his wife dead

---

2. **rebuffed:** refused bluntly; snubbed.

3. **misemotion:** a coined word used in Dianetics and Scientology to mean an emotion or emotional reaction that is inappropriate to the present time situation. It is taken from *mis-* (wrong) + *emotion*. To say that a person was *misemotional* would indicate that the person did not display the emotion called for by the actual circumstances of the situation. Being misemotional would be synonymous with being irrational. One can fairly judge the rationality of any individual by the correctness of the emotion he displays in a given set of circumstances. To be joyful and happy when circumstances call for joy and happiness would be rational. To display grief without sufficient present time cause would be irrational.

and friends murdered around him. Through all this delirium he decided that no one could ever help him, and after some effort plunged his sword into his heart.

On the death of his body he was bewildered and for forty-five minutes could not understand why he should be alive, and his body dead. He kept near his dead body for three hours, feeling the heat of the sun on the dead body and watching a soldier take the sword out of it. He had decided to stay with the dead body until it had been helped in some way. Now, detached from his body, he decided to use the body of the brother of the woman who poisoned him, as he was in the vicinity. He wanted to feel bodily emotions again and also to feel the experience of seeing the woman who poisoned him through another person's body. During the time he was in that person's body he experienced the emotions of that person and also that person's profession.

He did see the woman again and later on in the evening left her brother's body and went back to take a look at his old dead body to see if it was all right. He sensed the "cheesy" smell of the body.

Three years later he came back to that area still without a body and was surprised to find a man sleeping in the same spot where he had left his dead body. End of incident.

During the running of this incident pieces of the incident began to fit together like a jigsaw puzzle, until the whole of the incident knitted together.

For a large part of the time the preclear went through and felt she was actually in the incident, and went through degradation, unconsciousness, effort, pain, physical agony, emotion and thoughts in the incident. Later the preclear could view the whole incident objectively and take full responsibility for it.

The act of suicide was not easy for the preclear to confront, but with some prompting, she did it all right.

Case 4

Preclear's Report

Former Condition

Could not face a present time picture or a past picture. Could not create a good imagery. Would not act (do) because I thought, "What would other people think?"

Mental Outlook

I am willing to face a lot more of my incident.

Physical Improvement

Movement of body has improved.

What You Attribute Improvement To

The willingness of the auditor to face the reality of an engram and to allow me to be cause over and willing to face (confront) part of the incident. My confidence in my auditor which made me willing. My auditor's knowledge of the subject of Scientology and his ability to duplicate a command[1] during

---

1. **command:** in auditing, the exact question an auditor asks a preclear which is to be answered by the preclear.

auditing. Ron Hubbard's interest in improving the application of Scientology to make a better planet for people to live on.

The Engram

This took place nine galaxy periods ago. I was a male, born of space parents. I seem to have had two or three mothers who died or were killed. At the age of five I was already on the lookout for brothels.[2] At nine years of age I asked my father if I could join the space academy, but did not actually join until I was fourteen. At fifteen, I went with other boys and girls for three months to learn all about sex and homosexuality. When I was sixteen I killed my father while fighting on the planet and I joined a spaceship. It seems I had a journey there and rejoined the ship when I was nineteen. Then I learned all about spaceship drill, takeoffs, etc. There was homosexuality, as only officers were allowed women.

I did not care for homosexuality and soon gained the title of captain and so was able to have a wife of my own. She had a baby and a few days later I found the wife enjoying pleasures with another officer. I put her and the officer up for trial and they were condemned and burned (zapped with special ray equipment). I killed the baby because I thought it was not my child. I wanted to go back home so I went to see the captain who was in charge of all the spacecraft men and who knew where the ship was going. I asked for the spaceship to be turned around and he said "No." I went mad and killed the captain with my hands and broke up his body. Next I went into the main hall and pressed a button to ring the bell for assembly. I asked for votes on turning back the spaceship for home. Sixty-five percent said "Yes." As I was talking to the crew members I felt a gun at the back of my body and I was led off by officers along the corridor. I was screaming and

---

2. **brothels:** houses of prostitution.

struggling as I did not want to go to the zap machine (a ray gun to destroy bodies).

However, I arrived and my body was held against the wall by clamps, hands were outstretched against the wall. This wall was made of special ray-deflecting material about a yard to two yards thick. I felt the warmth of the ray until it grew so bad that I left the body. As soon as the head had been burned off, the clamps were automatically opened and the body fell in a trench in the floor—arms outstretched. A large trap door made of metal was slammed on my arms cutting them off. The arms were swept into the trench when the trap door was lifted up again. As it slammed tight again, my body fell into a space container and was thrown outside by tremendous pressure. A space coffin had its own power to fall away from the ship.

That is all I remember for this was written by me ten days after I found out most of the story. The story is still disjointed so one day I hope to recall the whole story of my life in that incident.

Case 5

Preclear's Report

Former Condition

Inclined to be anxious about others and not asserting myself enough.

Mental Outlook

Much less anxious and more willing to accept even unpleasant situations as they are. More outspoken and less afraid of the disapproval of others.

Physical Improvement

My back is more able to resist a temptation to droop and ache with long sitting. I seem to need less sleep. Head is freed from a pressure.

What You Attribute Improvement To

To simply contacting past life and present life incidents and simply scanning them.

The Engram

I had the heaviest meter reaction on a space incident 78,000,000,000,000 years ago, 2,000,000,000,000 years further than

I had ever heard existed and this was not encouraging. So much of it was so fantastic that it seemed like dub-in but I am pretty sure now that the incidents were, in the main, real.

There was a fantastic space factory with gold animals hanging concentrically[1] from it all around, mainly elephants and zebras, by the necks. These appeared solid but periodically imploded[2] or exploded. There was no gravity even near planets. Inside were four great bronze grinding wheels. During the incident, I look at time both ways as well as seeing it as a kind of circle from outside time. Therefore, it is hard to say whether discs were ground up and made into small animals (which I think was the case) or whether animals were compressed into discs. I think the animals were subsequently inflated after blowing up through a totem[3] and a cat devil and then broadcast (via the outside animals?) to other planets.

This was so fantastic I was unwilling to run it and considered it dub-in. The main and most awful part, and the most impenetrable, of the incident was the feeling of waiting and counting thirty to press a button. What was to happen then was uncertain. Either I was to blow up a planet, had blown one up or failed to prevent it from being blown up. For this I felt I was punished by a bearded priest to whom I was betrayed by colleagues, by being compelled to work the grinder. There was also, toward the end, the stronger idea that all this appeared to happen in a robot body.

The incident was so heavy and so confused that a lighter

---

1. **concentrically:** arranged so as to have a common center, such as circles one within another.

2. **imploded:** burst inward.

3. **totem:** a representation of a natural object or an animate being, as an animal or bird, serving as the distinctive mark of a clan or group.

process had to be run. During this, which lasted the remainder of the course, many lighter incidents were scanned such as Chinese tortures, meeting Christ, a crucifixion, a heart operation, a hanging, rape and attempted murder. All of these, and especially an arrow in the eye and the death of a pope, a Carthusian,[4] and a girl were extremely real, but I was not sure they had happened to me, because incidents run from this present body's lifetime proved to appear, to my astonishment, less real than any of the above mentioned. This may be because of drugs I have previously taken, since the face of a person known intimately to me in this life appeared less real than all these earlier incidents.

---

4. **Carthusian:** a monk or nun of a very strict order founded at Chartreuse, France, in 1084.

Case 6

Preclear's Report

Former Condition

Scared of looking at any past life time track[1] and of taking responsibility for the game of life on a *knowing level*, letting past failures on the track sidestep me into a lot of phenomena and mystery, allowing it to overwhelm me.

Mental Outlook

Reality on what an engram is and how it takes control of you when in actual restimulation, and what the mind is capable of doing when in restimulation with an engram. Also more confident in confronting a person's reactive mind,[2] and not letting it overwhelm me to the extent of communicating to it instead of to the individual himself.

---

1. **time track:** the consecutive record of mental image pictures which accumulate through a person's life or lives. It is very exactly dated. The *time track* is the entire sequence of "now" incidents, complete with all sense messages, picked up by a person during his whole existence.

2. **reactive mind:** that portion of a person's mind which works on a totally stimulus-response basis, which is not under his volitional control and which exerts force and the power of command over his awareness, purposes, thoughts, body and actions. The *reactive mind* is where engrams are stored.

Physical Improvement

Much lighter and more vitality.

What You Attribute Improvement To

With having confronted the pasts of myself and lots of other people, and not just certain parts but the bad and good as well. Getting the actuality and distortions of an engram, getting an idea of what the thetan[3] uses for souvenirs of a life experience. Also to three good instructors who like the captain on his bridge would keep it on a straight course somehow no matter what's ahead.

The Engram

It all started on a planet of perfection 1,600 years ago. By that I mean everything was orderly and routine. My part on this planet was a sort of engineer in a big powerhouse[4] that supplied the energy by means of beams to feed the machines that were in use for the welfare of the people.

One of these machines being a sort of god, it being the big boss giving us our orders by the use of a beam. And no man having the right to originate a thought, other than a copy of what the big boss (machine) says.

Anyway, something goes wrong with the powerhouse and the machine doesn't get enough energy, and the people put

---

3. **thetan:** the person himself—not his body or his name, the physical universe, his mind, or anything else; that which is aware of being aware; the identity which is the individual. The term was coined to eliminate any possible confusion with older, invalid concepts. It comes from the Greek letter Theta (θ), which the Greeks used to represent *thought* or perhaps *spirit*, to which an n is added to make a noun in the modern style used to create words in engineering. It is also θ^n, or "theta to the nth degree," meaning unlimited or vast.

4. **powerhouse:** a building where electric power is generated.

the blame on me, and give me a dose of this energy which is shot through a kind of pistol; this puts me out for the count.[5] I am then transferred to a space station where I am left to look after things. No one returns to the space station, and eventually everything breaks up through the lack of this energy to keep it together. And my body breaks up into bits and pieces, having no energy to feed it with, the spaceship not having returned with the supplies needed to create this energy.

5. **out for the count:** knocked unconscious. Comes from boxing, where when one of the opponents is knocked down during a match, the referee counts aloud the seconds from 1 to 10. If the boxer stays down for the count of 10, he is declared defeated.

Case 7

Preclear's Report

Former Condition

I had insufficient subjective reality on mental image pictures and insufficient understanding of others and their subjective realities. I had a fear, but did not know what the fear was, nor had I recognized it as a fear. Sometimes I seemed to be cruel, other times I was kind and gentle, and yet thirdly I felt I was being victimized and "others" were "doing it to me."

Mental Outlook

Correction of the above statement on realities. I'm more easily able to have a grief charge.[1] Am now more able to audit despite my own condition. I recognized I had a fear, now I couldn't care less. No longer scared, even though the reason for the fear is still unknown. I found out that these states were all three in the engram. I am now able to be myself much more and can recognize any of the three states. I feel more stable.

---

1. **grief charge:** an outburst of tears that may continue for a considerable time, in a session, after which the preclear feels greatly relieved. This is occasioned by the discharge of grief or painful emotion.

Physical Improvement

I'm much more capable in intercourse and ability to experience pleasure from the company of my wife. Body generally more relaxed. Hair and fingernails seem to be growing faster.

What You Attribute Improvement To

Confronting and handling my mind (i.e., pictures) and the discovery of an incident which when discovered had all the symptoms of my hitherto "present" disabilities that I was "aware" of (though not aware of them to the degree of being able to discuss them or verbalize them to myself). This takes into consideration that the mere fact of being partially aware of what might be in the incident has caused these improvements.

The Engram

This incident started off with a door that was shut and I was looking at it as if hypnotized by it. Nothing else occurred. After working around this door for some time and nothing happening, I then began to get some vague impressions of other things such as a woods and the fact that I was a burglar and that I had burgled this house. After this a facsimile[2] of a little girl turned up. She seemed to have a knife wound in her chest and I was convinced that I had murdered her. After finding this out I then had the idea that I was by the door ready to make a break for freedom but that I heard a carriage coming to the door. I then began to experience fear.

My auditor made me go over this again and again, taking pieces and going over them. As this was occurring various other things began to show up and fill in until in the end, I

---

2. **facsimile:** a three-dimensional color picture with sound and smell and all other perceptions, plus the conclusions or speculations of the individual. *See also* **mental image picture** in the glossary.

discovered several things which had their counterpart in my present life. During the recounting of these present life things to my auditor, another as yet unmentioned and unexplained incident in present life came to mind, and immediately I was filled with petrifying horror which within seconds became a violent grief charge. This was a grief that I had never before experienced. Not only was my body crying and weak with no strength, but I was crying with anguish in every part of me, for I had found out that the thing behind the door that I was afraid of was my daughter's body as it was thrown into the hall of my house.

After what seemed an eternity, I was able to tell my auditor about this realization and a lot more besides. It would seem that I had been a statesman and that I had been "under pressure" to prevent a humane law from being passed. I had refused and this was a method of retaliation. After my daughter's body was thrown in through the front door I went into the lounge where I was beset by some people, whom I presumed to be a stepbrother, some brothers or friends and a woman who was either my wife or my sister, who were blaming me for my child's death. Overwrought, I am next in a woods, crying. I have found what seems to be a white mist floating before my eyes and a feeling of the most abject helplessness and that life doesn't matter anymore. The next thing I know is that I have the idea I have committed suicide and then that I seem to be a long way above the scene of the corpse and the house.

I was all set with this engram but, on checking this over with my auditor, I found that in truth I was not sure that this man hanging from a tree was me. After this I went into a confusion. Later, when I came out of this confusion I seemed to have collected more data. The engram still seemed more or less the same except that I was a girl and that I was being chased by an intruder who caught me in the lounge and raped me and beat me. Then I seemed to see this from a man's view and the man was being tortured and forced to watch the girl being tortured. After this there was more confusion, I seemed to go unconscious, and my body was heavy and seemed to be devoid of any energy. The main thing I could see was a white rug. When I looked at the rug I seemed to spin, and pictures that made no sense appeared and blotted out the rug. Eventually I was able to look at the rug. When I did I found out that I was to all intents and purposes the girl being beaten. I had all the pain of being beaten, and then miraculously I seemed to be the man with all the pain of having my wrists and hands tortured. Being the man I would then feel very dizzy and end up being the girl.

This went on for some time. Afterwards, in order to stabilize things, we scouted[3] earlier and found I had recall of being a girl in France and coming to England, ending up by coming to this house to meet a brother or lover, and being tortured by some people to reveal my brother's (or lover's) location. By this time, unfortunately, time was running short. On the last day everything seemed to be unreal. I recognized all the parts of the incident as present life things—the fireplace, settee, rugs, etc., as coming from a friend's house; the paneling of the walls from a re-creation of an old English house I had seen in a museum, and so on.

This is how the engram has ended for the moment. However, so many things in it that have appeared in my daily life which have never before had an explanation or seemed

---

3. **scouted:** sought, searched for. In doing a meter *scout*, the E-Meter is used to search out areas of charge.

reasonable, now seem to fit. What is more, though in the past I could not handle these things, now I can to quite some degree. I now look forward to really clearing up this engram and being able to fully handle my life in the way in which I want to handle it.

Case 8

Preclear's Report

Former Condition

I did not feel too bad. However, fairly uncertain and sometimes a little obsessive in communication about some subjects concerning present affairs.

Mental Outlook

I am more confident in learning. I was never good in learning verse; this has improved as I can now remember the new processes much better. The ability to apply these has, however, increased many fold.

Physical Improvement

Less stomach pain—next to nil.[1] Fewer somatics.[2]

---

1. **nil:** nothing.

2. **somatics:** physical pains or discomforts of any kind, especially painful or uncomfortable physical perceptions stemming from the reactive mind. *Somatic* means, actually, "bodily" or "physical." Because the word *pain* is restimulative, and because the word *pain* has in the past led to a confusion between physical pain and mental pain, the word *somatic* is used in Dianetics and Scientology to denote physical pain or discomfort of any kind.

What You Attribute Improvement To

Tips and hints received during the lectures, mainly the ones teaching how to handle people and banks.[3] The demonstration sessions which gave me more understanding of how to relax during processing. The processing before the engram was run eased off some effort.

The Engram

The incident was located on the E-Meter and had happened 3,225 years ago. I was positioned in North Africa near the coast. I was the leader of that sector of the Roman army. There were only five such sectors in existence, reaching round the coast to Europe.

The chief leader is always the first one to go anywhere danger is present and also where danger might be present. He is the first volunteer. At a distance of three days' marching time from the major camp to the east along the coast was a small outpost for communication and observation purposes. A nice looking well-built stone cave plus an enormous tropical tree were the major points of that outpost. There was a small outlook basket on the top of that tree from which messages were conveyed during sunrise and sunset.

This outpost had been found not working. I took off with fifty men to examine the breakdown. At arrival three men entered the cave and did not come out again. I stopped any further actions in that direction. With the aid of a rope tied around that huge tree I managed to work myself in a circular motion to the top of it. I discovered that the basket was vacant.

---

3. **banks:** mental image picture collections of the preclear—the reactive mind. It comes from computer terminology where all data is in a "bank." *See also* **reactive mind** in the glossary.

As it was early morning, I acted as a signalman, transferring all the messages and adding my own. Then I climbed down. Later I gave the highest ranked person the command to take the men to camp. After they left I worked myself through some very high grass at the back of the cave toward the near native village. I made a jump on my spear into the grass to avoid traces. It was hot and hard work. When I arrived at the village I found it empty. I hurried to the cave now on the usual pathway. However, I stopped at the side of the cave cautiously in the high grass and waited for a few hours. During that wait my chest started to ache.

I decided to have a look inside without being seen from the inside by looking through some grass on the side of the entrance to the cave. I inhaled some very sharp powdery smell, which had a floral odor and gave an acid taste in my mouth. I saw a white circular object in the passage of the cave. I leaned back and felt very weak, giddy and got a headache. My chest hurt very badly, I started coughing and sank to the ground. At that moment I left my body. After twenty minutes the whole body was burned up, turned black and vanished. There was only the breastplate left on the ground. I was very disappointed and sorry that this should have happened to me. I scanned the district and lessened the loss by the idea that the breastplate would be a warning to my people which meant that a part of my mission had been carried out by me. There was no other regret present. After this I left that place.

Case 9

Preclear's Report

Former Condition

Body somatics in left side of chest. Headaches seemingly originating from right side.

Physical Improvement

I still have some somatics but running the engram has reduced them.

The Engram

The incident that has been run on me is one that started with the feeling of falling. The feeling itself was very real and after the actual fall the reality of anything else tapered off. I was falling through space and fell onto some barren rocky surface.

We again went over this and after a few times all of a sudden a hole appeared in the ground which had a tremendous suction power. I went down this hole at tremendous speed and after awhile something (unidentifiable at this stage) bashed into me. I experienced a real urge to pull back very fast from it but couldn't do so. After that experience I had the impression of being in a calm wide space.

Now, as one obviously falls from somewhere, I looked around and had the idea it could have been a spaceship from which I had fallen. This time (and here things were only concepts and ideas of possibilities) I had the idea of being pushed and falling to the rough rocky surface. On being questioned what was on the rock, some ideas of lizards, etc., came up but these later on fell away. I also then had an idea of me having a catlike body, although still retaining abilities to think and decide, etc.

After going over this a few times we backtracked past the spaceship to some strange place where none of the buildings had windows and were apparently made of some metal which was smooth all over like a cement covering or skin. Here apparently I was (now) a mountain lion and got captured. A gas was released in my cage which made me quiet and I was given as a pet to a woman who was eventually aboard this spaceship. She took me into her room. I lay down next to the bed and she, taking a drug of sorts, lay on the bed. However, she died and I was dragged out and thrown from the ship.

This part of the incident, however, became lost again as we went through the pattern again. The next time it appears I was in the spaceship's observation room at the top. I pressed a button for an astral[1] dome to go up to take some visual navigational checks and a meteorite smashed the dome. As the ship was pressurized I, along with all the other loose things, including a few other guys, was sucked out of the hole at the top into space. All of a sudden, down from my right, I had the impression of something big coming at fantastic speed. It later transpired this was a large meteorite which slammed into me and carted me off at a mere 500,000 miles per hour. I then had the idea I was sitting atop it and my body

---

1. **astral:** of or relating to the stars.

was stuck on its lower edge. After a while I decided it was no good hanging onto things and slid off, letting it disappear. I was next back at the spaceship and after again deciding it was no good hanging around, went "down" and found a maternity home on another planet and got myself another newborn body.

Some of the details of the incident have since changed but the last coverage is still the same. It appears I was navigation officer aboard that ship and while sleeping the alarm bells rang. I jumped up and ran into the main control and plotting[2] room, found out we were off course and close to a meteorite stream. I ran upstairs and the rest was the same as before.

2. **plotting:** marking the position or course of (a ship, etc.) on a map.

Case 10

Preclear's Report

Former Condition

No reality on past lives. Good health—no somatics.

Mental Outlook

I can think constructively—envisage scenes of great variance without refusing to look. I now know that by looking I can resolve my difficulties and by confronting attain to[1] a beingness[2] of my own.

Physical Improvement

Smell keener and most likely improved the body's tolerance to radiation.

What You Attribute Improvement To

Realization of a past track. Encouragement and success in being able to look at possibilities of past happenings and to confront the weirdness of same, the confusion, and absence of

---

1. **attain to:** to succeed in reaching or coming to.

2. **beingness:** the assumption or choosing of a category of identity. Beingness is assumed by oneself or given to oneself or is attained. Examples of beingness would be one's own name, one's profession, one's physical characteristics, one's role in a game—each and all of these could be called one's beingness.

---

direction in them. Glimmerings of understanding regarding confronting and creativity and some better ability to do both, from running the command "What part of that incident can you confront." I mainly owe my cognitions[3] to the fact of confronting, the many outcomes of confronting and to my auditor who confronted me sufficiently for me to do the process.

The Engram

Incident 55,000,000,000,000,000,000,000 years ago. There is not good enough perception in this to be certain of what happened. I was in the sea and had thoughts only for manta rays,[4] and for a long time in running this felt I was probably a manta ray. We went earlier and I was in a flying saucer over the ocean, a man and a woman were evidently my companions. I fell into the sea after suffering some ailment, maybe radiation, and was frightened out of my wits by a manta ray.

Later it seemed I was on land in an atomic war and could smell what seemed like the smell of death or burning bodies. Pictures of absolute chaos with people terribly burned asking for help and to be put out of their misery quickly. Roads completely blocked—no communication anywhere and a migration of people to the coasts where they lived on raw fish and bathed in the salty water.

Auditor's Report

Located the incident with the command "Have you ever

---

3. **cognitions:** new realizations of life. They result in higher degrees of awareness and consequently greater abilities to succeed with one's endeavors in life. A cognition is a "What do you know, I . . ." statement.

4. **manta rays:** large fish having a broad flat body with both eyes on top, wide fins which are horn-like when rolled up and a slender or whiplike tail.

died?" The E-Meter needle[5] dropped.[6] "Was it more than 100 years ago?" Needle dropped. "More than 1,000 years ago?" Needle dropped. "More than 1,000,000 years ago?" Needle dropped. Carried on like this and finally located it at 55,000,-000,000,000,000,000 years ago.

"Be in that incident." "What part of that incident can you confront?" and we were away. First picture that came was of the sea, great deal of unreality but by discussion and continuing the question "What part of that incident can you confront?" various other pictures and sensations uncovered which eventually added up to a section of the incident concerning a giant manta ray type of aquatic creature which the preclear had seen while underwater. Had been killed by the manta ray and had then assumed the identity of the manta ray. What had happened before and after this was hidden for a good while. In searching the area previous to the sea incident, a picture of a flying-saucer type of spaceship brought a marked drop on the E-Meter. Investigated this further to find that the engram started on this spaceship. The ship had needed an outside repair. On going outside, the preclear had been hit by a meteorite particle which had not punctured the suit. At this point an acute pain, under the arm where the meteor had struck, occurred. The pc[7] clambers back into the spaceship. Later the atomic engines of the ship break down and the pc has to repair these and apparently receives radioactive burns. He finds that he has to leave the ship and so falls from a ladder into the sea where he encounters the manta ray.

5. **needle:** a slender rod with a pointed end which is used as the indicator on an E-Meter dial, such as the type of indicator often seen on the dial of an electronic instrument. *See also* **E-Meter** in the glossary.

6. **dropped:** fell to the right. When an E-Meter needle drops, it is an indication that an area of charge has been located.

7. **pc:** abbreviation for **preclear.** *See* **preclear** in the glossary.

Case 11

Preclear's Report

Former Condition

I sometimes took instant dislike to people—and didn't know why. Also there were certain types of people I didn't like talking to.

Mental Outlook

Feel lighter, better able to communicate, more able to realize what I am thinking and feeling, and when this is not optimum, to do something about it.

Physical Improvement

Feel wider awake and more able to have my attention on what I am doing. Had a nosebleed after discussing a punch on the nose, and my nose felt less blocked afterwards.

What You Attribute Improvement To

Realized that someone I know who made me curl up inside when he spoke to me was like the villain in my engram—as soon as I realized this the condition vanished, and I spoke to him at the first opportunity, feeling very friendly toward him. Feel lighter as if a big weight has been lifted from my mind—just by having taken a look at what was there all the time.

Auditor's Report

Preclear a young girl of twenty-four, student. The incident was located by using an E-Meter, asking for a previous death and by questioning on how long ago, pinning it to 6,254 years ago. On asking what happened then, the pc had a violent twitching in the left leg and saw a mental picture of a male body on a slab with the left leg moving slightly.

Further questioning on the earlier events leading up to this brought out the following story:

The preclear was a carpenter, aged about thirty-five when the story began, had been married for twelve years and had three children. He never earned enough money and was constantly reproached[1] by the wife for this. Close by lived a man (about forty) who was always prosperous but rarely seemed to work, who habitually "dropped in" to the workshop and hinted at easier ways of earning money. After a quarrel with his wife one afternoon, the carpenter poured his troubles out to the neighbor who suggested he meet a woman friend who would provide some solace. He arranged for the carpenter to visit the woman the same night. She became his mistress and over the next six years he was alternately happy and frustrated—there was still never enough money. The woman became more shrewish[2] and demanding and eventually he wished to break off the association. She demanded a large

---

1. **reproached:** accused of and blamed for a fault so as to make feel ashamed.
2. **shrewish:** like a nagging, bad-tempered woman.

sum of money on the threat to tell his wife the whole story. The "friend," hearing of this, offers an easy way of getting the money and arranges a meeting for the carpenter with a man who wants a small job of "acquiring" an official document done. Two days later the carpenter meets this man in the marketplace (a tall, thin man about fifty-five years) and is told to go to a certain street on a certain night about a week later, watch for a man coming out of a house and get from him some papers in a leather pouch, hidden under his robe.

The carpenter keeps the assignment, attacks the man, but the man manages to cry out. In panic the carpenter kills him, takes the papers and runs back to the appointed place—a spot outside the town (a cave). He delivers the papers but is refused the money by the man who employed him (several people were in the cave—presumably the political group involved). He returns to his mistress's house—a quarrel ensues because he doesn't have the money. He nearly strangles her then goes to his own home in despair.

A week later officials arrive at his workshop to arrest him and he is taken away for questioning. The woman, who betrayed him out of spite, now identifies him. He confesses to the murder, but the officials are more concerned about the papers—who did he give them to? He has never been told the names of the group involved or the purpose of the papers and can only protest that he doesn't know. Interrogation continues with beating and periods of solitary confinement. During this his wife and children are brought in and one by one killed as he continues to say he doesn't know who employed him. Eventually his eyes are burned out with a hot iron brand[3]—then his body stretched on a rack and placed on the

---

3. **brand:** a metal rod heated and used for branding.

marble slab where it dies. The last sign of life is the twitching of the left leg.

Auditing of the Engram

Period of incident—three weeks. Events leading up to it covered six years.

This incident was difficult to enter as questioning of any kind was very restimulative to the pc. Her whole body became stiff and nervous and the eyes flinched constantly.

It was opened up by questioning on the early track of the lifetime, before any pain was encountered. Much secrecy (on the mistress and the arrangements with the political group) had to be uncovered before these terminals showed up and became real. Repetitive work on the two main people to whom she had assigned blame for the series of painful events (the man who introduced him to the woman and this woman who became his mistress) brought up the data on the sequence of events over six years—leading to torture and death.

The latter part of the incident has not yet been reexperienced—merely told in a flat, apathetic tone. The early part produced changes of emotion and some reexperiencing of slight somatics (e.g. the strangling episode with the mistress, the fight with the man when stealing the papers). The handling of the man who originally subverted[4] the pc, and who was assigned main cause, brought on aching and sharp somatics in all parts of the body—mainly stomach, legs, arms and neck, and dark circles appeared under the eyes (presumably the burning out of the eyes beginning to get more real).

---

4. **subverted:** made weaker or corrupted, as in morals.

The incident has been covered on "confront" fairly well up to the point of the interrogation. The latter part needs much more auditing and should be easier to get into when the interrogation with its repeated "I don't know" postulate is thoroughly run.

The incident may take place in Babylon.[5] Long, mostly white, loose robes and sandals are worn. Male personnel are dark and bearded with longish hair. Poorer quarter of the town has rough stone buildings—doorways but no doors.

A ring worn by the main villain was very upsetting, emotionally and physically, to the preclear. Pc has had a great antipathy[6] to rings with jewels in them in this lifetime and to dark, bearded men. Both these manifestations have now disappeared already.

Should need about 15-20 hours to complete.

---

5. **Babylon:** the capital of an ancient empire called Babylonia which was located in southwest Asia and flourished from 2100–538 B.C.

6. **antipathy:** a strong dislike.

Case 12

Preclear's Report

Former Condition

I was in capable condition but still tending occasionally to have unreasoning fears of certain persons and objects, occasional headaches (not so many as before earlier auditing), and a considerable occlusion[1] of any past life track, a tendency sometimes to be over-withdrawn and uncertainty on my personal worth and place in life.

Mental Outlook

Happy beginnings of confidence in having a true place in life. No psychosomatics.

Physical Improvement

Difficult to state at this stage, I have always been proud of being healthy. If I grow my hair and diminish my waistline a bit as a result of running this engram (a possibility) *I call that* physical improvement.

---

1. **occlusion:** the state of something being hidden or forgotten and not available for conscious recall.

What You Attribute Improvement To

Locating of personnel found in engram and their various significances, exhaustion of pain in the incident and the looking at a thoroughly comprehensible, if complex, story that is real to me and that I know occurred to me. Dignity recovered by realizing that it isn't true that the only lives we've led are degrading to one's personality. That life was a pretty excellent example of worthwhile living, ended only by overwhelming forces.

Auditor's Report

The engram was located by requesting from the preclear the date of a past death on a snap of the fingers. The date was checked on the E-Meter, as was further information to the effect that the incident (death) occurred during a naval battle aboard a British man-of-war.[2] The preclear considered himself to be a naval officer of high rank (perhaps Lord Nelson[3]).

The preclear was requested to return to the incident. He got a picture of a naval battle and was asked, "What part of that incident can you confront?" As the picture became more real, the preclear identified himself with a person in the incident and experienced the feelings and emotions of the person he had identified himself with. The command was used repeatedly throughout the first part of the therapy. First the preclear identified himself as the officer in charge of the ship (Lord Nelson) but after several hours this identity became unreal and the preclear identified himself in turn as another

2. **man-of-war:** an armed naval vessel; warship.

3. **Lord Nelson:** Horatio Nelson (1758–1805), English admiral. Nelson was most famous for his naval victory over a combined French and Spanish fleet at Cape Trafalgar, off the southwest coast of Spain.

officer, a marine,[4] and finally as a small boy attending one of the guns.

At this stage the story (it was related with much coincident pain) was that he was helping on one of the guns during a naval engagement, when the gun was dislodged by enemy fire. He attempted to flee but was brought back by the marine who proceeded to assault him with great ferocity. His head and chest were stove in[5] by a musket butt and the preclear was killed to the accompaniment of "you stay here," which explained the preclear's violent dislike of naval officers, particularly marines, in his current life. The body was then sewn up in sailcloth and the next day buried at sea.

The story gradually changed and expanded: a new consideration[6] that the marine was not really cruel, but only doing what he considered to be his duty and not being completely responsible for preclear's death. Preclear next discovered that he was killed in the explosion of a cannon which warranted his injuries. He passed through a period of unconsciousness and pain. The explosion brought complete unreality to the incident, which persisted until the preclear picked up decisions that he made during the explosion that "everything was unreal." When this was picked up and run through, reality returned. The story was now that the preclear was assisting on a gun when an enemy shot caused an explosion, which wrecked the cannon and severely injured the preclear. The preclear was picked up by the marine, who carried him to a safe spot where the preclear died. I now noticed that the preclear had assumed a rigid position during the auditing session. Searching round and round, the preclear had found

4. **marine:** member of a military force at sea.

5. **stove in:** broken or crushed inward.

6. **consideration:** a thought or belief about something.

the spot he had been placed in by the marine so comfortable that, after the confusion of the explosion, he had decided to "stay right here and never move again." When this was picked up the preclear resumed normal sitting position. Other stuck points located were where the preclear struck the deck after explosion, on the cannon which had hit the preclear and on the deck after death. Each of these were located and run out, thereby freeing preclear from the incident.

About this time the preclear became very angry and antagonistic but when angry and antagonistic parts of the incident were handled, these emotions disappeared. More information continued to come up. The stuck point after death was released by locating the decision of the preclear that he had not completed his life and therefore could not leave. He explained this as "I seem to be like a little ball of Saint Elmo's fire[7] floating in the air but when I made the decision I settled gently onto the deck and stuck there." Another point that really stuck occurred when the preclear considered, when he had been overwhelmed by the cannon, that it was good to be a cannon. At this point preclear straightened out into a good imitation of a cannon. Throughout the running of the incident the preclear had periods when "it was a bit unreal" and had to be nursed through these to increase reality.

The final story of this life which began in 1790 and ended in 1804, was that the preclear was born to French aristocrats and at the age of three was smuggled from that country to England. Both parents died in France. At about nine years of age he returned to take over his father's estates, which had been managed during his absence by a half-brother of his

---

7. **Saint Elmo's fire:** a visible electric discharge from charged, especially pointed, objects, as the tips of masts, spires, trees, etc.: seen sometimes during electrical storms. After Saint Elmo, patron saint of sailors.

---

father's. The preclear's uncle, who had grown fat on the income from the estate, was not pleased to see the preclear return, more especially as the preclear treated him with contempt. Further reason for the uncle's dislike of the preclear lay in the fact that he was a rejected lover of the preclear's mother. The uncle decided to be finally rid of the preclear, and had him taken aboard a British man-of-war as a cabin boy. The preclear's duty was to keep the deck about the cannons wet during action and whenever a cannon was fired. On one particular evening he was bringing these buckets of water in preparation for the firing of the evening cannon. He was abused by the bosun,[8] and running from him, tripped and fell into the rear of the cannon at the moment of firing. His ribs and chest stove in and he died in a few minutes. His body was buried at sea next day and his last view of the ship was from an immense height from clouds above the ship which appeared as a white speck in the blue of the sea.

At the end of the auditing the preclear had excellent reality on past lives.

---

8. **bosun:** a ship's petty officer in charge of rigging, boats, anchors, etc.

Case 13

Preclear's Report

Former Condition

Happy and fit. Tendency to be confused over directions and confused in thoughts. Unwillingness to control others. Unwillingness to use force.

Mental Outlook

More reality on my mental state. Feeling happier about my ability to control confusion. More willing to use force. A better understanding of responsibility. More reality on past lives and myself as a spirit.

Physical Improvement

No additional change, in generally good physical condition.

What You Attribute Improvement To

Finding out about the confusion mechanism and finding out how willing I was to be responsible for causing havoc.

Auditor's Report

The auditor contacted several engrams, but on final recheck the engram with the most charge was one not previously contacted which appeared by chance and was ready to be run. The pc had lost a robot body 468 million years ago. During the first five hours running, the pc was coaxed to look further back at how he obtained the body. He had at first a stick body on Mars, and later he decided it was a doll's body. Some parts of the incident were dub-in, but even some of this, reshuffled, fitted into the final form, only slightly modified.

The story, as near final as possible, runs as follows: The preclear was on Mars without a body 469,476,600 years ago, creating havoc, destroying a bridge and buildings. The people were called by an alarm to a temple. The pc went and broke the back pew, and the temple tower. He wandered into town and saw a doll in a window, and got entrapped trying to move its limbs. People seized it, beat it up, and threw the doll out of the window (thirty-foot drop). The doll was taken roughly to the temple, and was zapped by a bishop's gun while the congregation chanted "God is love." When the people left, the doll, out of control, staggered out and was run over by a large car and a steamroller. It was then taken back to the bishop, who ordered it to be taken (in a truck with others) to dig trenches or ditches for 2,000 years. (The whole incident took nearly 2,000,000 years.) Then it was taken and the body was removed and the pc was promised a robot body. The thetan (pc) went up to an implant station[1] and was put into an ice cube and went by flying saucer and was dropped at Planet ZX 432. He was drawn to a building by an emanator.[2] Pc was interiorized[3] by spinning and confusion into a dummy training and indoctrination robot body. In some way not very clear, a

---

1. **implant station:** a place or installation in which implants were administered. *See also* **implant** in the glossary.

2. **emanator:** a large, glowing body of radioactive material which hangs magically in thin air, a sort of a god, an all-knower. Its outpulse puts one into a trance.

3. **interiorized:** went into something too fixedly, and became part of it too fixedly.

transfer was made to another robot body and the pc was told to look after it forever. It reported to a village (after a doubtful encounter with a giant, and heatstroke) and was set to supervise unloading of saucers. It zapped and killed another robot and the pc took over its body to prove it could work. The pc was punished in the first robot body in a saucer and shipped off. The saucer exploded en route and the body of the robot was in space falling in two parts with pc vainly endeavoring to take care of it and the second body. This was sucked down by departure of a saucer into water in a dock. Divers brought it up, but the pc left it, he thinks, to attend the other body.

There were other less real incidents of space stations and zapping and many engram command phrases. On final recount it came out the pc threw the doll out of the window (only fifteen feet) and got stuck, then was beaten up on the ground. There were body jerks and head throwing at intervals throughout processing, and eye fluttering. During the fall of the doll the body and head jerks were much more violent.

Case 14

Preclear's Report

Former Condition

Although the amount of chronic dispersal in my mental makeup is not particularly bad, it is still the biggest block on my mental efficiency, whether it's momentarily increased or at its chronic level. This is how it seems to me and it corresponds with the personality assessment of the Oxford Capacity Analysis,[1] nine traits of which are rated high and one lower, the latter being related to dispersal.

Mental Outlook

Optimism; persistence; logical; not easily pleased by poor standards; happy; sociable; a strong urge to survive and improve; and strongly ethical.

Physical Improvement

None. Mental improvement—less dispersed.

---

1. **Oxford Capacity Analysis:** a test which consists of 200 questions which measure personality traits. These tests are used to evaluate preclear gains.

The Engram

I did exercises in confronting logically produced imaginary pictures and in confronting nonsequitur[2] mental pictures, some consciously produced, some not. There were present life memories, imaginary, and others, which subjectively (to me) were imaginary but produced unusual and unprecedented (for me) needle actions and readings on the E-Meter. The picture producing the most phenomenal E-Meter effects was one of a machine, boxlike, with proportions of one wide, three high and four in length roughly. Approximate height was twenty inches. Two circular apertures were on the front at a guess.

Other pictures included tigers, gladiators, blackness, stars, interior scenes of a spaceship, a green humanoid with a trunklike proboscis,[3] who seemed to have some connection with the above-mentioned machine, the planet Venus, a damp room lit by a dim, diffused green light and a web-footed female. I get the impression, or imagine, I'm strapped to a chair in the damp room, to my front left is a table upon which is this ray machine. Seated at the table is the green humanoid. Originally I saw only the machine.

There were two things I could definitely subjectively differentiate from imagination. One was the bodily pains that frequently occurred, one of which was a mild pain in the little and third finger of the left hand. The other thing was also something over which I had no control, no starting, changing or stopping. It was a few seconds long, a mental picture, a fast fluttering lightness and darkness effect in the shape of a square, usually, but once like an expanding beam directed at

2. **nonsequitur:** something that has no bearing on what previously occurred or does not follow logically from what comes before it. From Latin, meaning "it does not follow."

3. **proboscis:** a long flexible snout, as an elephant's trunk.

me. I had experienced this occasionally during the previous three and a half years—in a dark room at night, my head under the blankets, my eyelids shut tight with both hands over my eyes—and yet I had seen it, so it certainly wasn't my eyelids fluttering.

Case 15

Preclear's Report

Former Condition

I had an inability to concentrate, an unwillingness to accept other people's ideas, and a reluctance to be effect.[1] I also had difficulty confronting.

Mental Outlook

I feel better able to handle people. I enjoy confronting people. I have more definite plans for the future. Less concern, if any, what others will think.

Physical Improvement

Eyes in better condition. Better control of body.

What You Attribute Improvement To

Increased ability to hold and confront pictures. Cognitions concerning time. Realization that I had been expecting to see

---

1. **effect:** the receipt point of a flow (thought, energy or action). For example: If one considers a river flowing to the sea, the place where it began would be the source-point or cause, and the place where it went into the sea would be the effect-point, and the sea would be the effect of the river. A man firing a gun is cause; a man receiving a bullet is effect.

myself. Willingness to accept what other people say, irrespective of believing it. Better understanding of other people's universes.[2]

Auditor's Report

The incident with the biggest drop (greatest stress) located on the E-Meter was 1 million, 15 thousand, 550 years ago. It took place on another planet. Pc had no reality on the incident at first and then found he was a space pilot with a robot body. Something went wrong and his body burnt out. He found this out under my direction by looking at impressions which later turned into 3D pictures. Of course, at first he said, "There's nothing there, I could look at the incident if there was an incident there, but there's not."

From the robot body being burnt out, I asked him what he did next, (of course, now he was without a body) and found from him and with the help of the E-Meter that he saw something in the distance bright and glittering, liked the look of it and went to see what it was. When he wanted to leave he found he couldn't, for he felt sort of pulled into the "trap." Then he found himself being twisted round and round very fast, so fast that he was extremely confused and his present body, as I was working with him, was also twisting and turning. We found that the purpose of the trap was to make him "forget everything." On working with him on this part of the incident he was extremely unwilling at first to reexperience and look at this trap. A point of interest here, pc's unhappiest time in present life was when he was doing a job connected

---

2. **universes:** whole systems of created things. The universes are three in number. The first of these is one's own universe. The second would be the material universe, which is the universe of matter, energy, space and time, which is the common meeting ground of all of us. The third is actually a class of universes—the universe of every other person.

with diamonds and he felt he "could not get away" just as he "could not get away" from the glitter around the trap which pulled him into it. Apparently the diamonds restimulated the feeling of being "trapped." The next thing I found was that pictures began flying around in the trap covering the location where the incident took place—this phenomena is technically called a "grouper" and it is something, usually an object, that pulls things into it rather like a vacuum cleaner does with dust. My pc and I had to sort this out as the incident was disappearing with all the pictures landing on top of it. We rectified this by finding out what was putting pictures into it. We found this out by discussing what was happening and watching reactions on the E-Meter. The next thing to do was to get the pc to look at the actual grouper which turned out to be some sort of reflector, rather like a mirror and to "confront" it. The reflector would get covered over with pictures rather like a snowfall but eventually this ended and when it did the pc found the incident more real again, since he could see it again. Pc then found there was some time, some years, between him and the engram, whereas before, unknowingly, he had been carrying this incident around with him all the time, in present time. This, of course, meant now he was more separate from the incident and so would be able to have more of his attention in present time. We then looked earlier in the incident to find out what harmful acts, if any, the pc had committed against anyone. So far the pc had been the "victim." This part of the incident had a lot of confusion on it. First of all, pc said that the bad action he had committed was that he had jeered at a man who had later killed him; of course, this was not very logical. Later, the pc thought he was a girl attacked by a man, but we found out eventually that what really happened was that he had murdered the girl just for the fun of it.

The pc in this present life had continued to adopt the

personality of this girl. We straightened this out by running a drill of "What part of that girl can you confront?" This was difficult at first—the girl kept disappearing since he was being that girl. Eventually, however, the pc and girl separated and so the pc became that much more "himself."

On checking with the pc and by using the E-Meter, we found the pc had put up the theta trap[3] *before* killing the girl in order to have some excuse, and what really happened was that he killed the girl and then went to the theta trap which he did not mind doing very much, since he decided after killing the girl that what he wanted was to "forget everything."

More time is needed on this incident—it is not complete, but in brief this is what happened:

Pc killed a girl—having the idea of forgetting everything and being attracted to the glitter, and landed in a theta trap where he was "all jumbled up." Pc then took over a robot body which burnt out.

---

3. **theta trap:** a means used to trap a thetan. All theta traps have one thing in common: They use electronic force to knock the thetan into forgetting, into unknowingness, into effect. *See also* **thetan** in the glossary.

Case 16

Preclear's Report

Former Condition

Pretty good. But could not get going with my work. Had a feeling it was useless, someone would spoil (destroy) it. As a child I always felt somewhat unwanted and felt some sort of guilt. I think the father in the engram was represented by Jesus in this life.

Mental Outlook

Always thought it was pretty good, but after running this engram I suddenly realized (during one of L. Ron Hubbard's lectures) I had never *really* lived. I saw all the succumb attitudes all through my work and life. I suddenly became alive and felt marvelous, and much more confident.

Physical Improvement

Physically I feel very well. Far less tired than at the beginning of the course.

What You Attribute Improvement To

1. A good auditor

2. The instructors

3.   The process of "confronting" and also "being responsible for"

4.   Confronting misemotions, frustrations, postulates, e.g., "I can't, and no one ever helps," etc.

The Engram

The incident was 1,500 years ago — the first picture I saw was four arms sticking out of the earth. The next was a dead body lying on the back portion of a balcony with a huge piece of masonry[1] stone on its chest.

I was standing by another man, very tall and beautifully clothed in cream rich robes with a gold border. He had large, very white, artistic hands. He stood perfectly still gazing at the mountain, which was Vesuvius[2] in Italy. A beautiful bay[3] horse came dashing out from behind the building with his coat smoldering. I was in agony because the man neither killed the horse nor tried to help him, nor would he try to move the stone off the dead body. I was terribly upset and felt desperate. I kept saying, "I can't do it." "It is always like this, no one ever helps." I was very confused and angry with the man's white hands, which I felt had never done any work. There were two other bodies on the veranda, an old man, the grandfather, who had fallen as the house rocked and knocked his temple on the cornice[4] of the pillar. Blood was flowing. Behind him lay the dead servant with his mouth wide open and a look of complete surprise in his eyes.

The mountain was throwing up huge boulders of rock and ashes. Red-hot lava was pouring from its mouth. Flames of all

---

1. **masonry:** brickwork or stonework.

2. **Vesuvius:** an active volcano in the south of Italy.

3. **bay:** a reddish-brown color.

4. **cornice:** the ornamental molding that projects along the top of a pillar.

colors shot up. A woman and a child were trying to escape and got caught and covered with lava. I felt terribly upset and wept. An old man on a crutch ran as best he could. He fell and got caught by the red-hot lava. A herd of sheep with their fleece burning tore down the plain from the hills. They were "baa-ing" in terror; they got caught and covered up. They were followed by a herd of goats. They were trying to jump out of the hot lava. Their coats were on fire and they made a terrible noise. A large he-goat fell, rolled on his side and was immediately covered, all but one side of his face and one horn. He had great terror in his eye. I felt very sick. There were two olive trees; they withered up. The bay horse was lying on his side covered with hot lava. There was a horrible smell of burning flesh and sulfur[5] from the volcano. All the hair had burnt from his beautiful face—just one eye was left. I felt desperate. I went and looked at the dead body with the stone on it and felt terrible grief, guilt and despair. I realized it was my body. I looked at the tall man and realized he was my father. I began to come out of my confusion and to realize he could do absolutely nothing. I was feeling very grieved and guilty when the house rolled and tottered again and my father fell off the cornice of the pillar he was standing on. It bent right over and he was thrown off the balcony into the lava below—about four feet below. The lava immediately covered him—it was flowing very fast. It was about five miles wide, reaching nearly to the sea. I could see the foam of huge waves. One hand remained uncovered (the right). He was holding it up as if in forgiveness or blessing. It had a silver ring on the first finger. It stayed like that for a long time. I kept looking at it. I suddenly changed my considerations about him and felt a great devotion to him. I realized he could have done nothing. As that affection crept into me, the hand curled up and it fell by his side into the lava.

---

5. **sulfur:** a natural substance that exists in several forms. Most common form is a yellow crystal-like solid that has a suffocating odor when it burns.

I stayed by my body, hoping someone might come and remove the lava and the stone. The face was very beautiful. I stayed around for 1,426 years, and then some robbers in search of treasure came and cut up the lava over the mound of my body. I saw my body had turned to stone. The robbers threw the pieces into a pit. I did not care anymore. After 100 years, grass began to grow, and then blue and yellow flowers covered the plain.

After 1,000 years I noticed a little pond had formed in the lava deposit and a gray-blue bird, the size of a blackbird, came and sat on the edge and drank from it. I watched him for a long time and the apathy and guilt began to lift. I noticed a small brown beetle crawl over the ruins. Then a butterfly came, about three inches across, brown, with two yellow circles in the center of each wing. I began to get thoroughly bored with the place but still wandered back and forth because I had such a terrible feeling of guilt, and thought no one would want me.

The beginning of the story was as follows: I was the son of a very rich nobleman and twenty-five years old. The evening before the earthquake and eruption I took my bay horse and rode across the plain to the house of the villager who had six years ago been my mistress. She bore a son—a lovely child of whom I was very fond. I had not told my father. I went to see them that night because I had a feeling that her crippled father was going to blackmail my father over the matter. My father was building a beautiful city called the "City of Beauty" and I helped him by designing the houses. Everything was rather religious and I was rather bored with it all. When I got to the cottage I kissed the child, talked to the old man and gave him money. I felt out of communication with the girl, feeling she had talked to somebody. I stopped only a very short time. I was afraid to be late for the evening meal as my father might suspect where I had been if I was late. As I got on my horse, the sun was setting. The child laughed and I galloped back at full speed. I hooked the horse's rein onto a hook in the yard, washed my hands in a spout of water flowing from a small stream into an earthenware trough, then I walked slowly into the dining room. It was a large room with the balcony facing the plain. The mountain was at the end on the right. The room was supported by six pillars and three archways led onto the balcony, some five feet above the earth. The table was made of marble, also the stools. There were silver goblets, silver plates beaten at the edges into a design of ramping[6] horses. The grandfather sat in a chair by himself. My father did not speak. I felt very troubled and wished to goodness something would happen. As the servant began to hand my father roast chicken with green parsley on the top, in a silver dish, a terrific rumbling started and the whole house began to rock. I looked out onto the plain and saw a part of the land rising like a huge wave and then a large fissure[7] opened in the earth and many people who were running fell in and were covered up as the wave of earth subsided on the top of them. Four arms stuck out. My father said, "Harri, the mountain!" and he went onto the balcony. The servant went to help the old man out of the chair. I suddenly felt furious with the servant, who was the brother of my mistress, for I suddenly knew it was he who had given the show away to my father. As I passed out onto the balcony I gave him a terrific biff[8] on the jaw and killed him. He let go the old man he was helping, who fell, and was also killed. I went out onto the balcony hoping my father had not seen what I had done. I looked up into the sky and it was black with falling dust and ashes. I saw a huge block of masonry falling, it hit my left arm and shoulder, knocked me over and

6. **ramping:** standing upright on the hind legs.
7. **fissure:** a long, narrow, deep opening or crack.
8. **biff:** a blow; a hit.

landed right on the middle of my body. My right temple struck the marble floor. The stone weighed about half a ton. Everything in my body was crushed. I could not expand to breathe. The only acute pain was the stopping of all the circulation in my limbs. It was agony. My hands and feet swelled up. I went stone cold. The last movement was a slight waggle of the fingers.

I exteriorized[9] as the stone crushed me and in the confusion was for some time not sure whether I owned the body of the father or the son. My terrible grief over this body (the son) made me realize it was mine. I hung about in apathy and guilt, not because I had killed the servant, but because if I had not delayed going onto the balcony that stone would not have fallen on my body. I had no sense but to blame my father and then felt guilt for that. I felt no one would want to have anything to do with me.

During the eruption I was very excited about the volcano and went up to the mouth of the crater and looked in. It was a boiling cauldron of red and yellow liquid. The sides of the crater were like razed[10] vertical pillars. Smoke, steam and sulfur smells came up. Flames of all colors shot up high each time the crater gave a new thunderous roar. A blue gas came nearly to the top of the crater and then exploded, forming flame, and a blue light like the blue of lightning flashed each time over the boiling mass.

Auditor's Report

I located the engram by various reactions on an E-Meter,

---

9. **exteriorized:** went exterior to the body. The spirit has moved out of the body and is able to view the body or control the body from a distance.

10. **razed:** cut or shaved off.

having asked for dates and times of an incident of loss. Having done this I went ahead in getting the preclear to confront parts of the incident. She cried a great deal at the loss of her body and made many considerations such as "I can't go on," and "If I create it, it will only get destroyed, so I won't create." The pc was unwilling to confront the moment at which she knocked down the two men and killed them. She tried to ignore this part and this was completely occluded until the end part of the incident. Pc was very stuck on the "rest" points, i.e., the points at which there was no motion, such as the sunrises and the peace after the volcano had finished erupting and everything had been destroyed. Pc had very great reality at the end of the incident and had the time and place located. The incident took place just outside Pompeii[11] in Italy at 500 years B.C. Briefly the story is:

The pc was the son of a ruler who was building a new city. This son had a mistress and son in a village which was secret from the father for six years. At the moment the father was told of this, the son hit the servant, brother of the mistress, and killed him. The volcano then started killing everything and everybody. The biggest loss in the incident was the loss of the good, healthy body.

---

11. **Pompeii:** an ancient city in southwest Italy, which in A.D. 79 was destroyed (completely covered in lava) by the eruption of the nearby volcano called Mount Vesuvius.

Case 17

Preclear's Report

Former Condition

I was in good communication and felt I could handle life pretty well. Physical condition excellent.

Mental Outlook

Life is worth living, mankind is worth saving and I'm worth even more to all of them!

Physical Improvement

I'm much more relaxed and the engram made a great deal of difference to the carrying and the eventual birth of my baby. I found a postulate to "succumb" my body before the birth of my baby. This changed, therefore, I *do* have a physical improvement.

What You Attribute Improvement To

I attribute this improvement to having found a great deal of considerations on the area of sex and children, and my ability to be *willing* to confront. My auditor also did a good job.

The Engram

Events take place in Italian Somaliland[1] in South Africa in the seventeenth or eighteenth century.

I was the son of a small family and became a doctor. The brother and the mother were very angry about this as I was breaking away from family tradition. One day I had been home all morning and my brother had been out; when he arrived home he had on my clothes and boots, which were very muddy. I became very annoyed at him for always loafing around while I worked so hard, and my mother was very angry and told me to leave him alone.

So I went off to the hospital to deliver the baby of my wife. Just as I was getting ready for this I noticed my brother coming up the steps of the hospital with two men. I decided to take no notice of them until after the delivery. I ordered the nurses to get the patient ready and then followed them into the delivery room. The baby was born without much trouble and the mother was doped.[2] Just as I turned to receive the clippers for the cutting of the cord one of the nurses shouted, "She's dead, Doctor." I thought she meant my wife was dead, so I turned very quickly to see how the heart was beating and in doing so went out of present time for a minute and collapsed over the body, as I had not realized I had put my face too near the ether[3] pad and that had knocked me unconscious. In collapsing I accidentally stabbed my wife in the stomach with the clippers—this killed her. The baby had been born dead. I was taken to a room to sleep it off; on waking I went to see the sister, and in the room with her were the two men and my

---

1. **Italian Somaliland:** a former Italian colony and territory located on the coast of East Africa.

2. **doped:** drugged.

3. **ether:** a drug used to produce anesthesia, as before surgery.

brother. This put the cap on it.[4] I was questioned and arrested for a murder my brother and mother had planned (that's why the brother had been wearing my clothes previously) and was jailed for six years.

When freed, I met a girl whom I eventually fell in love with, but she was so much like my wife that one night I went psychotic and raped and killed her. I then ran off to my tent in which I practiced with the natives as a doctor and found a pet lion which I kept had been killed by one of the natives. This native also attacked me and I killed him. I then became very ill and went to bed with a heavy fever soon after. That night one of the large lions with the black manes entered my tent and we had a very hectic fight for survival. The lion attacked my face and ripped the body to pieces and, of course, killed it. That was the end of that life.

While running this there was a tremendous amount of unreality to begin with. At times I was totally unwilling to confront it but with a little help and pushing from the auditor we got the story more or less straight.

I found an amazing number of considerations made then which, until this week, I was still going around with, and of course, these were inhibiting me from doing many things in this life.

Auditor's Report

The incident my preclear uncovered and ran occurred in the seventeenth century. It was uncovered by using an E-Meter. I asked the preclear if she had experienced a moment of extreme terror and the meter indicated that she had, and confirmed the date of the happening as 1630.

---

4. **put the cap on it:** finished it; left nothing more to be said or done on it.

It was extremely difficult to get the preclear to confront the incident, and it was only after six hours of persistent questioning and directing that the moment of terror revealed itself as a time, May 16th, 1630, when she was attacked and killed by a lion.

At this point the incident became very unreal and many incidents, seemingly from several lives, came to view. The "time track" for several hundred years was apparently collapsed at this point. By the use of finger snaps and flash answers[5] the original incident was located more and more exactly, the track unraveled by keeping the preclear confronting "that incident" (the lion incident). After several more hours the pain, unconsciousness and death was run off and when this was accomplished other happenings in this life came to view, and in the end the preclear had reasonable reality on the whole of that life.

The unraveling of the incident was accompanied with physiological changes and body movement and position. For instance, when the lion was encountered the preclear's face and hands (the first body parts eaten) became very red and painful. Just before a poisonous spider bit her in the incident, her present body neck became red and swollen; and preceding the discovery of her dead infant (in the incident) she acted like a very young baby, her attention span decreased and she became very tired and stretched out in the position of a sleeping child.

It was fascinating as an auditor to run this incident and see the changes for the better in my preclear. It was an experience that I would not have missed.

---

5. **flash answers:** instantaneous replies, the first things that flash into the preclear's mind at the snap of the auditor's fingers upon asking a question.

Case 18

Preclear's Report

Former Condition

My health had been generally good—except for pain in my shoulder and neck muscles for a period of some four months prior to this course. Some business and domestic anxieties.

Mental Outlook

Undoubtedly I am more confident and optimistic than for the past four years. The feelings of anxiety have entirely disappeared.

Physical Improvement

Disappearance of pain, persistent over a period of some four months, in my neck and shoulder muscles. My posture became more erect.

What You Attribute Improvement To

I believe the decided gains I have made are due to the running of an engram. In particular because my ability to confront bodies, especially female bodies, was increased.

Other gains have been made due to the help and discipline given by the instructors, and from L. Ron Hubbard's lecture material.

Auditor's Report

I located the engram by asking the pc if he had ever experienced a moment of terror. The E-Meter, of course, was in use. A single picture of some dogs killing a fox flashed up. The time in which this incident occurred was traced by E-Meter questioning to being September 19th, 1672. This particular incident was chosen out of some half dozen others, since there was obviously more charge connected with that particular life.

An entrance was made by asking pc "What part of that incident can you confront?" For some time the pc was extremely confused about his own identity in this incident. Nevertheless, the pictures expanded further, more countryside, more people, yet no apparent sequence to be seen. Some little time later the pc ran into a death of a girl (aged fourteen) in attempting to jump a fence. After some further confronting and questioning, the pc knew that this was his identity. Before this point was reached the pc went through a great deal of reluctance to look at this dead female body. The idea of his being a woman in a past life was, to use his own language, out of character, quite impossible and a final breakthrough into an acceptance of his own experience.

Processing was now directed at clearing up the death fall. A trace-back was done to two minutes before the accident. Here the pc was riding sidesaddle across this stretch of countryside, when the hunt horn[1] sounded. On hearing this and knowing this was the kill, she urged the horse on, hoping to be in at the kill first. The shortest route was over a fence. Just as the horse jumped, she saw the pack of dogs some 200 yards

---

1. **hunt horn:** a signal horn used in the chase while hunting.

away, and almost the same second the horse hit the top of the fence. This was the moment of terror, since at that moment she was catapulted from the saddle. Her horse went one way, her body the other. The death came about by her head striking a rocky part of the gully. Head injuries, a broken neck, broken right arm and ankle and multiple bruises were sustained. From exhilaration riding the horse, to death in a few seconds — a section of the incident which was tricky to run.

The emotion was shut off, so I tried for the physical pain of the engram. To get the pc to confront this was difficult. Shifting the pc backwards and forwards from the jump to the death loosened the frozen area. Pains in all the areas of the body which were injured showed up and were reexperienced and felt as if it were all happening now. The blinding pain of the first impact, the shock and finding herself outside her own body came off first. Then came the falling sensation, the terror and the blind panic, all reexperienced by the pc. This was one of the trickiest patches of the incident to run, since the pc was attempting to get out of looking at what happened. However, psychosomatic pains of some years in duration lifted off the head, spine and shoulders, and have not returned to date — nor do I expect a recurrence.

From this point a fairly straight run was made up to the funeral. A brief résumé here is as follows. The people in the hunt came across to the scene of the accident. Naturally, the pc is now viewing the incident from outside her own body. The master of the hunt poured some whiskey down her throat, found she was dead and made up a stretcher with coats and poles to carry her back to her home.

At various times up to the funeral, the pc, while exteriorized, took up the viewpoints of some eighteen odd people. A good deal of loss was experienced by the pc at no longer being a member of the group.

The scene moves through the journey back to the house. Nuns clean the body up and prepare it for the funeral, the girl's aunt having taken charge of the proceedings now. The body is clothed in a white gown, the hair combed, etc., and placed in a coffin the following day.

The girl's father (Sir Hugh Henning) returns that night. The pc views her father's grief somewhat remotely—which gives a clue to some yet to be found facts. Father remains for some hours buried in grief by the coffin, the pc still watching. The funeral takes place a day or two later. Here the pc watches the cortège[2] move off, and attempts to confront the nanny who sobs bitterly at her loss. All to no avail. Apparently the last act is the pc waiting around the garden, hanging around the statue of a boy, sometimes moving around the garden (for a period of about ten weeks) enjoying the freedom of not having a body.

A further scout through the incident brought up some further data. The beginning of the hunt takes place that day with the pc (named Agnes) persuading her father to let her have Ra, a high-spirited horse, to use on the hunt. This is done with some wheedling.

A quick run from here to the fall—the pc is looking at some pigs being born, alone with a friend, Marjorie by name. Following the birth, the pig eats the placenta.[3] The pc at this point starts to shy[4] out of the incident and has to be held in hand.[5] Some restimulation has occurred of something which

---

2. **cortège:** solemn procession, as at a funeral.

3. **placenta:** an organ within the uterus via which the fetus receives nourishment as it is developing and which is discharged shortly after birth.

4. **shy:** to react negatively; be or become cautious or unwilling; draw back.

5. **held in hand:** caused to stay in control.

the pc does not want to look at. Finally, I manage to get some more facts. A huntsman nearby had said, "Wait till your turn comes." The pc apparently has no desire to be a girl and would rather be dead than have children.

There is something around here which is too glib,[6] and a little too pat.[7] For an expert horsewoman to attempt such a fence sidesaddle is almost self-inflicted death.

So a check back was made to the birth. The mother died of some form of milk,[8] or some other fever three months after childbirth. Steep drops showed on meter, the pc becoming more obstinate and recalcitrant[9] the while. A further check back on the mother's pregnancy was done. Birth was on March 7th, 1672 — a marked meter drop was found on August 22nd–23rd, 1658. A great deal of checking and rechecking was needed here. Pc was obviously unwilling to look around this area.

This was the key point of the engram and the possible real beginning. The pc as a spirit took over control of the mother and father. Such an incident is usually termed "blanketing" or possessing two people and monitoring their thought and behavior to some nefarious[10] end. From the fall back to the bedroom scene follows a train of demonical possession, overcoming the will of both people, the pc as a spirit throws them

---

6. **glib:** done or spoken in an easy manner, too easy and smooth to be convincing.

7. **pat:** smooth and clever but superficial, as in a *pat* solution to a complex problem.

8. **milk:** short for *milk fever*, a slight fever sometimes occurring in women about the beginning of lactation, originally believed to be caused by a great accumulation of milk in the breasts, now thought to be caused by infection.

9. **recalcitrant:** refusing to follow direction, etc.; stubborn and defiant.

10. **nefarious:** very wicked; evil.

into sexual frenzies and an orgy results. The pc's intention was to degrade these people to the uttermost limits. Any extent would do, the intention being to kill the mother and child through the father. The mother becomes unconscious after the third coitus[11] and a hemorrhage[12] ensues. Pc hangs about and tries again and again to engage the two in further sexual perversions. The mother holds out and comes through to birth, all the while being tormented by this disembodied spirit. The fetus has been injured but the damage is not permanent.

The pc decides to take over the body of the girl at birth. In feeding the child this incident is next isolated. The pc, still detached from the body, is still intent on injuring the mother. The mother died still being tormented by this decayed spirit.

This was apparently the entirety of the event. A further check showed up an earlier attempt at debasing[13] the mother as a young woman of twenty years. The incident concerned an attempt by this spirit to ravish[14] the woman with a dog.

This may or may not be complete. The original intentions of the spirit to kill the mother and child succeeded. The original injuries to fetus head, neck and spine correspond to death injuries of the girl at fourteen.

---

11. **coitus:** sexual intercourse.

12. **hemorrhage:** heavy bleeding, as from a broken blood vessel.

13. **debasing:** making lower in value, character, dignity, etc.

14. **ravish:** to rape.

Case 19

Preclear's Report

Former Condition

Sometimes vague and confused, and difficulty in receiving an inflow of communication. Eyes lose focus and fog over easily (during last eighteen months only). Pain acute with this.

Mental Outlook

Reasonable, optimistic, often irritable.

Physical Improvement

Eyes a little improved—less pain.

The Engram

This happens in Tibet in 1500 A.D. I am a male of about thirty, son of a local politician, married, wife expecting first child. Father secures a diplomatic negotiation for son to carry out. I'm called before a council and given my order; aware of some dissension at proposed negotiation with neighboring state (Nepal). The scene is a council chamber, dark, lit with butter lamps;[1] there is a tiled and tessellated (checkerboard pattern)

---

1. **butter lamps:** lamps which use butter for fuel instead of oil.

floor. Embroidered hangings behind the carved seat of the president. He is an old man, stout, with bald head, no neck, a suave voice. His hands are on dragon heads at the end of the chair arms, his feet are on carved and embroidered footstools. He is wearing a long embroidered silk robe. Myself, I have a large long robe with a gilt sword and soft leather boots. I am five feet nine inches tall, fair, and more aquiline[2] than the usual Tibetan. I am conscious of a difficulty backing out, bowing and maneuvering my sword down a narrow passage into a sunny earth-floored courtyard where I say goodbye to my father.

I step across the street to my own house opposite. It has a narrow passageway leading to a large pillared room with no glass in the window openings. A large leather (yak skin) chest contains clothes and sword. I bid farewell to my wife, who has long black plaits and jingles on her tunic, with yellow underskirt and turquoise and cornelian[3] necklace. She has a simple submissive air. I am strutting about somewhat at my own importance. I put on a heavy sheepskin three-quarter-length coat for the journey and felt boots over the leather ones. I leave off my sword, I stride along the dark passage into the sunny street, and I leap onto a pony from behind (like a leapfrog game). There is no saddle and only a simple halter and rein, with patterns in color on the latter. It's a brown pony, long black tail and mane. I wave goodbye with my right hand and leave the city—Lhasa.

I amble across the plain outside it, which is covered with coarse brown grass, and notice the river winding to the left, with the hill and the white buildings of the Potala[4] behind.

2. **aquiline:** (of the nose) curving; hooked; prominent, like the beak of an eagle.

3. **cornelian:** a red or reddish type of translucent quartz used in making jewelry.

4. **Potala:** an eleven-story, gilt-roofed palace in Lhasa, the capital of Tibet. The Potala is so large that it can be seen from miles away. It was built in the 7th century as the residence of the priest king of Tibet and its name means "Palace of the Gods."

Some way out of the city I am going along singing and swinging my legs, very content, when I look back and see three horsemen galloping toward me in the distance. I feel certain they have been hired by the dissentients[5] to waylay and kill me. So I put my horse to the gallop, leaning flat over his neck; his mane flicks my left cheek. I look back and see the men have weapons (spears). They are too far off to see clearly. I ride madly and decide to outwit the men by riding off the track in a westerly direction, instead of southeast where I want to go. I turn the pony into a very rough, rocky ground and make toward high boulders and hilly country to get cover. We are still riding hard and it is not easy to decide the route. I go to the right around a huge rock formation, only to be faced with a sheer drop of thousands of feet, and only a ledge of at most two foot six inches wide, which ends abruptly within twenty feet. I rein in the pony, but he panics and trips and I fall, luckily away from the precipice[6] onto softish ground. The pony's leg is broken, I curse and push him over the precipice with my right foot, pressing my back against the earth behind. He whinnies and stones rattle as he falls. I scramble up the hill to the left which is slippery and very steep, and foothold is difficult. I hang on to the rocks which are rough and painful to my hands. I take cover behind a tall chimney of rock, not sitting or resting, the blood pounds in my ears, and I am sweating, my leg muscles are tautly braced. After an interval I decide the men have lost my track and I crawl across the steep fall of the hill to flatter ground, whereI rest for a while among rocks with veins of quartz[7] in them.

---

5. **dissentients:** people who disagree with the methods, goals, etc., of a political party or government.

6. **precipice:** a vertical, almost vertical or overhanging rock face; steep cliff.

7. **quartz:** a brilliant crystalline mineral which occurs most often in a colorless, transparent form, but also sometimes in colored varieties used as semiprecious stones.

I then try to find landmarks and make my way due south, but I am hopelessly lost. After hours of rough walking, night suddenly falls. It is very cold. I wander on, hoping to reach a village, but I stumble often and my felt boots get torn. I hold my hands in front to feel my way. I find myself in front of a great boulder. It is higher than I can reach, and the hill slopes up to the right. The face is ridged, but has smooth places on it. I decide to feel my way to the left, downhill, but my left foot slips into a crevice and I pitch forward, hitting my head on a sharp overhang. I slump backwards and spend the night semi-conscious, with my head on my right hand leaning against the rock. It is bitterly cold and I get a lot of dream pictures of my home and wife. I long for her.

I wake with the dawn and unstiffen my limbs. My head aches, and it is still very cold. I have no food in my huge pocket. I totter along a rocky ridge, and the beauty of the dawn over the hills revives me. I feel a little crazy; I have the idea I must get to the snow. So I trip and tumble over the rocky ground reaching snow; it is August and so it is very soft. I sink deep and drag my legs through it leaving a long track. I cannot go far, and totter forward using my arms and toes. Finally, I flop down deep into a drift and lying face downward quietly fall asleep, thinking and longing for my wife and home. As I leave the body, I notice the clean-cut wall of the snowdrifts sparkling in the sun, and deep blue shadows at its base. The body has its left arm extended, showing the big turquoise on the ring. I look at the virgin snowfield, the peak and the snowy mountain 18,000 feet high, with pink and blue lights on it from the rising sun, and the hills behind are still dark and the ravine beyond, very deep.

I linger there a long time; it's free without the body, I can roam the hills easily. When I look at the body now it disgusts me because every cell is congealing[8] with deep freeze. I feel it will be there for hundreds of years.

Auditor's Report

On questioning the preclear on having lived before, I got a sharp reaction on the E-Meter and was given the year 1500 A.D., the month August, his age thirty-three years; sex, male. The preclear was slow to begin with, reviewing certain parts of the incident, but began to look more closely later.

The scene is a large city near the mountains in Tibet and the story begins when the son of a rich man interested in politics receives his first official job. The boy talks with his father for a while, outside the hall where everyone had gathered, bids farewell to his wife, puts on warm clothing and gallops away. Soon he is pursued by three men on horses, and has to quicken his pace. This is near the foothills and he decides to put the men off, and so he goes in another direction and comes across a big ravine. As the horse stumbles the young man throws himself on the edge, and later pushes the maimed horse over the edge. He climbs up a slippery slope to a rock where he rests, and hearing no pursuers he continues on. He came to a plateau covered with sharp little rocks and as it was cold and night fell, he began to feel very miserable. Fumbling around, he slipped, and moving up again he banged his head and slumped down into unconsciousness until morning. Still not too alert, he stumbled on, looking for snow and feeling hungry. He felt in his large pocket for food, but found none. The snow was soft as it was the month of August, and he left a deep trail behind him as he sank into the snow. There he died and there the body froze.

---

8. **congealing:** changing from a soft or fluid state to a rigid or solid state, as by cooling or freezing.

Case 20

Preclear's Report

Former Condition

When angry people spoke to me I couldn't understand what they said. I could not stand the thought of anyone seeing me naked. I was being compulsively responsible about men. I had the victim's outlook. When I knew I was right about something I could lose that certainty if another person brought logical argument and data to prove me wrong. I would agree with them. I had to see big effects on people and could not see small effects.

Mental Outlook

I can now observe small effects on people. I don't go "away" mentally when an angry person is talking to me. I face up to the engram and handle it. I am no longer ashamed at being seen without clothes. I am not compulsively responsible for men. I feel that I am here in 1958 rather than in 1603. I don't have the victim's outlook, because I know I have some responsibility in being made a victim. I know myself to be a real person and I am not made uncertain of myself by other people talking theory or ideas at me. Life is now more like a play than some serious heavy thing. I know now that to look at truth is not hurtful, and that to admit one's failures and to accept responsibility is better than denial. I take responsibility for making sure that other people understand exactly what I say and no more, then I don't get come-backs. I have learned to take on as much responsibility as I can cope with and no more. I understand people more and I also understand how a person can be influenced by past ideas which they don't even know they still possess. I can be interested in another person and not try to impose my understanding on them. I can respect them and their ideas and not try to run their life, it is theirs. If they need help I give it and if they don't I don't impose it on them. Before embarking on something new I ask myself, "Is it worth it?" If it is not I don't do anything, I don't rush into things now. I have found that to pull someone down takes more trouble and effort than to pull them up. All these things are new to me, and I keep them to myself and use them in my life.

Auditor's Report

In 1603 during May the preclear, a young girl, went for a horse ride in the grounds of her father's house. He was a well-to-do merchant. As she rode away she noticed some of the women servants looking at her through a window, and felt a slightly irritated curiosity at being looked at and watched. She met in the grounds a military gentleman known to her parents, who continued his way to the house. That evening the gentleman was at dinner with them, and he and her father in conversation discussed politics and the man said something to the effect that some trouble was brewing. The girl was bored and paid little attention to the conversation.

Next morning she was playing a piano, described as a "sort of organ thing" with higher sound than present-day pianos, when guns started firing. A woman servant came in and asked the girl to go with her to a cottage in the country until the trouble was over. The girl said she couldn't go out without her papa's permission (Papa had gone out earlier that morning). The woman coaxed her and seemed to be in a state of anxiety. They drove out of the town and along a country road, in a closed coach (not the family's coach) and arrived at the cottage. She stayed all day, very impatiently, and slept there. The next morning after breakfast, the woman went out. Then two soldiers came with a carriage and said they had come to take her to the military gentleman's house, where she would be taken care of. She agreed to go, all the time wondering, as she had been doing all the previous day, what it was all about and what it had to do with her. She did not like the servant and was angry at having to drive beside her and stay at the cottage. She expected to be taken home and by the time she arrived at the military gentleman's house, she was in a fine fury. Taken to a room in which she sat at a desk, she stormed a flood of questions at him. He replied very little but soothingly, and suggested that she had better have lunch. He took her to another room where he and she and some other officers had a meal. They didn't talk much to her. Afterwards in another room sitting on a sofa he intimated a liking for her as though sounding[1] her feelings. She had been aware of his liking of her previously, but her parents had not encouraged him and she had little interest in him, nor in any particular man. She had gone to balls, ridden horses, learned French and the piano, and had a few romantic ideas, but seemed to have little understanding of the realities of life. He maintained the customary respect awarded to young ladies of good family. She now showed by some disdain and coldness, and laughing at the man, how little she had ever thought of him. He left her suggesting that she had better have her rest, and she dozed on the sofa until a soldier tapped her on the shoulder and told her to follow him.

---

1. **sounding:** trying to find out the opinions or feelings of a person, as by roundabout questioning.

She expected to have been taken home and was surprised and annoyed and not a little bewildered at being taken down to a small cell-like basement room with a window onto the courtyard. There was nowhere to sit, so for some hours or so she stood tapping her foot with anger on the wall.

After dark a man came down the steps that jutted out into the room, carrying a lamp. She saw that it was one of her own family's men servants, and thought that at last she was to be taken home. Near the top of the stairs, she was stopped short, and instead of going on up further on the stairs that she had previously come down from the living room, she was turned aside into a small windowless room containing a table, a chair and six male figures with black hoods. She was pushed into the chair and questioned about a piece of paper with figures on it, which it was said was her father's. She knew nothing of this and said so, so was punched four or five times between further asking, until her head spun. She spun out of this and then back in. She was wanting to urinate and had some thoughts about having to "pull it up" and "get out." She also got stubborn and silent.

Then she was jerked to her feet and her clothes torn off. She felt very ashamed at her nakedness and had a feeling of shock; verbalized by "That's the end," "I give up if this is what happens to you." It was a surprised culmination of a rising incredulity,[2] interspersed with irritation and stubborn refusal to recognize an incredibly unpleasant reality. They put her on the table. One man, a shortish man nearest to her, did most of the talking and bullying. They threatened to cut her and deprive her of her womanhood if she did not produce the paper. She had given up. A knife passed, a cut was made down the

2. **incredulity:** unwillingness or inability to believe; doubt.

center of her genitalia and she just gave up and died, after having slipped out of the body once and into the head of the bully and then back again.

When the body died she got out again, put its head over to one side and hovered above. The men went away, but she believed that they didn't intend to go so far. She hovered, considering such things as "So that is what you got if you had a woman's body." She felt grief and loss and anger, and a desire to be strong and "show them." The men returned and took the body back to the cell and left it on the floor. She stood near it, and later they took it back to the table and cut it still more, and took it back to the cell. She retired to the courtyard outside still watching it. She does not know if they ever buried it. She recalls the light dawning in the sky, a fire burning in the town, two men being shot in the courtyard, and a tree there. She waited some days. The body was never brought out and buried. She thinks they must have buried it in the earth floor of the little room where it was left. Eventually she drifted away and talked of "hoping and looking for a quiet place" and then going to a place she called "Alouika."

When run on responsibility the preclear took over responsibility for her stubbornness and stupidity, lack of sensitivity, refusal to recognize reality, and also for her snobbish dislike of the servants; and says that she was at least part cause of the death, forgetting easily that she was bored with that life.

The preclear had difficulty with running responsibility. In the engram during the most aberrative section when she was half conscious from the bullying and fear, the tallest of the six men had said something to the effect that she was only an irresponsible woman. She was very confused in this life about her own ideas and responsibility, and seemed to be using her husband's and other people's ideas theoretically, and theoretical ideas in general. A lot of work had to be done on this, and then she worked well on the clearing of the engram. It is interesting to note that in this life, this woman gave birth to her daughter when she was 18 and that she fought the obstetricians[3] and refused to open her legs to allow the baby to be born. It had to be born with her lying on her side. For six years after the birth she had continuous bleeding from the womb and had six operations on the womb for this without improvement. After earlier Scientology processing, the condition cleared up, without the preclear understanding why. Running this engram seemed to provide her with a satisfactory explanation; she said, "The high sort of bed table I was on in the hospital with the light overhead, and the men all standing around in masks and things, was like the other room only they were wearing black, and the room was darker, and I fought like a tiger not to open my legs, and I never understood why."

---

3. **obstetricians:** medical doctors who specialize in the branch of medicine dealing with the care and treatment of women during pregnancy, child birth and the period immediately following.

Case 21

Preclear's Report

Former Condition

I was in fairly good shape physically but somatics in ankle occasionally bothered me.

Mental Outlook

After the conclusion of the course I felt that my goals of being a better auditor and of being Clear[1] were more realizable.

Physical Improvement

More energetic and eyes more relaxed.

What You Attribute Improvement To

Running engram undoubtedly has helped my case to some degree.

---

1. **Clear:** the name of a state achieved through auditing or an individual who has achieved this state. A Clear is a being who no longer has his own reactive mind. A Clear is an unaberrated person and is rational in that he forms the best possible solutions he can on the data he has and from his viewpoint. The Clear has no engrams which can be restimulated to throw out the correctness of computation by entering hidden and false data.

Auditor's Report

The past life was contacted by asking the preclear for operations, past deaths and incidents of heavy emotion or loss, each incident being asked for singly, with the preclear connected to a Hubbard Electrometer (or E-Meter), and its existence confirmed by reaction of the E-Meter needle. The exact time of each incident was pinned down by asking for dates and checking the E-Meter reaction. In this way, a number of possible incidents were obtained and listed.

Several days later, this list of incidents was checked over with the preclear on the E-Meter. The one which produced the largest needle drop when mentioned by date and brief description was taken to be the most suitable to explore. In this case it turned out to be an operation, dated September, 750 B.C. The exact date was not established, probably because calendars were different then.

The preclear was asked to be in the incident, and he immediately perceived a red patch. When questioned further he recognized this as the open wound of an operation on his own neck, seen from above the body.

The incident was opened up somewhat by repeatedly asking the question, "What part of that incident can you confront?" This brought to light a number of pictures of the operation, in which a growth was removed from the back of the neck by surgery. An interesting feature of this was that all the views were as seen from a point exterior to the body, and, in fact, it was only after many hours of working on this incident that he would view events from within his own body during the more unpleasant parts of the story. Also at this stage he felt no pain.

Next step was to develop the story a bit more, so I questioned him on events leading up to the operation, largely with the purpose of establishing the beginning of the incident. We did not find the true beginning until we had been working on the incident about forty hours, but in these early investigations, a very large amount of the entire lifetime opened up. His visual perception of the scenes was fair, right from the beginning, but perception of sound, touch, smell, etc., was rather poor and somewhat fleeting. Also the certainty that these things had really happened was not high. All he knew was that he could find these pictures, which might or might not be an accurate record of what was happening.

The story which came up was that he was an inhabitant of some small state in the Middle East, the son of a general. He lost his mother at the age of ten. She used to punish him, then kiss him on the back of the neck to make it up to him afterwards. In his teens, he had a fight with another boy over a girl, and had the back of his neck injured. Later he became a tax collector working in the palace of the local ruler, and remained a palace official from then on. He had a knife fight with a man over the man's daughter, and received a knife wound in the back of the neck. The neck later developed a growth, so he had it cut out. Hence the surgery.

This is the story we got early. It seemed to fit together fairly well, but there seemed to be occluded parts. For one thing, he would or could not feel pain in the operation, and yet there was no evidence of anesthetic being used. Apparently he survived the operation, and yet what happened after it seemed rather obscure. We kept working the incident over and over, particularly in the part involving the operation. He was connected to the E-Meter at all times in order that needle reactions could be observed as a check on his verbal statements.

Eventually he got a fleeting perception of two staring eyes, but rejected it as not being part of the story. The meter, however, said otherwise; so, being suspicious, I threw the question at him, "Is there any hypnotism here?" Immediately he went very deeply into a previously hidden part of the story and picked up a very strong picture of being hypnotized prior to the operation, the surgeon saying to him words to the effect of "Sleep, sleep, feel nothing, feel no pain, forget," and so forth. We only succeeded in running off some of the hypnotism at this time, but it was sufficient to allow more of the story to lift after the "forget" command came up. Also the reality of the preclear increased and he started to get improved perception, particularly of sound, touch and, to some extent, pain. His perception of sound later became good enough so that he was able at times to give me words of the actual language used, which seemed to be something like Persian, a soft liquid language with an almost musical sound.

The incident had to be worked over and over, lifting a new bit of the story each time, and discarding parts here and there as not belonging. The worst pain in the operation did not show up, except as a very faint sensation, but I am pretty sure we got just about everything else of importance. We did establish with good certainty the beginning and end of the story, which turned out at the finish to be quite different from what it first appeared to be. Here it is:

The story begins at a feast in the palace of the local Emir or Shah, or whatever the ruler was called. The preclear, named Pamur in this incident (pronounced Pamoor), was conversing with a foreigner—possibly a Turk—next to him, named Mustapha, a man with a hook-shaped nose. They were discussing the growth on his neck, which Mustapha said could be removed by a surgeon, a countryman of his living outside the city.

Pamur later discussed this with his girlfriend back in the palace, who urged him to have the growth cut out, as it spoiled his appearance.

Next day, he visited the surgeon and consulted with him on the matter. The surgeon's manner was rather hypnotic and as he examined the growth he tried to give hypnotic suggestions to ensure that Pamur would come back and get the growth removed. Pamur resisted this, and vacillated[2] for about three weeks, but finally, on being threatened by his girlfriend that she would leave him if he didn't get the job done he made an appointment with the surgeon and went along one sunny afternoon to have the operation.

He was taken into the operating room and almost immediately put into hypnotic trance by the surgeon in preparation for the operation. The hypnotic technique used by the surgeon is very interesting, but there is not space to recount it here.

At this point the plot thickens.[3] After hypnotizing the patient and shaving around the growth, the surgeon attempted to implant Pamur with suggestions to supply military information regarding the local ruler's plans to invade the surgeon's own country. The information was to be supplied to Mustapha who would relay it to the surgeon. Even though under hypnosis, Pamur's fear of the consequences of carrying out such an action, plus possibly his feelings of patriotism, were so great that he refused. The surgeon struck him and insisted in angry tones that he would obey. Pamur yielded and said yes he would.

The surgeon then strapped him face downward onto a

2. **vacillated:** wavered in one's mind; showed indecision.
3. **the plot thickens:** the story becomes more complex or involved.

narrow operating table, cut out the growth, sewed it up neatly, bandaged the neck and then put him to sleep for about three hours on a couch under a lion-skin rug. After waking up sufficiently, Pamur went back to his room in the palace and slept.

Apparently the hypnotism, though sufficient to enable the operation to be carried out without pain, was not totally effective, even though it had carried a command to forget what the surgeon had done to him. Pamur, on waking up, realized that the surgeon had commanded him to spy, and immediately went and had audience with the ruler. The ruler commanded that Mustapha be apprehended, but that Pamur should wait until he was due to have the stitches removed in a few days time, to arrest the surgeon.

The evening before Pamur was to revisit the surgeon, Mustapha revisited the palace and was accosted on one of the balconies by Pamur, who attempted to arrest him single-handed. Mustapha resisted and drew a knife. A fight ensued which would have somewhat horrified the Marquis of Queensberry,[4] and resulted in Pamur being wounded in the hand and Mustapha being savagely killed with his own knife.

Next day, Pamur went to the surgeon's house, taking with him a couple of sturdy soldiers and planting them outside the back door of the surgery to act as hidden witnesses and make the arrest if required. The surgeon removed the stitches and then asked if Pamur had got the information. Pamur replied that he refused to have anything to do with such a thing and the surgeon was liable to find himself in custody. The surgeon

---

4. **Marquis of Queensberry:** John Sholto Douglas (1844–1900), patron of boxing who supervised the formulation of Marquis of Queensberry Rules in 1867. The Marquis of Queensberry Rules are the basic rules of modern boxing, providing for the use of gloves and the division of a match into rounds, etc.

became abusive and reached for a knife. At this point the two soldiers rushed in and overpowered him and took him away.

This is the end of the incident, but it might be mentioned that the surgeon was later tried, found guilty and most unpleasantly executed under Pamur's direction.

Case 22

Preclear's Report

Former Condition

I felt myself to be in pretty fair shape: but not satisfied with my apparent lack of ability to cope with things outside of myself in my life.

Mental Outlook

Had some improvement—more mentally relaxed and alert.

Physical Improvement

Had some improvement—more physically relaxed and fitter looking in the face.

What You Attribute Improvement To

To the running off of some of the emotional charge in the engram and the contacting and reevaluating of my considerations made at the time I was beaten by my grandmother in the engram—I came out of her valence.[1]

---

1. **valence:** personality. The term is used to denote the borrowing of the personality of another. A valence is a substitute for self taken on after the fact of lost confidence in self. A preclear "in his father's valence" is acting as though he were his father.

The Engram

In this life I was born in 1666. My mother died in childbirth (my birth) and as my father had died three months before my birth I was raised by my grandmother. The relationship between my grandmother and me was a bad one and we were always at odds[2] with each other. For instance, she once came into the room (I was five years old) and caught me busy bending one of her metal knitting needles. She then promptly hit me very solidly across the mouth with the back of her right hand (on which was a heavy, silver, ornate ring) splitting my bottom lip. In a rage, I then grabbed hold of the fire tongs and snatching a piece of glowing hot coal from the fire threw it across the room at her, just missing her. She then came across, tore the tongs away from me, hit me across the back with them, took up the piece of hot coal and taking my right hand pressed the coal on to it, burning it badly.

I had a brother two years older than I whom I fought with often and always came off the loser.

When I was eighteen I lost my temper with my grandmother and almost strangled her. As a consequence I had to leave home (which was somewhere in London) and went into rooms in another part of town.

Note: From the above point until the time when I visit my brother's house and kill him is very vague, but I'll write what I have got.

It seems that whilst in that new part of town I meet and fall in love with a beautiful auburn-haired girl by the name of Anna. At some time following that I go away for a period of

---

2. **at odds:** in conflict or disagreement, opposed.

three months (for some reason) and on returning find that (somehow or another) she has gone off with my brother. She marries him two months later.

Apparently angry with my brother—our relationship was always pretty antagonistic, and has been made worse by a court case regarding possession of certain property (what exactly and why is pretty vague) and, on top of that, his marrying Anna—I ride on horseback to an inn in a village in Sussex[3] (close by his estate) and stay there the night (it is 10:15 P.M. when I arrive). I then ride over to his large mansion-type house the next day.

He is not there when I arrive, but Anna is, and I remonstrate[4] with her about things (just what, I'm not certain). My brother rides up on horseback after about two hours and (at her wish) I go to wait in another room whilst she speaks to him first.

After I have been waiting for some twenty minutes my brother bursts into the room and grabs hold of me angrily (why, I'm very vague about). Losing my temper, I draw my sword, having pushed him away from me, and kill him. Confused, I leave the house hurriedly and gallop my horse back to the inn, where I go straight to my room, and throwing myself onto the bed (still in a confusion of thought and emotion) eventually fall asleep. There whilst sleeping, I am stabbed to death by Anna.

---

3. **Sussex:** a maritime county in southeast England.

4. **remonstrate:** to present and urge reasons in opposition or complaint, protest.

Case 23

Preclear's Report

Former Condition

Somewhat undecisive, hypercritical and intolerant. Varying between inferiority and superiority complex; sometimes rather withdrawn.

Mental Outlook

I feel that I have more point to living now and things in general do not appear so difficult. Improved tolerance of stupidity. I have a better balance between inferiority and superiority which enables me to communicate with others in an altogether relaxed way.

Physical Improvement

Feel as though a weight has been lifted from my shoulders. A good deal of physical tension has been eased in the body, particularly in the region of the neck and shoulders. There is a sensation in the head which I can only describe as a feeling that it has been "washed clean." Bodily warmth and aliveness has increased. The whole body feels better.

What You Attribute Improvement To

This was undoubtedly an incident which has had a harmful effect on me. In the mental sphere it has posed problems which I had found unsolvable as I had died whilst in the process of solving them. By increasing my ability to confront these I relaxed on the subject, and it no longer was necessary that I should solve them. I realized whilst running through this incident that I had been unconsciously keeping some attention on it. I am not doing it now. In keeping some attention on it, I had restimulated the physical pain in it to a slight degree constantly. Thus I had developed tensions in the neck and shoulders and a minute aching awareness of the head, which I was only fully aware of when it disappeared.

Auditor's Report

Preclear, called Robert, who is twenty-four years of age in 1746, is a man of great charm. He is handsome and of good physique, of aristocratic origin, with a disdain for the less fortunate, such as lackeys[1] and "underdogs."[2] He has got the makings of a Don Juan[3] and is aware of his physical attraction and his influence on women. His association with them is, in fact, easy and rewarding. His favorite colors are black and white and he owns a black Arabian horse of outstanding beauty and performance.

Robert has been staying for four weeks at a large mansion as the guest of an influential family, situated somewhere in the

---

1. **lackeys:** male servants of low rank.

2. **underdogs:** persons who are expected to lose in a contest or conflict; victims of social or political injustice.

3. **Don Juan:** a man who seduces women (from the Spanish legendary character Don Juan, an immoral nobleman and seducer of women).

---

north of the Midlands (central part of England). He is in love with the daughter Julia whom he intends to marry. Politically they are in a different camp,[4] the family favoring the present ruler, she supporting the pretender or opposite party, but only Julia knows this, not his family.

So when on April 11, 1746, he had to fulfill a secret mission, he does not leave by the front entrance, but at midnight climbs out of a window and, on his own black horse, rides to a neighboring farm to meet the special messenger. The latter treats him with great respect, addresses him as "lord" and hands him a handwritten scroll, provided with a blue seal. Its contents are of a disquieting nature. He is informed that owing to his undesirable or treacherous activities he is doomed and will have to pay for it with his life when caught.

He leaves the secret rendezvous but on the way back to the mansion where Julia lives, he has a fall while going through a wood, and loses his valuable Arabian horse. Walking back to a neighboring village, he finds food and shelter at an inn, with the proprietress, who is well known to him and with whom he has been on terms of intimacy. He is provided with other clothes and another horse and rides back to the mansion.

On entering he is confronted with a near relation of Julia, an uncle with whom he has now become good friends. This man is forty-five years of age. At that moment he is dressed as a monk, although actually he does not exercise the profession of a monk. The monk's cloak is therefore more in the nature of a disguise. This so-called monk makes a remark which Robert interprets to be hostile, and reveals that he is aware of the fact that Robert belongs politically to the other side. Robert becomes irritated and, being weary and tired, is drawn into a

---

4. **camp:** a group of people who support some cause, opinion, etc., together.

useless argument very much against his will. The monk draws his rapier,[5] which is a stupid thing to do, because the monk is a bad duelist. Robert hesitates, knowing full well that he can finish the monk off with the greatest of ease, being far superior in skill. After some short skirmishing, Robert pierces his chest, which scene is witnessed by Julia, who is horrified and screams. The uncle dies.

Without paying a great deal of attention to Julia and realizing that he now has got to leave the premises hurriedly, he saddles his newly acquired horse, a brown one, to make off for London. In spite of everything that has happened, he is full of zest, vigor and the joy of life. While galloping south through the fields in damp rainy weather, he notices at one stage that he is followed by two men whom he recognizes as Julia's brothers, and whom he always disliked because of their poor speech and conduct.

(The above is the introduction, the actual incident started here.)

He spurs his horse on to greater effort, and takes one high fence successfully. The chase is fast and exciting, he feels the big horse's supreme staying powers and large movements, and approaches another fence. This time the jump is miscalculated, the horse takes the jump too early and hits the fence with his front legs. He is thrown, the horse comes down on top of him, one of the horse's rear hoofs hits the right side of his skull in the region of the ear and his left foot is twisted and hurts badly. He loses and regains consciousness several times. Meanwhile, the two brothers have arrived on the scene, pick

---

5. **rapier:** a small sword with a narrow blade, especially from the 18th century.

---

him up, rig him onto another horse, and whilst he is suffering great pain and discomfort, ride him to a nearby cottage.

After entering the cottage, they put him onto a sort of bed or table. Whilst withering in misery, pain and agony, he is aware that they are preparing some sort of an operation, and is under the impression that they are going to help him.

But he is to realize quickly that nothing of the sort is going to happen. Whilst the one brother is hurting his head on the left, the other approaches with a red-hot and flat-headed iron, the kind of branding iron used for branding cattle. He now realizes that they are going to brand and torture him. He sees the iron approaching and feels the red heat. The agony of being thus finished off fills him with indescribable horror. The first branding, followed by one or more others, produces indescribable pain, agony and body convulsions. When the branding is stopped, the right side of his face is horribly mutilated. He has been trying to resist, but all to no avail. The two brothers have had his face tightly gripped, his face is now a horrible mess, he has lost the sight in his right eye, the room is filled with the frightful stench of burning flesh and hair and he can stand it no longer.

He feels that he is gradually "unhooking" himself from the body and exteriorizes for good. A man comes into the room and remarks "Good God, he is dead." He sees the body some three to four feet away, horribly mutilated and unrecognizable. He feels sad for this body and for the loss of it, it was so attractive and full of promise. He feels he should not have met that kind of horrible fate. But he realizes that in that condition it is not much good to him anymore and he can now abandon it without much regret. He stays around for some time, for more than an hour. When the body is carried away, he leaves the scene and blackness ensues.

Case 24

Preclear's Report

Former Condition

Fairly good condition, no body illness.

Mental Outlook

I had a changed consideration that I have been looking too much at counter-effort[1] instead of looking at my own efforts. I am of the opinion that I have made gains in responsibility.

Physical Improvement

Have not noticed any change; mental outlook improved as noted above.

What You Attribute Improvement To

When looking at the engram I have been running, it seems somehow to parallel my struggle in this life. To me it is steady confronting of the facets of the engram which has improved my ability to confront, as I noticed quite a change in confronting.

---

1. **counter-effort:** effort is divided into the effort of the individual himself and the efforts of the environment (physical) against the individual. The individual's own effort is simply called effort. The efforts of the environment are called counter-efforts.

The Engram

This engram occurred in the year A.D. 54 I believe, some-where in Europe. It concerns the decision of myself (a fair-haired boy of 18 years) coming under the influence of an older person of some influence to undertake a mission to obtain, possibly, a manuscript. The journey was started a year and a half later and entailed long hundreds of miles across country, possibly in the direction of Greece. The course of the journey was through towns, rough country and the crossing of rivers, but the arduous part of the journey seemed to be while going through forests, when I would lose my way or when I had to go miles out of my way to cross a lake or bog. The first serious mishap on the journey was being attacked by thieves at night in a town, whilst going through a tunnel-like opening which was bridged by a house. The injuries I got in this attack were mostly to the head and seemed to put a grim aspect to the rest of the journey as, from there on, everything connected with the journey was of the grimmest character. Further along on the journey whilst crossing a bog I went down a hole and almost drowned, and compulsively exteriorized from the body for the first time at this event. After this near death I must have been in an emaciated or weak condi-tion as the consideration was that this body could not handle itself very well. Most of the journey seemed to be of a furtive[2] nature as I seemed wherever possible to avoid people or dogs. The objective of my mission seemed to be a castle or abode of monks as when I did get within sight of the place I seemed to take every precaution not to be seen. When I reached the vicinity of the walls of the castle I was quite fearful, and my main concern seemed to be to find a secret entrance into the interior of the castle.

All crevices in the rocks on which the castle walls were

2. **furtive:** done by stealth; secret.

built were examined for a secret entrance, and this meant searching along the shore as the castle was built near the sea. Finally, in a small ravine near the castle a secret entrance was discovered and, after a lot of squirming through underground passages, an entrance to the castle was obtained.

There was evidence of incarceration[3] in a dungeon, the bed of which was a ledge cut out of rock, with hardly any movement that could be made in the confined space. Later, three monks did something to my head whilst I was strapped in a chair. This consisted of placing a metal cage over the head: during processing this brought on an earache and head somatics, and the heavy dopiness I went through seemed to indicate a period of unconsciousness.

A final scene, where the body was concerned, was being strapped to a table. Three more monks were present, but only one of the monks present at the aforementioned scene was there. At this point of the engram the death of the body took place, as one of the monks removed a circular portion of the top of the head. Whilst being processed on this part of the engram, considerable apathy, head somatics and dopiness occurred. Final exteriorization from the body occurred at the body death, and I seemed to go to a considerable height and distance from the castle area, only to return to try and locate the body. There seems to be a period where I was stuck in a position a few yards outside the building from where the body died and could not move from same. Whilst being processed at this stage there was a period when I felt acutely the loss of the body, that it had been a good body, and that I had not done the right thing by the body. Also it might be mentioned that when the monks were doing something to the body in the first stages of the engram, it seemed very dramatic. A considerable

3. **incarceration:** imprisonment; confinement.

amount of perturbation[4] was present, as was deep apathy and a form of amazement at the monks not seeming to realize that what they were doing was an injury to the body. At this stage in the engram I was unable to tell whether the monks were trying to operate on me or torture me; as far as I can see, it seems the former.

---

4. **perturbation:** being worried or upset; being disturbed or troubled greatly.

Case 25

Auditor's Report

This incident was first contacted by asking the preclear for a "time when she lost the body." This produced a large reaction on the E-Meter. Further questioning, using E-Meter technique, produced an unmistakable reaction on the time of three million years ago. The repetitive process[1] "What part of that incident can you confront?" was immediately started. This resulted in the preclear seeing large quantities of jumbled mental image pictures. This confusion was accompanied by a great deal of grief and convulsive body movements. Persistent use of the process, with interpolations[2] of questions on specific details, developed after several hours a fairly consecutive narrative of the incident, which was found to contain torture of the body of that lifetime. The torture consisted of compression of the body in a casing similar to the "iron maiden"[3] of medieval times. This was designed so as to allow the body to be

---

1. **repetitive process:** an auditing process which is run over and over again, with the same question of the preclear. The preclear answers the question and the auditor acknowledges him. The process is run until it no longer produces change or a reaction in the preclear.

2. **interpolations:** insertions of statements, remarks, etc., between or among others.

3. **iron maiden:** a medieval torture instrument, fashioned as a box in the shape of a woman, large enough to hold a human being, and studded with sharp spikes on the inside.

subjected to electronic shock. During this period in the casing the body was also twice mutilated by electronic cautery.[4]

It was necessary in running this incident to direct the preclear's attention to her efforts to resist all the compression, shocks and pain. This resulted in a great deal of body movement, actual pain in the areas concerned and swelling of the lower limbs. These physical manifestations ceased completely as the incident was thoroughly contacted and confronted; although, in order to obtain this result, it was necessary to make an E-Meter "scout" for two separate occasions prior to the main incident, when the preclear was responsible for committing similar hostile acts against other beings. When these were found and confronted, it was found that the main incident ran very easily. More details came to light, and the preclear was able to confront them satisfactorily.

During the running of this incident, there were periods when the preclear was unwilling to confront certain details. At these times the preclear felt that the whole incident was "unreal, imaginary, etc." but, by getting the preclear's interest in the details which were "confrontable," she was persuaded gradually to confront the difficult part. This resulted in the incident becoming completely real to the preclear and she realized that many of her thoughts during the torture had been "stuck" in her mind and had been the cause of much of her present-life behavior and physical condition.

---

4. **cautery:** The operation of cauterizing. *Cauterize* means to burn with a hot iron, electric current, fire or a caustic substance (one that is capable of burning, corroding or destroying living tissue), especially for curative purposes. An example of the use of cautery would be pressing a hot iron against a wart to burn it off; another would be to sear an open wound in order to form a scar and stop it from bleeding.

Case 26

Preclear's Report

Former Condition

I got on[1] quite well. I tried to the best of my ability to keep myself and my reactive mind separate. I didn't look at my reactive mind much for fear of not being able to handle it. Too much uncertainty on my part.

Mental Outlook Now

My bank now looks very impressive to me. I have more respect for it—it seems more real to me. There is a tremendous amount of uncertainty and "maybe I'm wrong" in the engram which fits in with my present-life personality so well.

What You Attribute Improvement To

My increased acceptance of my recorded past-life track is due to being run on "What part of that incident can you confront?" plus the instructor's reality on it.

The Engram

The incident was rather confusing as I had two deaths in the

---

1. **got on:** got or made what one needed; managed.

same house on the same bed. The first death was as an old man.

The other death was in 1903. I am a child about eleven years old. I am in a four-poster bed with a green coverlet and drapes, in front is a window, to the left a fire and on the right a marble-topped table and a door.

There is a housekeeper who I feel wants me out of the way and, although I am told this is just a "childish fancy," I wonder if it is so.

I don't feel I can get away from the house because I will be brought back and no one will believe what I say about the housekeeper. I feel I must be careful not to be ill, and must always be on my guard. The housekeeper gives me some medicine to dope me; I am wondering what she is going to do, but take the medicine. I fall asleep and wake up to hear heavy footsteps. She comes in, she tells me she is going to kill me and takes out of her dress a kitchen knife. My attention is not on her but on the glittering knife. She stabs me just above the heart.

Auditor's Report

This engram was selected out of five incidents detected five days previously by finding the one that reacted the most on the E-Meter.

For the first three hours there was a lot of confusion and unreality for the pc. By the end of five hours it appeared as if there were three deaths in the same room, with confusion over changes of furniture and period. This all seemed "make believe" to the pc, but by use of the meter one incident was disentangled and worked on for a further two and a half hours with increasing reality and increasing ability to face up to what was going on.

Briefly, this was the pc's death as a girl of twelve on May 31, 1903. This was in a four-poster bed in a room she had apparently died in, in three different lives, possibly by being knifed, after being drugged or with diphtheria.[2] Being given the drug or sleeping draft was very real and pc has *in this life* the period[3] spoon with which this was administered in the incident. Also in this life, she has a carved box which was at the end of the bed in the room in the incident.

The following morning it was very difficult to keep the pc in-session.[4] The incident flicked to and fro between the dread and unreality of her mother's death, fear she was to blame, the funeral and being in the stables with her pony.

Much of this time her body was restless, as if feverish, and, all the time, tense. On the slightest pressure from the auditor the pc would become very alert and very aggressive. Phrases like "I might as well give up" leveled at the auditor were found to be in the engram, as also, "I will not speak about it." And certainly the sense of "I'm making it all up," and "It can't really be true," said to the auditor, derived directly from the little girl, incredulous at her mother's death and the machinations[5] of the bossy housekeeper.

---

2. **diphtheria:** an acute infectious disease that causes a sore throat, high fever, and the formation in the air passages of a membrane that can block breathing.

3. **period:** of or like that of an earlier time or age.

4. **in-session:** the condition necessary for successful auditing, defined as preclear "willing to talk to the auditor and is interested in his own case."

5. **machinations:** sly or secret plots or schemes, especially evil ones.

A further day's hard work elicited very little gain, and at the auditor's insistence that there was something keeping the pc unable to confront so much charge, the chief instructor came and agreed that it would be best to run the far more general process "What can you confront?" This brought up some present-life problems which were handled and the pc went willingly into session. The pc was confronting much better and was less fearful of "going out of present time."

Case 27

Preclear's Report

Former Condition

I knew that I was always looking at something, listening to and thinking about someone or something unknown. Most of my attention was kept elsewhere than here. Having ideas I knew did not come from me, but from an unknown source. Felt at times uncommunicative and strongly desiring to be elsewhere than on this planet.

Mental Outlook

Walking less as if on eggshells. I have less feeling of having to hold something down or keep from exploding. I have more attention in the present time. I feel very certain that this incident has a great deal to do with my present time life.

Physical Improvement

My face looks clearer. Varicose veins are slowly disappearing. I have more energy and less tension in my abdomen where my operation was performed. Less heavy feeling (not change in weight—just feeling). Less fear around me (there was lots of terror run off the incident).

What You Attribute Improvement To

To having found out part of the wording of the implant[1] and also the "ideas" of having been made into a monster.

Knowing that this incident is the engram that will really change my life when completely run out. The instructor helped me to have more interest in my engram and to have again a desire to run through the incident.

I also attribute my improvement to the perseverance of my auditor.

Auditor's Report

The scene is 11th century Norway. This person was the unwanted male child of a woman "who lived in ships." Abortion was attempted during the third month of pregnancy and the baby's right eye blinded by the instrument, while the mother was saying to the man, "You're no good, you're driving me crazy." The boy was not loved by the mother nor by the man she married. "Nobody likes me" was a recurring phrase in processing.

Scene II was at seven years old on a hot day when the boy and stepfather were walking along the cliffs. The child was verminous[2] and scratching and the man got angry, saying "dirty little bastard, I will kill you." He pushed him over the cliff, mother consenting. The boy lay semiconscious halfway down and later ran away to sea.

1. **implant:** an enforced command or series of commands installed in the reactive mind below the awareness level of the individual to cause him to react or behave in a prearranged way without his "knowing it."

2. **verminous:** infested with small, objectionable parasites such as fleas, lice, etc.

Scene III was at age thirty. He got drunk, went berserk and killed the captain of a trading vessel bound for Iceland. The crew set on him saying, "You're crazy. We're going to kill you." His head was clamped into a metal frame and his left eye blinded with a hot instrument and his eardrums pierced. Now there is a gap in the story. The next recall is of the body in the sea still alive, washed up for awhile onto the beach, and finally swallowed by a huge monster (whale?) with a gaping mouth, vast rib cage and intestine half full of water. Exteriorization took place at this point and there were many pictures of sea and coast from above. The pc said, "I've the idea I've been there for a very long time."

On account of the pc's great unreality, "Look around here and find something you would permit to vanish" was run, which produced the following much earlier incident (ca. 3 trillion B.C.).

Change of Sex Incident

Pc dopey, reclining posture, nostrils dilated, somatics in groin, back, left eye and between eyes. She had impression of revolving circle above head and beams of light hitting center of forehead. Much teeth clenching, voice change: "I felt like a girl, now I feel like a man"; "I feel I'm being hypnotized." Audio of voices: "You will kill whatever you are told to kill"; "You will be crazy if you are a girl."

Undersea Incident (not finished)

Disconnected pictures of huge "fish-craft" and smaller ones with four "engines" in front and one at rear. Pc felt like a cat, saw her hands as claws. The atmosphere was damp and heavy. She was underwater.

Case 28

Auditor's Report

This incident was located by another auditor by flash answer, and further checking as to accuracy of the place and type of occurrence by meter. At the point of my taking over the pc, he had run about twenty hours and, owing to unreality and some reluctance to run the incident, had not been able to view anything of the sequence (story) of the incident or locate any pictures which would indicate what the incident was about.

The amount of data available at this stage was that there seemed to be something to do with a stork eating the pc, which on further checking got unreal and left the pc with a somatic in the forehead. The somatic came on consistently at the contacting of the established time of the incident 5,100 years ago. Further scouting around this time elicited the fact that "There was a feeling of some sort of operation done on the forehead." This was not real enough to see, but, as this did not change in content and read consistently on the meter, it gave a starting point to the incident.

It was at this point that I took over the case.

We established the time of the incident and, from the

pieces of data to hand, gradually widened the content of the operation to being done in an antechamber of a temple by a chief priest. It was being done as an initiation into priesthood. This had some confusion about it, however, as on further viewing it appeared that during the ceremony and with his body lying on a marble slab and having some object inserted into his head, the body ceased to live. Therefore, why perform an initiation ceremony which defeated its main purpose?

On further confronting the area of the place of operation it very slowly became real enough for the pc to piece together more of what actually did happen. His forehead was opened and an operation done with drugs and hypnosis as control medium, in which the "soul" (the pc himself as a being) was extracted from the forehead and placed in some container, sealed in and placed with other such containers in a cupboard. Later, this is removed by another priest who has a private purpose to practice black magic with it. In doing so, the pc in the container finds that owing to an accidental mishandling, the container explodes, he with it, and he is left in a dazed but free state and at an apparent end of incident.

With further running of the incident, however, the pc discovered that the object he is placed in is a type of lamp in which he is hypnotically told he is to stay for all time and to keep burning to "Light the gates of hell for the Prince of Darkness." The lamp is really left in the outer chamber and he in the lamp until he is suddenly aware that there is an explosion in a 17th century drawing room. On going over this again the story resolves into the fact that he did remain in the lamp 4,800 years and gradually became so unaware that his removal from the original place and the elapsed time had gone completely unnoticed.

At this point in running the incident a lot of unconsciousness started to interfere with confronting and an earlier portion of the incident was opened up. One in which an initiation
of a different nature is experienced , which he is tricked into
by being given a drugged liquid to drink. During this time he
is haunted by an ape which one of the priests uses to perform
part of an enforced personality change.

As no more data was available at this juncture in the
incident, a very early part of his life was contacted and a rapid
scan done up to the beginning of the incident proper. This
brought the pc to view the fact that he had led a comparatively
normal early life as an Egyptian, of a royal household, hunting, chariot racing and spear throwing, the latter making him
become slightly lame (a manifestation in his present life in a
very slight form in his right leg).

He later becomes involved with a mistress. At the time of
his first initiation at the age of twenty he is very powerful
spiritually, though not wise, and is feared, hated and partly in
disgrace in his household, owing to his general attitude to
others and their standards of living. He constantly challenges
those who stand in his own personal path, frequently to their
demise, and often kills his opponents by willpower, which has
the effect of weakening him too.

At this point the fact is uncovered that at his first initiation he is operated on with drugs and hypnosis and has
inserted into his forehead a jewel which causes much of his
later trouble. Its purpose is to increase his powers of will over
others and make him a member of the priesthood, which it
very effectively does. At the same time it makes him a party to
their purposes right or wrong, as well as to some degree
changing his character to partly that of the ape experienced
some time earlier.

The effects of these experiences lead to a fairly short and temperamental life, which is terminated when he is attacked by lions whilst hunting and the wounds go gangrenous.[1] As he is dying he is taken to the antechamber and removed from the body, placed in the lamp in which he remains until his freedom 4,800 years later. After the lamp's explosion he is very dazed and, for a period of seven years, gradually recovers from his complete unawareness to take up life again, very reduced in ability and with no memory of his free life and the fall into unconsciousness.

This incident is not quite fully viewed and many small pieces of it, although mostly in sequence, are still unconnected. However, during the running of it the pc realized that many unwanted effects in this life (such as an occasional slight weakness in the right leg) were traceable to the incident as the source of their origin.

---

1. **gangrenous:** decay of tissue in a part of the body when the blood supply is blocked by injury, disease, etc.

Case 29

Preclear's Report

Former Condition

I was in very good shape.

Mental Outlook

I have certainly noticed an improvement in my ability to confront situations. This is apparent in my business life, where I have been able to direct employees to the roots of problems without any tendency to feel "sorry" for being too direct with them. Two gains here, of course: one, to confront problems better and, two, to better confront people.

Physical Improvement

My appetite has increased somewhat.

What You Attribute Improvement To

I had processes run on me which were undoubtedly therapeutic.

The Engram

The story starts with my first being aware of a leather-aproned bearded man. As it developed, a group of people became apparent standing around a pinkish-colored stone post. This was about four feet high. It was square in shape, each side being about eight inches wide. I was led up to the stone, chained to it, and the leather-aproned man proceeded to burn out my eyes with a red-hot rod. I hastily got out of the body, and followed it when it was taken down to the edge of a nearby lake. All the time I was trying to get back into the body but considered I couldn't do so. However, I maintained some control and let it fall into the shallow water, where I pathetically bathed its eyes. I turned the body on its side but then decided to abandon it. Incidentally, some distance away in the lake was another body but, try as I would, I had no ideas about it. I returned minus body to the stone and group of people and, feeling lost, seemed to shoot up into the sky from where I regarded the scene with very mild interest, and then passed into oblivion.

I could not get any earlier recollection as to why I was so cruelly treated.

Auditor's Report

This engram was located on the E-Meter as having occurred in the year A.D. 856. The beginning was walking as in a trance toward a stone where two people stood. The preclear's hands were tied behind his back and when he reached the stone a chain was tightened around his neck, binding him to the stone. One of the two persons who appeared to be like a blacksmith then heated some irons in a fire and hammered them out on an anvil. The red-hot irons were put into the eyes of the body chained to the stone. (At this stage of the processing, the preclear briefly experienced some somatics in the eyes, throat and head.) As soon as the red-hot irons were placed into the eyes, the thetan exteriorized from the body. The body was taken down to a nearby lake or sea and was thrown into the water. The thetan returned to the body and turned it over in the water, and while doing this he looked at a castle on a hill in the distance. He then returned to the scene where the eyes had been put out and, seeming to find nothing there, went to a considerable height overlooking the entire scene of the death of the body. When the preclear was processed on the attitude he had when walking up to the stone where his eyes were put out, he doped off,[1] and during the processing this lasted for a period of over four hours. The scene of this incident was near a lake or sea, and lying in the water was another dead body. No explanation was given for its being there.

---

1. **doped off:** got tired, sleepy, foggy (as though doped).

Case 30

Preclear's Report

Former Condition

Emotionally unstable, insecure with regard to holding positions. No physical disabilities.

Mental Outlook

Fluctuating between positive outlook and negative.

Physical Improvement

Ability to do with less sleep, despite very heavy schedule.

Auditor's Report

The incident was found by asking the preclear for the date of a past death and snapping my fingers.

The preclear gave me a number and I pinned this down to years, months, days and hours by means of finger snaps. I got a number of incidents like this; some were this life and some were of previous lives. I made a chart of these. I then asked him about each incident on the chart and chose the one which caused the preclear the most discomfort and showed the most charge on the E-Meter. I then told the preclear to return to the incident in 3 A.D., June 10, at 1 A.M. He said that he was strangling a girl by means of a cord—this was quite real to him. I then went straight in and ran this process "What part of that incident can you confront?" After a few commands of this the preclear found himself in an arena being attacked by a lion. This was at first real to him and then became less real. This was the first time that he complained of the unreality. I continued with the process, keeping his interest up by asking questions and gradually the details of the incident came to light, although the preclear complained bitterly that he didn't want to look at it anymore.

The preclear was a Roman soldier in 3 A.D. He meets a girl at a party and marries her soon afterwards. Shortly he is sent off to fight at the border with his regiment; while there he is sent out on a scout of the enemy camp and returns to find that his own camp has been attacked. He leaves the location and heads back to Rome alone. The trip is long and uneventful, except that he spends the night at a farmer's house and makes love to the farmer's daughter. He leaves the next day. On arrival in Rome, he finds sentries on the road to the city, so he falls in with some marching troops and slips away once inside the city.

When he reaches his home his wife is not there. He beats a slave and finds out that she is living with another man. He goes over there and kills the man by throwing a spear and hitting him in the back. He then strangles his wife with a cord. As he is leaving, a servant tries to stop him, so he kills the servant with his sword. On the way home, a couple of officers in a chariot stop to ask him his business there and notice the blood on his sword. They take him in for questioning.

He is brought before the presiding officer and he is beaten

across the face with the handle of a chariot whip until he confesses to the murders. He is sentenced to the lions. He is taken, chained, to the arena in a chariot, and put into a cell. Some hours later he is unchained and pushed out into the arena; the lion is then let loose.

The preclear stands in the arena frightened, but knowing that to be a good Roman he must not be afraid, so when the lion comes toward him he does not run away. The lion jumps at him and knocks him over backwards. He rolls over on his face to protect it, but the lion puts its front paws on his back and chews off his head and neck. The preclear exteriorizes from the body and the body dies. The preclear then watches from a few feet above while the lion plays around with and paws at the body. Later the body is taken away and burned.

While the incident was being run, the preclear dramatized many of the happenings. In the early stages it was mostly the effort showing up in the form of tenseness in the body. One particular time the preclear's body went stiff as a board. He lost his voice and his mind went blank. This lasted for three quarters of an hour and I continued, by repeating the command and getting him to continue the process. Somatics turned on many times in the preclear's body in the running of the incident, especially when going over the parts where he was beaten, and where he was mauled by the lion. The somatics were pains in the head, a stiff neck, a sore face, the pressure of the lion standing on his back, and others.

Emotions showed up in the form of anger, fear, boredom and others. The preclear picked up many of the thoughts, considerations and postulates of the incident and saw how many of these affected his present life. Most of the perceptions were picked up in the incident, such as the smell of the lion's body and the sound of his snarl.

The preclear's reality on the incident fluctuated throughout the running of it. Many times when he was in doubt as to the authenticity of it I would get him to look around by asking questions concerning the environment of the incident, thus getting his interest up so that he would keep going. There was some difference between the original and the last version, apart from new details coming up all the time, but as the incident gradually developed, things fell into place.

Case 31

Preclear's Report

Former Condition

An unwillingness to change in myself, with a strong tendency to destroy people with whom I associated.

Mental Outlook

I feel free, and am willing to change—if I want to.

Physical Improvement

I have lost some excess weight.

What You Attribute Improvement To

Knowing what I was doing and why I was doing it.

Auditor's Report

The engram run on this preclear (a male) was located by the use of an E-Meter. I had asked the preclear for a moment of death and he gave me the first thing that came into his mind. I next checked for the time of this incident by asking him if it was before or after certain dates, and then checked into his responses. When a full date was established, I asked whose death was this and found out that it was a woman that he had murdered. Having located this incident, I next inquired as to whether or not the preclear had any pictures of this incident. He had; it was a picture of a large nude woman on a bed. Taking this still picture, I then began to run a process on it. It was not long before the preclear began to say that this incident was a figment of his very good imagination; that it might have happened, but actually the preclear was just making it up. The preclear then treated it as a game, adding pieces here, taking pieces away and building a story around this original picture.

After a while this story of "imagination" begins to make sense and suddenly the preclear is telling me that in his present life many years ago he had an affair with a lady friend that ended in the same way as this "made-up" story, except that he did not murder her. The preclear was a little surprised to find this, as he had definitely not been thinking of this particular episode in his life. Furthermore, on discussion, the preclear found out that he had not realized before that, with large women, something happened that always made him feel that he had broken faith with himself. Shortly after this, while running a process, the preclear's voice, which had been very deep and froggy, became more normal. He also developed many somatics in his neck, shoulders and back. Even so, he still said, "This is all silly, it is all my imagination."

The next thing that happened went further to convince him that this was nothing more or less than giving rein to his imagination or fancy. He had established his story as that of being a coachman and driving his coach up to a pub. He made a date with a maid servant, and had an affair with her that was rather disappointing and the maid taunted him. His temper being what it was, he put his hands around her throat to silence her. She screamed, there was a knock on the door, the maid was struggling madly, so he picked up a gold candlestick and smashed it on her head. The next instant, the door opened and a man came in. He then hit the man, got out of the door, found a horse in the yard and rode away. Now his story changed, and this time he was taking his mother to get the coach, and he killed the maid for her money. After making these additions he added that no maid would have money enough to warrant killing her for it. And, besides, she had a bookcase in her bedroom and that was highly improbable.

Despite these protestations I had noticed that he had watched the coach for quite long periods, and that he was most meticulous about the details of the coach and that they did not change in any way, so I began to concentrate on the coach. I kept asking, "What is so special about the coach?" "Where had it come from?" "Where was it going?" "Where had he sat in it?" etc. Eventually I had him giving me a detailed description of the coach from every angle. Nothing happened until I had him do it from the driver's seat. Immediately he changed his physical body position in the auditing chair to sitting back a little more, legs stretched out in front of him, and he swivelled the E-Meter cans that he was holding so that the leads were going away from him to the E-Meter. A perfect picture of a happy coachman with the reins held easily in his hands. We carried on with a description of the coach for another five minutes until the preclear said, "Ah! that's it, I'm the driver of the coach."

As soon as he knew this, it was as if his memory had suddenly returned. For he was then able to answer my question of, "Well, what is this incident all about?" He replied, "You see, I'm the coachman and this is an overnight stop. I have been having an affair with the landlady. This night I got there and went to her room, across the roof, and stole the money from the bookcase. She woke up and went to scream. I put my hands around her throat. She struggled, there was a knock on the door and I panicked and bashed her head in with a candlestick. I got out of the window, and shut it behind me. The catch was a bit stiff and fell into place, locking the window from the inside. I got back to my room, hid the money and went out and joined all the others who were aroused by now."

Having recalled all this, the preclear was delighted. We talked it over for some time and then I got him to go over this incident again. After getting up to the point where the horses were removed from the coach, he had a great reluctance to get down from the seat, and then, without any warning, he said, "That's funny, I now seem to be in a barn, but I am still on top of the coach." I had him look around and describe his environment; this he did by saying that this was an old, dirty, unrepaired barn and that, horror of horrors, the coach was covered in cobwebs and rusty. Furthermore, he seemed to have the body of a young girl about twelve. This did not all come out at once but gradually developed as we ran the process. The next thing that seemed to happen was that she (the preclear) fell off the coach and broke her neck.

At this moment the preclear became his old self, and said, "See—engrams, huh!—past lives, huh!—my imagination is real wild. Now you try to make sense out of that." To get him back into session at this point was a little hard going, but we made it. I ran a snap check for the time of this incident of the little girl and found it to be January 1st, 1800, the same date as the murder of the woman in the pub. This really set the preclear laughing. "Now what are you going to do?" he said. Fortunately, there was an answer to that: With two different incidents showing up at the same time there must be something contained in both incidents that is very similar and "holding" them together. So, getting back into session, we set to work to find the "holder." Eventually we found that the link between the two incidents was the driving seat of the coach. With this established, I then ran a process and got the two incidents separated, then located the incident of the child in time and found it to be 1815.

We then went back to the original incident and traced it from the murder to leaving the pub and going to Portsmouth, where he left his coach and managed to get on board a ship as a seaman bound for either Australia or America. Aboard ship he was flogged[1] for stealing food. Then he left the ship for a new country, got married and had a daughter. And he killed his daughter by pulling her off the top of a coach in a barn in a fit of temper. This was fine, but not good enough. We had found out why the incident of a girl had suddenly shown up, and the fact that he had killed his daughter would explain why he had believed himself to be a young girl (trying to live her life for her). But both I and the preclear were intrigued as to why he had killed his daughter. Previously he had mentioned that he was in a temper. Well, why? So we set to work using the pictures that he had of killing the girl, and we ran the process that we had been running all along.

After one and a quarter hours nothing had turned up, my preclear began to get agitated, and he began mumbling about the stupidity of it all—that once again it was all his imagination, he had made it all up—and, as we continued, he became more and more agitated until he was eventually quite annoyed and began to demand that we finish "mucking around"[2] and get down to some serious work. But we still carried on. The preclear then became quite belligerent[3] and angry with me. I was told that I didn't know what I was doing, that he was

---

1. **flogged:** beaten, or punished by being beaten, with a strap, stick, whip, etc.

2. **mucking around:** wasting time, puttering, going about aimlessly.

3. **belligerent:** showing readiness to fight or quarrel.

quite sure that this was a waste of time, and from that moment on, as far as the preclear was concerned, I couldn't do a thing right. I was talking too loud in one command; the next command, I was too quiet; and then I disturbed him if I moved a finger. He couldn't concentrate because of all the noise in the environment, I held my head wrong, we should have a break—all of which was stated in a very loud, angry manner, which was curious because we were looking for something that had made him angry in the incident when he had killed his daughter in a fit of temper. The preclear couldn't recall what it was but it was surely having an effect right now in the auditing room, for my manner had not changed since we had begun auditing, and the environment noise at this moment was less than it normally was.

The only conclusion to be drawn from this was that we had found what was making the preclear mad in the incident. But that it was not available to his normal memory could only mean one thing, and that was that something or someone was withholding something from the memory of the preclear. And that someone or something was contained in the incident. So I quietly asked the preclear, was somebody withholding something from him in the incident. Instantly his face became beetroot[4] red, his hands gripped the cans he was holding very, very hard, and he sucked his breath in. "Yes," he managed to say, "Jack was holding the gold from me"—and out poured another part of the incident. Apparently he had a friend called Jack. They had robbed a bank; he had been shot while robbing the bank. They had got back to the farm and his wife had dressed the wound. Then when he saw Jack, Jack had refused to give him any gold or tell him where it was. He had been too scared of Jack to do anything about it, and had stalked off into the barn to get his horse. When he got into the barn his

---

4. **beetroot:** (same as beet) a reddish colored root vegetable.

daughter was on a buckboard[5] and had some reins in her hand. She threw the reins to him and asked him to pretend to be a horse. At this, his suppressed anger had broken loose. He grabbed the reins and gave them a tremendous jerk that pulled her off the buckboard. She fell headfirst and hit her neck on the iron rim of the wheel and had then fallen onto the cobblestones of the barn entrance.

At this moment the preclear said that he had felt tremendously angry during that incident especially when I mentioned the gold. He also mentioned that sometimes while fighting in the ring he had felt like this, but had never known why.

As for the anger with me, why, this had totally disappeared and we were now the best of friends. What is more important, though, was that the incident was now once again very real to him. Now we checked over the incident and eventually found out that the story was this: As he was passing his barn, he heard some giggling, went in, and found a worker on the farm, a young boy of nineteen, on top of a haystack with his daughter of twelve. He became very angry and called the boy down. The boy came down grasping a pitchfork. He went for the boy, and the pitchfork pierced his own shoulder (at this moment he felt the full pain of this happening). He then pulled the pitchfork out and knocked the boy unconscious with it. His daughter screamed and he threw the pitchfork in her direction and said, "I'll deal with you later." He was horrified to see the pitchfork hit the girl in the chest, all three prongs going in deep and sticking there. Just at this moment the boy moved, and he looked at the boy and blamed him for being the cause of the girl's death.

---

5. **buckboard:** an open, flat-bottomed, four-wheeled carriage.

Two of his farm workers came and they led the boy over to a post and flogged him. As they did this, the boy shouted out that he would tell all about it. The preclear thought that this meant about the murder of the fat woman, so he had the young boy hanged from a chain from the seat of the buckboard. Just before they hanged the boy, the preclear himself was knocked unconscious by hitting his head on the buckboard seat. While unconscious he seemed to be looking down at all this. He saw the body of his daughter and thought of the murder of the fat woman. He next saw this boy struggling and the chain around his neck. He knew the boy was being hanged, and he thought he himself ought to be hanged; then he didn't know which was his body and so decided that he must be the boy because he ought to be hanged. In a hazy way after this, he came to, but had no recollection of these thoughts. He then proceeded to hang the boy. After this he rode away, but then changed his mind and returned to make amends. But his wife shot him in the back, "like a dog," and he died. When he died, he seemed to be looking down at his body, his horse dying (for the bullet had gone through him into the horse), his wife, and the full scene.

The preclear on viewing this went into a violent grief. He was crying about being betrayed. He had decided to change his way of life and be what his wife wanted, and she had shot him "like a dog in the back." Then we began to pick up further decisions he had made at this time, such as "I'll never change," "I will destroy and no one will ever stop me," "I'll destroy everybody and nobody will ever get at me," "I'll be inside a tube (cylinder) and no one will ever hurt me but I'll be able to destroy them," etc. When we had cleared this up, the preclear said, "So that's what it was! Boy, is it true! Have I destroyed things! (And then related all the things he had been destroying.) And I sure wouldn't let anything have an effect on me. God, isn't this stupid! Fancy living like this." Whereupon, he promptly changed his decisions, having regained the abilities to create and change which he now can do with ease.

Preclear's Report

The engram was picked as the murder of a woman at a hotel somewhere in England on New Year's Day 1800. I seem to have killed a woman for money which was hidden in a cupboard. I escaped to Australia and bought a farm with the money, then married and had a daughter. When the Australian part of the incident was picked up the year was 1815, I had been married for thirteen years, and the daughter was about four years old. The story this time was that I had robbed a bank, been shot during the robbery, and my accomplice had escaped with the loot. He defied me when I asked for my share, and pointed out that if I killed him I would never get it anyway. In a rage I flung my daughter off the high seat of a wagonette (a type of carriage) and she was killed by impact with the cobbled[6] yard. Still angry, I rode away; but a couple of hours later I changed my mind, decided I shouldn't have done it and came back to make amends. My wife shot me in the back as I took the saddle off my horse and, as I died, some man from the bank I had robbed came and hanged my dead body.

During the running of the incident, it became unreal many times, so that I doubted that it ever existed. The location, however, remained stable irrespective of how the incident twisted and changed. In turn, as the story unfolded, I was first

---

6. **cobbled:** paved with rounded stones (cobblestones), formerly used for paving streets.

myself as the murderer, and then the woman I had killed, then the boy who later became part of the story and then the wife I felt regret about. The final story was as follows:

I was walking alongside the barn, on the farm (location of the incident) when I heard a scuffling in the hayloft. As I reached the doorway and looked up I saw a boy of about nineteen years of age, whom I had befriended and who lived with us on the farm, kneeling beside my daughter, who I have now established as being about twelve years old. I was angry and shouted to the boy to come down. He picked up a pitchfork and threw it at me, it hit me in the shoulder, and he then slid down the hay and came toward me. As he approached I took the tine[7] from my shoulder and hit him on the side of the head with the handle. My daughter screamed out not to hurt him, and, enraged, I threw the pitchfork at her and hit her squarely in the chest. She fell backwards out of sight on the top of the hay. I was dismayed at what I had done but blamed the boy for the occurrence. Two of the convict workers on the farm had been attracted by the uproar and I ordered these to handcuff the boy to a nearby post in order that I could administer a flogging. On the first stroke the boy said that if I did anything to him he would tell everyone about me—meaning, I thought, that he would tell people about the murder and robbery in England. I knew then that I must kill him. The three of us got him into the back of the wagonette, but in the struggle I was knocked out.

During the resulting exteriorization I saw the top of the hay with the dead girl lying on it. And I blamed the boy for her death, and said to myself that he deserved to hang; but, knowing that I had really killed the girl myself, I actually

---

7. **tine:** a slender, projecting part that is pointed at the end; prong.

considered I should hang and to some degree identified myself with the boy. I saw my body get off the wagonette and fix a chain to the beam over the doorway, I saw the chain placed about the boy's throat and experienced the sensation of hanging when he was hung. After this incident, several times I picked up the decision that "I should hang there," and from then on became myself again. After the hanging, I rode to a lookout point and there decided that I was sorry for what I had done, and I would go back and make amends. The recovery of this decision brought a flood of tears. I rode to the farm, and as I took the saddle off the horse my wife shot me through the lower part of the back. The ball passed right through my body and hit my horse in the stomach, eventually killing him too. This produced further tears, and after the body was dead I remained poised over it and decided that I would never change: I had changed, and this was my reward. I decided that I would put a tube around me to protect me, for I would never trust anyone or change ever again.

At this point, the auditor requested that I return to the clearing. As I rode up the hill I said that I had never had a chance anyway; that the decision about changing had been made a long time before. I felt as though I were moving rapidly back in time. I felt stuck to a post, and amid a feeling of terrific indignity, anger and grief, said that "I had decided never to be curious, and then I had changed and been curious, and here I was, stuck to a post." Immediately this decision was recovered, I was freed from the post and once again flew back in time. Quite suddenly everything felt still—the anger, grief and indignity disappeared. I said, "This is where it began. I was perfect and I made a perfect tube. It was a perfect creation and I decided that I would never change it," but since it was *the* perfect creation, I must be less than perfect, and so to be perfect I became the tube and it went on from there. Then I saw where the mistake lay. I had said I would never change the tube and then confused the decision into never changing my-self. The engram had lost its importance except as an interesting validation of past lives.

Since then I see that always before I was *being perfect*. But I don't have to be anything, I only have to *be*. This seems to have been the restricting feature of this life and doubtless of many other lives, too.

Case 32

Preclear's Report

Former Condition

I was truly willing to be effect, but only secondarily to be cause. If I wanted to be cause, I had to get someone else to want, need or flatly tell me whatever I wanted to do. Or I had to think that someone else would be happier by my act. I went to extraordinary lengths to avoid being primary cause, and especially as I have a great deal of enterprise, this was evident to me, but I could not pin it down.

Mental Outlook

Searching, and being fairly certain, I am still in a male valence.

Physical Improvement

None, but there was formerly nothing wrong.

What You Attribute Improvement To

Putting into words the decision of my engram: "I will accept whatever comes." Thus, in 1958 "I can cause whatever I decide to cause," whereas, in the engram, at the time of my decision, this would have been pointless as I was entering a period in which I knew I would be a pure effect.

The Engram

The incident took place in February of 1703, and I was attached to some fighting group, possibly around the Pretender[1] to the English throne.

I was a healthy young boy of about fifteen and had been given my first solo assignment. My father seemed to have been an important person, probably first in command, and I was extremely anxious to do a good job and very excited at this chance. I started out from the royal encampment about 5 A.M. I was on horseback and thoroughly enjoyed the cold wind and the feel of the horse beneath me crossing country which I knew well. I arrived before dawn near a hermit's cottage. I tethered my black horse to a bush near some trees, some distance from the cottage. I left him in a place where there was plenty of fodder. We were great friends.

I think my message was to my father, to warn him of our force's approach, and speed was second to safety, so I had to remain in hiding until nightfall, when I would continue my journey.

I walked to the hermit's cottage with spring in my step, and tapped a significant rhythm on the door. The hermit was expecting me, and first opened a peephole in the door, to ensure that I was a friend. I entered, and while he was rebolting the doors, I went directly to the fire which awaited me. After a few moments of warming myself I took off my cloak

---

1. **Pretender:** James Francis Edward Stuart (1688–1766), English prince of Wales who claimed the English throne and led an unsuccessful revolt to obtain it.

and sat down on a stool by the fire. Meanwhile, apart from inquiring what was happening, and how things were, the old man had been preparing something like porridge in a wooden bowl.

He was wearing a sack-brown monk's habit[2] with a cowl (hood). After I had eaten and gotten thoroughly warmed through, I took off my jacket and went over to a wide bench bed and snuggled up under some rugs and went off to sleep. I had a young and active body and was thoroughly tired out after a hard ride, apart from the strain and excitement of riding through the quarter-light of night. I slept until about midday, then I remained for a few moments more in the warmth before I arose and resumed small talk with the old man, who attentively hovered attempting to forestall[3] my needs.

Then I got up and stretched my light young limbs, and tried to restrain the exuberance bubbling to the surface. The old man was faithful and I didn't want him to suspect how restricted I felt in his small house, but at the end of the day the physical limitations imposed by my imprisonment were too strong for me and I was pacing the floor, counting the seconds until dark. At last dusk fell, our goodbyes were said, and I had expressed my reassurances to the old hermit who had shown me such hospitality. And so I set off with an easy stride, enjoying the fields and the feel of the leaves around my feet, as I trudged over the little hills to where I had tethered my horse. As I approached, the horse whinnied audibly and I broke into a run to see what was the matter. While releasing the lead I patted and stroked him and talked reassuringly, thinking that he must have felt lonely because I had left him all day.

---

2. **habit:** garb of a particular rank, profession, religious order, etc.

3. **forestall:** to act in advance of; get ahead of; anticipate.

But I was suddenly aware of the true reason as I felt my shoulder grasped, and with one swift stroke I slapped my horse soundly on the flank and whispered "home." Off he went at a gallop and I prayed he would reach my father who would draw the correct conclusions from my message.

The man who had first grasped me had me more firmly now, and he and his companions tied my wrists together behind my back and set me on course towards a group of trees not far distant. They held me by a lead, long enough to permit me freedom of my legs, though I knew they were too close to make it worth my while to attempt to escape. I kicked the leaves and breathed deeply as I made my way through the descending darkness. I could still move freely and thus kept my courage, and used some of my repressed energy.

Blackness descended and we entered a group of trees which surrounded a small stone dwelling, and my hopes sank. The door opened and for a moment I was transfixed.[4] In that instant I felt suspended in time. I realized that liberty was no longer mine, that freedom of movement and the joy of living were at an end. I saw objects which could only mean torture and captivity. In that moment I grew from a carefree youth into a man, and I made a decision to fit me for the role in these circumstances. I would accept willingly whatever they would do, and so I took my first step into the room and into my manhood.

They put me behind bars so that I could not lie or sit. In the morning I was sorely tired and aching. Something about my clothes must have given me away for they made little attempt to question me. And the third man who came then just ordered my captors to get on with it as if my treatment

---

4. **transfixed:** unable to move.

were a softening up process to prepare me for questioning. So they put me on some kind of contraption I can only describe as the rack. Slowly from a horizontal position the head and feet were descended until I suppose the support described an arch. The descent was very slow, and I was kept there for maybe half an hour, and the rise was even more painful.

I was more or less unconscious at this point, and someone's attempt to raise my head was useless. They lifted me off and put me in a chair. Perhaps an hour later I was led outside and in the bitter cold in only my shirt and tight black trousers, I was tied onto a kind of flat cartwheel, which was lifted onto a post and revolved slowly. This, with a dip where the surface was irregular to add to the rhythm, made me feel very sick, but my being kept flat by my bonds prevented me from relieving the inner agony and thus many minutes passed with waves of sickness coming and going. There was some sort of upper disc with spikes projecting that did not revolve but gradually descended and I was not sure whether it would stop descending before it had taken slices off my face. I did not so much as let out a murmur of disapproval—I was truly willing effect, and grateful for having made such a decision, for I could never have endured such horror and still remained my father's son if I had once begun to express what would have previously been my reactions.

Thus came the moment when the spikes ceased to approach my face. They removed this contraption, lifted the wheel off, and released my body. I remember little more than that I was violently and lengthily sick. I was led back to the room and put into a wooden chair with arms to which I was tied and left for some time in solitude. With bare time to remuster my courage, a man with similar bearing to my father entered and drew up a stool to face me. In that first moment he knew that I would never reveal any useful information, and we both knew that mine was a hopeless (political) cause, and it was only a matter of honor that my side held out. Somehow I managed to withhold my father's name and my questioner was so convinced that no further torture would get more out of me, we almost talked as equals. As he left he gave me the impression that we would soon be meeting again, no longer as enemies. This all seemed a bit vague and unreal, but feeling as ghastly as I did I suppose it is not surprising. They tried to put me back behind my bars, but I suspect I was too weak to remain upright and I was soon returned to a chair and here ends all I know at the moment.

Case 33

Preclear's Report

Former Condition

I was somewhat stale and stuck. I seemed to have come to a standstill psychologically, while continuing to have unwavering certainty. I decided to launch a fresh onslaught on my case.

Mental Outlook

Before course, worried and depressed. After course, general gains and feeling of expansion. I'm determined to get continued auditing along the new lines.

Physical Improvement

Improvement in neck and head somatics.

What You Attribute Improvement To

Two-way communication[1] with my auditor and gains in the earlier part of the course. Seeing the processes working steadily;

---

1. **two-way communication:** a two-way cycle of communication would work as follows: Joe, having originated a communication, and having completed it, may then wait for Bill to originate a communication to Joe, thus completing the remainder of the two-way cycle of communication. Thus we get the normal cycle of a communication between two people.

mostly running (probably about 50 percent) the "resolution of the case engram."

The Engram

The story is set in Shropshire (England) in 1792 when I was born an only child, son of a local squire.[2] Father was apparently a waster[3] and mother a bitter and disappointed woman. My grandmother was my very chief ally,[4] inculcating[5] the idea of service and leadership to the local community and giving me the love and understanding that my mother lacked. Clark, the gamekeeper, provided the training of outdoor sport and knowledge of the estate. He was always there to answer the thousand and one questions of a small boy and was steadfast but unimaginative. The first incident is myself, at age five, being summoned to my grandmother's bedroom. I am shocked to see how ill she looks. She says, "I am glad that you have come, boy. I am going away on a journey and I will not see you again for a long time." She then slumps back on the pillow and I am led away hurriedly. Next day, Mother says, "Would you like to see Grandmother?" I agree with joy, because I have decided on seeing her just once more and imagine her dressing for the journey. Mother takes me into the cold, locked bedroom and suddenly confronts me with the scarcely recognizable corpse, laid out with flowers and candles. After a bewildering moment she hisses at me, "She's dead." I am put out of the room to wander away alone.

---

2. **squire:** a country gentleman in Great Britain, especially the chief landowner in a village or district.

3. **waster:** a person who wastes money; spendthrift.

4. **ally:** a person who associates or cooperates with another; supporter. As used in Scientology, *ally* means someone who protects a person who is in a weak state and becomes a very strong influence over the person. The weaker person, such as a child, even partakes of the characteristics of the ally, so that one may find that a person who has, for instance, a bad leg, has it because a protector or ally in his youth had a bad leg. The word is from French and Latin and means *to bind together.*

5. **inculcating:** impressing upon the mind by frequent repetition or persistent urging.

The next item is at the age of ten. I am dressed up for a house party and expecting to dazzle my girlfriends. I wander out into the orchard, and on an impulse climb a favorite tree, slip in my new shoes and fall ten feet headfirst into the soft, wet turf. Bodily hurt, half conscious, and with clothes ruined with muddy water, I stagger back to the house. The old nanny fetches Mother, who says, "Disgusting boy. Put him under the pump, nurse, and put him straight to bed. I don't want to see him again." No one realizes or even asks if I am hurt, and the sentence is duly carried out.

The next episode is as an officer in the cavalry, where I see a cannon burst when on maneuvers. It blows some of the crew to pieces and kills the commanding officer to whom I am particularly attached. I feel so shaken that I retire from the army and go home more or less as a result of this.

I am by now so pushed in that I fail to take responsibilities properly, although wanting to and feeling baffled by my inability to cope. In 1821, when inspecting the forefoot of a treacherous horse, it seizes my ear in its teeth and swings me by it. The pain makes me faint. Mother greets me with a snort saying, "What do you expect from that beastly horse. You should have shot it long ago." In 1834, when riding the same horse, I allow it to rush me into a tree, a branch smashes in my lower forehead and eyes and breaks a collarbone. I am unconscious for about a day and a half and die. Exterior, I see the local doctor's grief, and realize that he is my real father. I had great grief over the fact that there was no real communication with Mother, in that she and the doctor had not told me I was really their son. As I exteriorize over the locality I realize what a beautiful fertile countryside it is, where all life lives to the full. I have failed to marry, failed to raise a family, failed the faithful Clark by not running the estate properly. I have also failed the doctor and Mother who had hoped by raising me to achieve this through me. I have also failed my employees, and the villagers in their need to get a fair deal from the local farmers.

Case 34

Preclear's Report

Former Condition

Fairly good mentally—tendency to disperse. A lot of fear repressed which I had not been able to get rid of.

Mental Outlook

Probably very close to being entirely clear of all junk (i.e., inhibitions and aberrations).

Physical Improvement

Much healthier and brighter and more in control of my thoughts, actions and life, and can do much more work on much less sleep with practically no physical discomfort whatsoever. I was overweight and have lost at least five to seven pounds, which is a great improvement. My color is better and complexion is clearer and eyes very bright.

What You Attribute Improvement To

All credit goes to my auditor who has been direct and well controlled. I've never experienced better auditing and my trust in my auditor's ability to help me could not have been higher from the minute we sat opposite each other—consequently my willingness to work with and for her and for both of us, could not have been more. That is the most important factor of the lot.

Also I was not too aberrated in the first place, so consequently was able to work quickly and achieve the maximum results in the minimum of time. It was a team job and, although the going was tough at times, "my head was always above water" and I never was unaware of what I was doing or saying or thinking at any time.

The Engram

23,064,000,000 years ago I was a very happy being who, with many others, strayed to a planet called "Nostra." All that we had there to show what we were, were little gold identity discs.

On seeing a great number of robots descend from an immense spaceship, we wandered down and started teasing these robots. The robots seized our discs and took them from us by clamping their big claw hands upon either side of them —by then we were unable to exert a great deal of force as, though happy, we had lost a great deal of our power. The chief robot told us via telepathy[1] that if we helped them manufacture a new type of body they were trying to form, they would, at a later date, return our original identity discs to us. We did help them, but I never got my identity disk back.

My actual incident started 64,000,000 years later, and the part that was run took place over a period of four months and twenty-one days.

Apparently we were all issued with similar type prototype bodies about five feet tall. By this time we were all so thoroughly hypnotized that I thought I was the only being present;

---

1. **telepathy:** a communication between minds other than by speaking, seeing, etc.

but I discovered on running the incident that there was a being with each body and that we were all completely and thoroughly enslaved to the beings who ran the robots. Their story was that we were to help form bones and organs inside these bodies by different types of experiments. I worked on this, but others were used to develop the mechanical ability of these bodies.

There were two types of beings running the robots—orthodox[2] and progressive. The orthodox wanted to retain robot bodies whereas the progressives wanted these new-type bodies developed. As our powers were greater than theirs, they enticed us to do the work for them, so we were really entrapped.

The story opens when rows of us were standing outside a big temple-like whitish building, and when we were telepathed we walked forward, one at a time, up the steps into this building. At the far end was a long white table where five similar bodies to my own were sitting. I progressed to a certain spot where I stood and energy flowed around me up from the floor. Its light was reflected onto two mirrors on each side of the wall in front, in the center of which were vertical reflecting bars of metal and, right in the center, a round flat disc. The mirror showed mirrors within mirrors and drew the attention inwards and the vertical bars gave the illusion of whirling inwards until the attention was fixated right in the disc which seemed to be a long hole extending into nothingness. When hypnotized thus, one was given the order "go do as before" telepathically, then one bowed, turned and left. This was a split second occurrence and could only be seen at one spot and gave the impression of an infinite power, so that one was led

---

2. **orthodox:** conforming to the usual beliefs or established doctrines; approved or conventional.

to believe a powerful being was present, while, in fact—as was discovered later—no one was present, and the bodies behind the table were not motivated at all. It was a "being substitute" machine—another method of entrapment.

I then left, climbed on board a spaceship with five other similar-type bodies and a twelve-foot-high robot to watch over us, and left for outer space to do my project. I sat in a chair inside the door and immediately lapsed into an unconsciousness which lasted for two months.

On awakening, I walked to a control room, lay on an "operating type" table and caused the body I was motivating to be impregnated by radiation from a lamp, whose rays I resisted, to make the body resistant to radiation. I gave myself a bit of an overdose, but in doing so awakened a bit of awareness within myself and had to summon the robot to carry the body to a bunk near the end of the spaceship. I was aware at the time that he was suspicious of my being more aware than I should have been and that I was being a bit too much the effect of my body, and I thought that I mustn't get caught. Here was another trap—becoming the effect of the body, i.e., traps within traps under the guise of experiment.

I went unconscious again but soon was aware again and left the body and the spaceship, which by this time had landed on another planet. The other bodies were outside getting practice in using the mechanics of their bodies in an atmosphere in which they had to use extra spacesuits for breathing. Lungs were being developed by them.

Then I left, as a being, and went to another part of the planet and took over a walrus body for about twenty minutes.

I had great fun swimming and gamboling[3] with it and then left it and went back to the spaceship—my short allowed "holiday" over. I couldn't escape, as both my identities, i.e., body and disc, were in the hands of the robots and I thought I couldn't get along without one or the other of them.

The spaceship soon took off again and this time, after collecting my body and moving it to a type of lounge, I went unconscious for another couple of months or more on a settee. Just before I did so I caught the robot eyeing me again and felt he knew I knew more than I should have. After this I awoke and went to another room where I performed an experiment on the body. This entailed placing the body in a dentist-like chair which, when motivated, jerked up and down on a back rod; I exerted pressure against limbs and chest, forming ridges of energy which helped to form bones and lungs, nostrils and air passages. This I overdid, too, and felt weak but aware as before, and the robot caught me again, but I was strong enough to stagger the body back to my bunk myself where I lapsed into unconsciousness again. However, I soon awoke to find a white gas seeping into my room. This was used to catch unwary beings with bodies who had become too much the effect of them, and started one coughing. Very foolishly I got up instead of staying where I was (which was another trap) and staggered to the ship's control room, at the end or stern. I was surprised to see that there was no one there. I activated an electronic beam, which I should have turned off, and so gave the alarm that I was there.

I turned to find the robot coming for me, dodged and tripped him up somehow, and on recovering saw the other five bodies motivated by beings of my type (although I didn't know it then) standing there. One of these, motivated by long

3. **gamboling:** playing; frolicking.

distance telepathy control over himself, shot me and completely disintegrated the front of my body with an energy gun. I convulsed forward and then backwards coughing, breaking my neck in the spasm backwards. I writhed on the floor for a split second, saw the collapsed body of the robot where I had tripped him, hated him for finding me out and causing the complete loss of my identity of which I had become too fond, and left the spaceship and body and floated in space.

My body was released through the air lock and I was left contemplating my fate. I had a body but it was no use to me in the state of no solidness to use it against, no gravity, etc. I bemoaned[4] my loss and degradation and the beautiful sadness of it all. I investigated the body, found it no use and just sat around. The body was finally hit by a meteor and carried off and I sat around there for 22,999,500,000 years before going off to find a new life and a new game. What a performance!

So much of this incident was related to my present life. As I left the spaceship I felt, "Well, now you can't hurt me." But of course I hurt—the body doesn't feel except if I make it feel. I have always had to watch myself for being just a bit too clever. I've had trouble with chest coughs, especially with fogs; trouble with blushing and curious energy and heat somatics associated with my face; a tendency not to want to get too fond of bodies and get too much sensation from them (so I thought); a tendency to be all alone. I have loved to gaze into space and I enjoy big spacious countries like Australia (where I was born) and Rhodesia (where I have lived), but I find England too cramped.

I was always being made the first to do things at school and couldn't understand why. I had trouble with seasickness

4. **bemoaned:** grieved over.

and vertigo[5] on board ships and in confined spaces like them and felt I was trapped and couldn't get off. Seasickness could be attributed to the illusion in the temple place, which also impelled awe. I got my compulsion about religion from there.

As a whole, this incident could in many ways be a complete prototype of my present life. Also my biggest pleasure has been in swimming and diving (see the walrus).

I always had complete reality on the pictures in the incident and the occurrences and on being further run on it was able to assume complete responsibility for getting myself into such a situation in the first place and got all situations, happenings and ideas put in their proper perspective.

Many of the somatics, for example, coughing and blushing, are practically nonexistent now. I am very concerned about the enslavement of humanity and know that as a being "I am" and need no further identity than my knowledge of my own existence. Further changes, I've no doubt, will be noticeable in my future attitude towards situations but, as the incident was only finished on the day on which I write, I haven't had a chance to put it into practice in everyday life.

---

5. **vertigo:** a dizzying sensation of tilting within stable surroundings or of being in tilting or spinning surroundings.

Case 35

Preclear's Report

Former Condition

I was in good condition, except for unaccountable easy invalidation of myself by others. Upsets always took place on misunderstandings.

Mental Outlook

Brighter, calmer, more certain. Less influenced by entheta.[1] I'm not distorting other people's opinions communicated to me and am assigning correct significance to these opinions.

Physical Improvement

Slight constipation over one year now cleared.

What You Attribute Improvement To

I attribute improvement to the discovery and the handling of the distortion sphere aspect of the incident contacted.

---

1. **entheta:** enturbulated theta (thought or life); especially referring to communications, which, based on lies and confusions, are slanderous, choppy or destructive in an attempt to overwhelm or suppress a person or group.

The Engram

Seventy-six trillion years ago, being in space, and totally at knowingness[2] I decided to create a game. I closed down to having "a space," and created blobs and geometrical forms. My considerations were about a "to create" postulate, a no-creation and a duration—namely, time.

I mocked up[3] a pyramid, and was most pleased that this was the perfect form, since at all times there were four sides, no matter how near to the point one went. I found some others to whom I could demonstrate this. They were interested in pyramids, but they had become rather degraded. They could not appreciate the simplicity of the pyramid, and wanted to see the "point" of it. Investigating the point, they became smaller and smaller, and finally "vanished."

Enjoying this joke, I went on a "grand tour," doing the same thing with others, but finally grew bored with the ease of deception, and decided to find someone in a group who would be a little more difficult to fool. I tried the same game, and this time the person "found the point," became confused, and rapidly pulled out so as to discover "what was wrong" with the pyramid. I decided to improve it by enclosing it in a distortion sphere, thus making it more difficult to solve. Having done so, I adopted the view of someone who had never seen the pyramid before. Becoming fascinated by my own

2. **knowingness:** awareness not depending upon perception. One doesn't have to look to find out. For example, you do not have to get a perception or picture of where you are living to know where you live.

3. **mocked up:** as used here, it simply means "created." In Scientology, the word *mock-up* is used to mean, in essence, something which a person makes up himself. A *mock-up* is more than a mental picture; it is a self-created object which exists as itself or symbolizes some object in the physical universe. The term was derived from the World War II phrase for miniature models that were constructed to symbolize weapóns (airplanes, ships, artillery, etc.) or areas of attack (hills, rivers, buildings, etc.) for use in planning a battle.

creation, I interiorized to check it over. On exteriorizing again, I saw an image of self in the pyramid and was pleased.

I moved to another group and presented the pyramid, rather than myself, very quickly. The pyramid, not I, received a lot of admiration. I was concerned at this, and located myself at the receipt point of admiration. Due to the now forgotten distortion sphere, the admiration was turned to scorn and "deadness," so I checked up by exteriorizing, and again read the emotion as admiration and respect. Interiorized, I once again received scorn. That was painful, and I was overwhelmed by the "wrong emotion," passing through pain, degradation, woe, shame, regret, blame, unconsciousness and despair.

After two trillion years I decided that the only way out of this was to return to the time when the pyramid was created. I tried to do so, but succeeded only in coming out of the sphere. Again I saw the pyramid, and grew angry, blaming it for all the trouble. I ejected it, hoping to explode it as it left the sphere, but as it did so the distortion passed from it, and it was restored to its valuable and pleasing original form. I tried to prevent the explosion, and flipped back to the position I was in before, namely, in the distortion sphere, in a part of the hollow where the pyramid had been. I was looking at a distorted picture of the explosion, which I refused to accept as having happened. I was unable to compute the factors of this situation; neither could I go back or sideways in time or space, since I would be forced to see the destruction of my own creation, so I decided to hold everything as it was, and one day to sort it out.

This has been the state ever since: sitting in a distortion sphere not knowing that it exists, fastened to a pyramid that is not there, and looking at a distorted view of an explosion which I know happened, but which I am trying not to look at.

Case 36

Auditor's Report

This engram is actually not one single incident but more like a part of a series of lives ending with the completion of that series.

It was located by E-Meter reaction and the question "Is this the incident necessary to resolve the case?" An affirmative answer was noted on the meter. It was probably in constant daily restimulation and had been entered on briefly in earlier auditing six years ago. Because of this, the pc was anxious to have it completely run out. We contacted the time area and entered it with little difficulty.

Located some 2,000,000,000 years ago in an area of the physical universe many galaxies away, it is basic to the pc's major problems in current life, including a TB[1] condition and other intimate problems.

Using the process "What part of that incident can you confront?" with the aid of finger snaps to pinpoint exactly occluded portions, it opened up and the pc's sense of the

---

1. **TB:** abbreviation for tuberculosis, an infectious disease that may affect almost any tissue of the body, especially the lungs.

reality of the incident increased. At first there was reluctance to confront the pain. The pc overcame this in a few hours and the major somatics were located and confronted to some degree. The plot had to be located and straightened out, as the great force and violence received did not appear reasonable to the pc till this was done. Progress was held up considerably because throughout the period of the incident special implants were being used on the pc to bring about hallucination. It was difficult in these circumstances to get the story accurately and to be comprehensible to the pc; but though the incident cannot at this date be said to be entirely cleared, its power to dictate aberrated action can be said to be thoroughly broken.

Only the briefest synopsis can be given here. Pc, after a period of 440 years without a body, arrives in error on a planet which is being taken over by "black magic" operators who are very low on the ethical scale and using electronics for evil purposes. Having come originally from a "good" planet he battles for a long, long time against the forces of "black magic," which, like a fifth column,[2] are subverting the originally "white magic" populace. It is a losing battle, implant after implant gradually weakening his ability and control by causing hallucinated perceptions. Eventually, after a period of spiritual torment and grief, he abandons his former high goals and goes over to the "black magic" faction,[3] not having entirely given up the idea of outwitting it from within. This occurs some 74,000 years after his first arrival on the planet.

He now goes to another planet by spaceship, and here ensues the more aberrative part of the incident. A deception is

2. **fifth column:** any group of people who aid the enemy from within their own country.

3. **faction:** a group of people in a political party, church, club, neighborhood or other body or organization who stand up for their side or act together for some common purpose against the rest of a larger group.

accomplished by hypnosis and pleasure implants (rather like opium in their effects) whereby he is deceived into a love affair with a robot decked out[4] as a beautiful, red-haired girl who receives all his confidences for a period of fifty years. When he discovers the deception, a tremendous unreality factor is thus installed in his memory and now, reduced by this betrayal to ruin, he is softened up for the final implant and degradation. Many serious shocks and operations are performed on him. He becomes a very weak being and is given a final implant to "be good" and "obey" and never to return to the home planet.

He stayed around in the vicinity of the implant area for several hundred years in a state of apathy, and then came up sufficiently to go into action and move off to another planet about forty-eight galaxies distant.

---

4. **decked out:** dressed up or specially decorated for some purpose.

Case 37

Preclear's Report

Location: Planet Setus. Time: 3,750 years ago.

I started space training at seventeen years of age and when I was twenty-one years old, war broke out. I then married and left my wife with my parents and two sisters. When I was twenty-two I was given the task of destroying an enemy ship that had broken through the protective screen. During the attack my ship, a one-man attack type, was holed, so I pulled out of the dive, in spite of training which emphasized the danger of doing this.

My thoughts, activated by the shock of near death, turned toward the importance of returning to my now pregnant wife and home, and this, I believe, prevented me pushing on with what looked, at that time, to be a most promising attack.

I then became aware of a body in a spacesuit attached by a line to a damaged ship. This raised the problem of whether I should save this pilot or keep on going away from a disturbing situation, as I knew that with a holed ship my air supply in the suit would barely outlast the emergency. I was conscious of choking and the feel of hands pulling me through a hatch, followed shortly afterwards by the prick of a hypodermic needle in the upper left arm.

It was then that I realized that the body in question was my own, and that in pulling out of the attack I had suffered a direct hit which threw me out of the ship. This was understandable as this type of ship is a "sitting duck"[1] when turning away from an objective as I well knew. I recall further treatment at base and, after reporting, was given permission to return home although in rather poor shape with bruised legs and back. (Could have been a type of the bends;[2] seemed possible.)

I was aware of a strange attitude in those around me but felt that it was due to my recent experiences. From the "air car" my first sight of the home town was a collection of burnt-out houses and it was then that I realized the meaning of the attitude of my comrades. The city had been blasted with a thermonuclear[3]-type bomb by the ship that had *not* been stopped by me.

Up to now I do not recall having seen this type of burn, as the bodies of all my family were seared[4] rather than burnt. Light fabric, i.e., clothing, etc., had disappeared, but furniture and so on was still standing, although surface charred. My family were all dead—death was so sudden that from their location I could reconstruct their activity at the time. My wife was lying on the bed and her last act was an attempt to protect the unborn child with one updrawn leg.

---

1. **sitting duck:** an easy target. In hunting a sitting duck is an easy target, as compared to one flying.

2. **bends, the:** a condition caused by the formation of nitrogen bubbles in the blood or body tissues as the result of a sudden lowering of atmospheric pressure, as in deep-sea divers returning to the surface too quickly: it is characterized by tightness in the chest, by pains in the joints, and by convulsions and collapse in severe cases.

3. **thermonuclear:** of nuclear reactions that occur at very high temperatures.

4. **seared:** scorched or burned on the surface.

It was then that I made the consideration that sentiment was the greatest inhibitor of survival, i.e., if I had been ruthless in the attack on that enemy ship these people would have survived—obviously the cold, calculated efforts of the enemy had been the winning factor.

I threw the bed over on top of my wife's body and left.

Regarding the rest of the war, I recall the building of a reputation and rank on the basis of "efficiency in carrying out a task." I do know that a larger power's (the Empire for want of[5] a better term) intervention as mediator settled the war, although leaving us under their control—a situation which I actively resisted later. I joined the Empire's forces as a "mercenary"[6] and there seems to have been considerable "helling around"[7] as I contacted many incidents of a callous, destructive nature.

Around about the age of thirty-seven, I returned from duties earlier than expected and found a woman, who belonged to me at that time, in bed with one of the space-station personnel. His challenging attitude and the woman's pleas not to hurt him provoked a fight in which I felt that he was playing into my hands. I was watching his body twitching with a broken neck when I was struck from behind, and turning, saw this woman with the neck of a broken glass vase in her hand.

I threw her on the bed and scarified[8] her face with the broken glass—she had been very attractive. Afterwards I threw

---

5. **for want of:** because of the lack or absence of.

6. **mercenary:** a professional soldier hired to serve in a foreign army.

7. **helling around:** going around in a noisy and often immoral way; carousing.

8. **scarified:** scratched or cut superficially.

the man's body over the porch and left her lying on the bed. I left the building and never returned.

I went AWOL[9] for a month, was arrested and went before a court martial. The charge had as its basis information given by the woman on my subversive activities for self-government for Setus. The "director's" attitude was so unjust that I feel he was concerned personally with the lover I had murdered. I know that my attitude to the council, and particularly to the director (i.e., chairman), was most irrational, but this incident had similar content to a much earlier incident in which there is considerable charge. I had trouble in staying out of this previous one.

I was placed under restriction (i.e., constant surveillance) and felt that the game was finished, with the collapse of my career and second dynamic.

While at a "drinking dive"[10] I got interested in one of the women there who refused favors until I got myself straightened out. To do this I accepted "advice" to go to an old shrine belonging to an ancient religious culture. The whole interior of this shrine or temple was bathed in a glow emanating from the roof. I got the understanding that there was a better game to be had doing good and forsaking the life I had been leading. I didn't have much to lose, did I?

After dumping all I had with me into a box (thoughtfully provided) I was met by attendants who were to show me the

---

9. **AWOL:** away from military duty without permission (but without the intention of deserting). From "*absent without leave.*"

10. **dive:** a disreputable resort for drinking or entertainment.

way—I had terrific unwillingness to enter this "new way of life" of sacrifice of self.

The preparation was as follows:

I was laid on an operating table, given hypodermic injections through the corner of each eye, deep into the skull. A machine having an amber green lens was swung over my eyes and seemed to pull me into its interior. I later found that I had been fixated into a small, glass jar. The body was preserved and placed into a glass-type container, then taken away. It was when I tried to follow that I realized that I was located by this jar on the shelf of the theater. The taking away of the body and the fact that the attendants left without a backward glance, was responsible for a terrific emotional upset—especially when I realized that the "Council" representing the Empire had been responsible for the situation in which I found myself.

I was later dumped on Earth about 1750 years B.C.

This was followed by life as a Hittite[11] in Anatolia.[12]

What I have written here is as close to factual as I am at this stage able to get, and I have not included the cognitions that have come to me, in looking at this incident, apart from the effect of the implants. I do, however, realize that much of my past activity has been influenced by my experiences during this past life on Setus. An intolerance of the honesty of any authority, a desire to do good on my terms, coupled with

---

11. **Hittite:** any of an ancient people of Asia Minor and Syria (1700–700 B.C.).

12. **Anatolia:** ancient name for the part of modern Turkey that is in Asia.

"don't be a sucker"[13] are discernible in much of the past, in Cromwellian[14] times, and in convict days in Australia, to mention a few that I am aware of at this time.

I realize that I would not be in England now if it were not for this incident. Well, there it is—like all games, good while they last.

---

13. **sucker:** a person easily cheated or taken in.

14. **Cromwellian:** of or having to do with Oliver Cromwell (1599–1658), English revolutionary leader who overthrew the king and ruled England from 1653–58.

Case 38

Preclear's Report

This incident began 17,543 years ago on a "space command" post on Earth. I had the idea that I could go to Mars incognito to learn how they handled disorder. The government warned me, but finally gave me unwilling assistance and transport to Mars and through the protective field of force to its surface.

On landing I was immediately surrounded and interrogated by Martian automatons[1] who recognized me instantly because I did not broadcast the same vibrations.

I was taken to a massive hall with insulated walls, where I was seated in front of a gray-green curtain and bombarded with invisible particles which caused confusion. Then I was immediately transferred to a cigar-shaped metal holder and whirled around rapidly to further increase my confusion. At the same time I was told that if I ever did anything or remembered any of this I'd get "zapped," i.e., hammered, again. At the end I felt I was just a heavy little object with practically no life at all. After elementary and technical school I was given a

---

1. **automatons:** mechanical figures constructed to act as if by their own power; robots.

metal body fitted with every conceivable electronic gadget and put as a solitary observer on a space outpost.

When the monotony of the robot life began to bore me I began to give all my reports a double meaning to amuse myself. Without warning my replacement arrived and I was told to join the "Reserve." When I arrived at the barracks two official automatons came out, turned me around, opened my back and began ripping out all my apparatus, the flexes[2] from my legs, the batteries from my stomach, the computers from my body. Then they threw my empty shell of a body on a scrap heap.

I remained in the right lobe of my head, while my body rusted and disintegrated. When the head disintegrated I found myself outside the body. I hung around for a long while but finally decided I could leave, and I reported back to "space command."

---

2. **flexes:** flexible insulated electric cords.

Case 39

Preclear's Report

Former Condition

Good health overall. Shortsightedness and a tendency to colds in the nose, frequent but never serious. Difficulty in originating communication—always had to overcome all sorts of inner resistance to do it.

Mental Outlook

Have greatly increased subjective reality on past lives—had reality previously only from running a number of pcs and from having own psychosomatics (usually migraine) run out by techniques which did not at the time give reality on specific incidents. I expect improved facility in communication and much more free attention (see contents of engram).

Physical Improvement

The tendency to colds in my nose reduced. I have more energy.

What You Attribute Improvement To

The engram contained a disabling-type operation fixing my attention in my body and implanting "Only the body feels, sees, hears, emotes,[1] etc.; I am a body." In addition, there was brain surgery to make my body useless and deaf. The pressure in the center of my forehead and on my nose, presumably affecting colds and eyesight, has been much reduced.

The Engram

The incident was dated by the death 25,016 years ago, and occurred over the preceding 14 years.

From vague and fragmentary information, it appears that I was a member of a foreign ruling group in a civilization advanced in electronics, space travel and mind control—e.g., electronic irradiation[2] and brain operations were used for controlling people.

In some manner not yet clarified I appear to have been concerned with such control operations, although I was not in sympathy with the ruling group and was carrying on secret activities against them. I trained a slave girl (whom I had bought fourteen years before the end and with whom there was a strong bond of love) to be able to undo the effects of an electronic control operation, which I knew I would be subjected to if caught.

This duly happened, though the circumstances are yet vague.

The operation itself and the following three episodes have very considerable reality, as they ran with much pain, emotion and perception, though this was yet limited to my own body and to the person or machine immediately concerned therewith.

---

1. **emote:** to show or pretend emotion.

2. **irradiation:** exposure to radiation such as X-rays, ultraviolet rays, etc.

For the disabling operation, the body was strapped on to an operating table, above which a wheeled electronic machine, running on rails and having different projectors for hitting various points in the body and for diffuse[3] radiation over the whole body, was mounted. This was operated by a person standing on a raised platform, higher than the table and to its right, who adjusted the position of the whole machine and aimed the various individual projectors, and switched them on and off in the required time cycle.

The first part of the operation consisted of directing a strong beam at the center of the forehead and below. This I resisted strongly by counter-beams from the forehead which the machine, however, pushed back, forming a ridge.[4] During the presumably very brief time in which the impact point of the beams was pushed from the projector to the forehead, I was violently interiorized into the head, and enormous rage was experienced. This changed briefly to fear and grief, and then to apathy, confusion and unconsciousness as the radiation entered the forehead.

The radiation then proceeded to impose a stress in some painful way on all the bones of the skull including the teeth, making them light up, as it appeared, and the same happened to all the bones of the skeleton. All of this interiorized my attention. Other radiation produced similar effects on the soft tissues of the body. This was followed by an implant to the effect "Only the body feels, sees, hears, emotes, etc. I am the body. . . ."

3. **diffuse:** spread out or dispersed; not concentrated.

4. **ridge:** a solid accumulation of old, inactive energy suspended in space and time. A ridge is generated by opposing energy flows which hit one another, and continues to exist long after the energy flows have ceased.

A second stage of the operation directed beams at the solar plexus[5] and the sex organs, giving a pleasant sex-type sensation with the implant "I do as I am told." This was for laying in orders and suggestions concerning specific tasks later, by means of a small portable projector used in the army, to which apparently the subjects of such operations were later assigned.

This was the usual disabling operation, which I had trained the girl to undo, so in spite of the pain, I had not despaired.

However, imagine my shock and terrible despair when I noted that a leading member of the rulers, apparently a personal enemy, then stepped up and, lifting up first the right eyelid and then the left one, pushed a needle above each eyeball into the frontal brain lobes. This ruined the body as a communication mechanism. For good measure, the eardrums were also pierced, so that it was impossible to undo the effects of the previous operations.

This produced enormous despair and rage, and body convulsions which, although held down in the incident, came out in the running of it—apart from the pain of the actual operation.

The chronologically following episode—although it was the first in which I gained some visual reality—was that after I had been in the army, the girl had traced me and got me to meet her alone. She tried in vain to communicate to me, and finally, in her despair, could not do anything else except make love to me. However, even this was terribly disappointing as

---

5. **solar plexus:** a network of nerves situated at the upper part of the abdomen, behind the stomach and in front of the aorta. *Plexus* means "a network, as of nerves or blood vessels" and it is called *solar* because of the raylike pattern of the nerve fibers.

she got nothing except body reaction. So she went away, crying, and left me in a confused and desperate stupor of inability to communicate—unable even to show grief.

The next episode is that I am called to a briefing room in a spaceship by a "commander." There, by means of a projector beaming on the solar plexus and sex organs, I get an implant with orders for an individual scouting or perhaps bombing mission in a saucer-type craft.

In this scene, the projector and beams and the gist of the commands are most real to the effect: "They are only savages, easy meat.[6] Get the town. Don't ever tell about this. Forget it."

The final episode is that, seated in the pilot seat of this "saucer"—which largely runs on exterior or automatic guidance, but requires some little guidance from me at times—I manage to decide to crash the machine, in order to do some damage and to get away from this body which had become a terrible trap.

The crash, with the head in the helmet being pinned against a kind of dashboard and the legs crushed underneath this, got very real through the pains involved. Following this was an inrush of freezing cold air and then an explosion with an enormous release of heat. This, hitting the body from below and behind, burnt it up very fast, enabling me to exteriorize as it shriveled up to a white-hot mass.

---

6. **easy meat:** those who are easily victimized or defeated.

Case 40

Preclear's Report

Former Condition

Physically well and overweight, slight skin irritation between the toes. Mentally fairly alert, but a lot of trouble recalling.

Mental Outlook

I have cognited[1] that I have not been willing to accept responsibility because of the penalties of failure. I feel I am more willing to accept responsibilities now. Persistence has improved.

Physical Improvement

None.

The Engram

It appears that I was in charge of a sector of a star system and that I caused some destruction in this sector (like causing its disintegration).

The next part of the incident appears to be an observation sphere connected to a larger sphere. I have the idea that it is

---

1. **cognited:** had a realization about life. *See also* **cognitions** in the glossary.

through this black sphere that a wreck of a spaceship was contacted. The next scene is the spaceship wreck which seems to be some sort of a trap — the trap appears to be a ball of black energy. (I've got the idea I went to investigate this wreck.)

The next scene seems to be composed of television-type screens all over the place, which are handing me pictures. This appears to be in some kind of flying saucer. I get the idea that there is a special kind of screen that gives out a bright warm light in front of me and a block of ice behind me in this same incident. In this flying saucer everything keeps changing. I have the idea that objects in the room keep changing their shape.

I think that I am packed off to another flying saucer in a block of ice. In this other flying saucer a peculiarly shaped being appears — his head is shaped like a watermelon and his body seems to be matchstick thin. In this part of the incident I have the idea that this spaceship is for storing bodies or body parts.

The next incident appears to be on a planet similar to this planet Earth and the people seem the same except that they have very long chins. There are a few scenes in this part of the incident, and the end seems to occur when I see a newborn baby.

Throughout the running of this engram everything keeps changing. The one object that appears all the time is a frame of a television screen.

Case 41

Preclear's Report

Former Condition

1.   Light burning sensations in legs occasionally when in great tension. It did not bother me and would vanish after a few minutes.

2.   On the death of my father I had a "blank," not remembering anything from the moment the coffin was brought out of the house, though I attended the funeral and went to the cemetery.

3.   After the divorce from my ex-wife I could not mock up or recall her face.

4.   I had a sort of intolerance of gas smell—I had a gas poisoning with unconsciousness in 1922.

5.   I occasionally had a sort of pressure on top of my head and sensitivity there in the cold, when strong physically and not complaining about health.

6.   In recent years I had difficulty working with artificial light—a sort of intolerance of artificial lights during work—and I stopped working at night unless in the case of great urgency.

Improvements

After my below-described engram was run out:

1. On burning sensations, will report later as they were not often.

2. The "blame" on my father's death disappeared. Now I have recall of Father, funeral and burying.

3. The "blame" on my ex-wife's face disappeared. I can recall and mock it up.

4. I regained full tolerance of gas smell.

5. My ability to confront was considerably improved in every case.

6. Intolerance of artificial light during night, now entirely vanished.

7. More alert, more awareness.

8. On pressure on top of head I will report later, as it was not frequent.

Improvements 2, 3, 4, 5 and 6 I attribute to running out of engrams. However, improvements 5 and 6 I attribute also to the whole course.

A few years ago my father died. He was in a desperate condition. Members of the family wanted him to be operated on (Grandpa died during an operation for the same trouble). I objected and proposed that Father should be treated otherwise by a competent doctor applying different therapeutic methods. My opinion was finally accepted, but Father died during treatment. After a while a relative said to my mother that "I was responsible for Father's death" because I objected to the operation. This somewhat affected me. Later on, when doing the Hubbard Dianetics Auditor Course[1] I noticed a "blank"—a total oblivion on my father's death, as I could not recall at all the funeral which I had attended and the burying, from the moment the coffin was brought out of the door of the house. A glimpse of Father's coffin in the church was, for the first time, achieved during my first Advanced Clinical Course[2] in London in 1954, during the application of the process "Recall something you wouldn't mind forgetting." But nothing more.

In recent years, after my father's death, I started feeling burning sensations in my legs when in great tension. They were occasional, light and did not bother me, and lasted for a few minutes, vanishing as soon as I was relaxing or stopping work. Yet, they were there and they were unexplained.

During the recent 5th London Advanced Clinical Course (October 20th to November 29th, 1958), during the process "What can you confront?" these burning sensations appeared again, and for the first time they were developed all over my body.

Then a previous life engram was detected by flash answer and the assistance of the E-Meter. It was the engram containing the greatest charge and the biggest needle fall on the

1. **Hubbard Dianetics Auditor Course:** a course which, in the middle and late 1950s trained an auditor in the handling of Dianetics techniques and procedures. Today it is a basic course which trains one to deliver auditing as described in *Dianetics: The Modern Science of Mental Health* by L. Ron Hubbard. The course is available at all Churches of Scientology.

2. **Advanced Clinical Course:** one of a number of theory and research courses delivered by L. Ron Hubbard during the years 1953 to 1961, which gave a deep insight into the phenomena of the mind and the rationale of research and investigation. Abbreviation *ACC.*

E-Meter and it was closely associated with the above-mentioned:

   a.   Burning sensation of my legs.

   b.   "Blank" on my father's death and a sort of doubt, uncertainty and guilt about the treatment used.

   c.   Intolerance of artificial light during night work.

The engram was Father's death by fire (Father was burned to death) and my death in battle when trying to rescue Father, with a guilt feeling that it was too late. I died failing to save Father's life. The incident happened according to the flash answer verified by the E-Meter, during the year 549 before Christ, in the ancient town of Krotona of South Italy (Magna Graecia[3]) during the destruction of the Pythagoras[4] philosophical school, and the Pythagorean[5] order. According to historians it happened in the middle of the fourth to fifth century before Christ, yet the flash answer and the E-Meter located this incident in the year 549 B.C.

To run out the above engram fifty hours of "Scientology confront processing" was needed. Here is the incident:

My "father" was a great philosopher-mystic master, having an occult[6] philosophical school. A mob of fanatics put fire to the houses of people belonging to the same brotherhood or society. Just after we started processing the engram I saw a

---

3. **Magna Graecia:** ancient Greek colonies in southern Italy.

4. **Pythagoras:** (ca. 582–500 B.C.) Greek philosopher, mathematician and religious reformer.

5. **Pythagorean:** following the teachings of Pythagoras, the main tenets of which were the transmigration of souls (reincarnation) and the belief that all relationships in the universe could be expressed numerically.

6. **occult:** secret; disclosed or communicated only to the initiated.

living picture of Pythagoras walking in the garden of his school. Yet my father burning on the fire was not Pythagoras himself. I could judge from his characteristics. He was rather a little younger than Pythagoras.

The mob seized my father and brought him to a square to burn him alive on the fire. He was tied to the trunk of a tree and the fire started raging below his body.

I was in some town or suburb close to Krotona. A young man of our order rushed to my house, knocked fiercely on the door and told me that the houses of our order's members were put to fire by the mob, that the mob had destroyed and burned our philosophical school and were killing our people, and that Father was in great danger.

I rushed from the balcony into my room and put on in a great hurry the specified officer's uniform of the order for the case. Then I rushed to a nearby gymnasium–camping-like place where there were a lot of young men of our order and a lot of fine horses. I announced to them the grim news and I asked them to follow me at once to try to save Father and whatever else could be saved. In the twinkling of an eye[7] all of us were on horseback almost flying to the town. I led them to a square, on the opposite edge of which we were confronted by a horrible spectacle. A big fire was raging, and above it, tied to a tree trunk, was Father in agony, calling for help. All around the fire were soldiers guarding the area, armed with spears, and big, heavy shields. We attacked fiercely and a wild body-to-body battle took place close to the fire. I had penetrated into the enemy's ranks, fighting against a group of soldiers, and I reached too close to the fire. At that point a spear was shoved into my stomach and I died looking at my

---

7. **in the twinkling of an eye:** the time required for a wink; an instant.

burning father with a feeling of guilt because I came late and failed to rescue him. At that moment there were visible a lot of burning houses in different points of the town, as well as a big building with high marble columns—Doric[8] type, of a classical ancient Greek building style. Close to Father on the left was visible a big, empty cross, below which a big fire was raging, awaiting some other victim it seemed, to be crucified and burned. My initial impression was that Father also was crucified before being burned.

During the last twenty-five hours of intensive processing of the engram the whole firing was clarified, as it is given now:

My body was put on a stretcher, brought to a place outside a cemetery and buried in a ditch. The same night young men of our order exhumed the body and took care of it according to the rituals of the order, burned it and put the ashes in a nicely decorated vase in an atmosphere of devotion, respect and love. In this incident I was twenty-five years young, and Father was around fifty-five years young.

Previous to this incident, at the age of ten, I was in a gymnasium exercising with a bow. In a moment when Father was close to the target I shot an arrow to the target. At that moment Father extended his hand and was wounded by the arrow in his forearm. I rushed to Father, and crying, I embraced his feet, asking to be pardoned. Father pardoned me and sent me to bring a doctor. I assisted Father to lie down on a nearby marble seat and rushed to bring the doctor. I returned running with an officially dressed doctor. The doctor made four incisions around the arrow on Father's forearm and removed the arrow, rinsed the wound with water, put on some oil and herbs and wrapped it with a bandage. Father was

8. **Doric:** a classic order of architecture characterized by simplicity of form.

almost fainting and in great pain during the doctor's intervention. I was also in great agony with strong sorrowful emotion
and a sort of guilt for Father's suffering at the moment the
arrow hit his forearm, as well as at the moment the doctor was
removing the arrow. I was crying loudly with a lot of tears
during the auditing session, so real was this incident which
was at the root of the guilt feeling for failing to save Father in
time when he was burned in the first above-mentioned incident. This guilt feeling had its origin in the guilt feeling of
wounding Father with the arrow and was responsible for the
guilt feeling for the death of my present-life father. With the
marvelous process "What part of that can you be responsible
for?" the engram was entirely run out. With the recent Scientology confront processing, it seems that L. Ron Hubbard and
Scientology hit the nucleus[9] of human suffering and behavior.

I experienced lots of strong emotions, efforts, shaking of
the body and somatics during the running of both of the
above-described incidents.

I have to add that from early childhood I had Pythagorean
inclinations, and that my writings have the "seal" of Pythagorean principle and teaching, that I entered occultism twenty
years ago, that I quit practicing law (I was practicing law for
twenty-one years) and entered the "drugless therapy field"
and finally Scientology (besides naturopathy[10] and chiropractic[11]), having as a basic goal in my life "to help humanity
in health and truth on an international scale." Twenty-three

---

9. **nucleus:** a central part around which other parts are grouped or gathered; core.

10. **naturopathy:** a system or method of treating disease that employs no surgery or
synthethic drugs but uses special diets, herbs, massage, etc., to assist the natural
healing processes.

11. **chiropractic:** a therapeutic system based primarily upon the interactions of the
spine and nervous system, the method of treatment usually being to adjust the
segments of the spinal column.

years ago I turned to vegetarianism. My basic motive was that ancient Greek philosophical teachings, and particularly the Pythagorean ones, together with Jesus Christ's teachings, *applied* in everyday life were the highest form of human behavior and civilization. The above engram gave me one more vivid explanation of the "origin and the why" of my inclination and goals in life.

Conclusion

Conclusion

Now what do you think?

Forty-one conservative, well-trained Scientologists, the most effective practitioners in today's world of mental healing, have gone through these experiences. Forty-one sane people have some evidence that they have lived before.

What about the rest of the human race?

Epilogue

The Phenomena of Death

by L. Ron Hubbard

It has only been in Scientology that the mechanics of death have been thoroughly understood. Hitherto, the whole subject of death has been one of the more mysterious subjects to man.

We are actually the first people that do know a great deal about death. It is one of the larger successes of Scientology.

In the first place, man is composed of a body, a mind and what we refer to as a *thetan*—the Scientology word for the spirit, the individual being himself who handles and lives in the body.

A very effective way to demonstrate this is by saying to a person, "Look at your body. Have you got a body there?" Then tell him, "Get a mental picture of a cat." He will get a picture of a cat. That picture is a mental image picture and is part of the mind.

The mind is composed of pictures that interassociate, act and carry perceptions. While the person is looking at this actual picture ask him, "What's looking at it?"

Nobody ever asked this question before! It is quite an innocent question, but this particular phrasing and this particular demonstration of the parts of man were unknown before Scientology.

This procedure gives a person a considerable subjective reality on the idea that he himself is a being that is independent of a mind or a body. There is an actual separateness there.

Man thought he *had* a human spirit. That is totally incorrect. Man *is* a human spirit which is enwrapped more or less in a mind which is in a body. That is *Homo sapiens*. He is a spirit and his usual residence is in his head. He looks at his mental image pictures and his body carries him around.

What happens to man when he dies?

Basically, all that happens is that a separation occurs between the thetan and the body.

The thetan, however, takes with him old tin cans, rattling chains, bric-a-brac[1] and other energy phenomena that he feels he cannot do without and stashes this in the next body that he picks up.

In this lazy time of manufactured items and gadgetry he does not build a new body. He picks up a body that is produced according to a certain blueprint that has been carried through from the earliest times of life on this planet until now.

There is such a thing as a cycle of action:[2] create-survive-destroy. At the shoulder of the curve an individual is mostly

1. **bric-a-brac:** literally means miscellaneous small articles collected because they are antique or for their sentimental, decorative or other interest. Used figuratively in this sense.

2. **cycle of action:** the sequence that an action goes through, wherein the action is started, is continued for as long as is required and then is completed as planned. The cycle of action of the physical universe is create, survive (which is persist), destroy. For more information on the cycle of action, see the book *Scientology: Fundamentals of Thought* by L. Ron Hubbard.

interested in surviving. Early on the curve he is interested in creating. And at the end of the curve, he is interested in the disposition[3] of the remains.

This cycle of action occurs whether you are speaking of a building, a tree or anything else. When we apply this cycle of action to the parts of man, we get a death of the body, a partial death of the mind and a condition of forgetting on the part of the spiritual being which is in itself a type of death.

The first thing one should learn about death is that it is not anything of which to be very frightened. If you are frightened of losing your pocketbook, if you are frightened of losing your memory, if you are frightened of losing your girl or your boy-friend, if you are frightened of losing your body—well that is how frightened you ought to be of dying, because it is all the same order of magnitude.[4]

We strike the first observable phenomenon in death when we find out that the mind, in spite of mechanisms which seek to decay it and wipe it out, does maintain and preserve mental image pictures of earlier existences. And with proper technology and an understanding of this one can be again possessed of the mental image pictures of earlier existences in order to understand what was going on.

But unless *remembrance* is restored to the *being*, the mental image pictures usually just continue to be pictures. Without that remembrance, sending somebody into a past life and having him look at a mental image picture would be similar to sending him to the art gallery. He would not connect himself with that picture.

3. **disposition:** a getting rid (of something).

4. **order of magnitude:** how large or how small something is in relation to other things.

The restoration of memory is therefore of great interest, since all that is really *wrong* with a person is that things have happened to him which he knows all about, but won't let himself in on.

The restoration of memory is done as a matter of course in almost any Dianetics or Scientology processing. It is impossible today to process somebody well and expertly without having them sooner or later get recall with reality on a past existence.

Past lives can be easily invalidated because, without processing, it is difficult to remember them. An individual's own will has a great deal to do with this. One should not look for outside sources as to why his memory is shut off. Just as he must grant permission to be trapped, so must he grant permission to be made to remember. He is more or less convinced that a memory, remembering back past this subject called death, would cause him to reexperience the pain he already feels has been too much for him. Thus he is very reluctant to face up again to this mechanism, and in facing death almost always goes into a degree of amnesia.

Now, it is all very well to take a scientific attitude towards death, but after all it does carry with it a little shock and upset. Until you have been dead a few times you wouldn't understand how upsetting it can be!

We are actually indebted for a considerable amount of our material on this subject to the odd fact that I have been officially dead twice in this lifetime. I died in an operation one time back in the 1930s, and went outside above the street, felt sorry for myself and decided they couldn't do this to me. The body's heart had stopped beating, and I went back and grabbed the body through the mechanisms in the head that stimulate its heartbeats. I just took hold of them and snapped the body back to life.

The only reason I mention this is because it happens to so many people and they never mention it. They die and come back to life again. Then somebody invalidates them, and they never say anything about it again.

Ordinarily when a person dies, he backs out of his body thinking of his responsibilities, knowing who he is, where he has been and what he has been doing. If he is in any kind of condition at all this is what occurs. He backs out at the moment of death with full memory.

Something kills a person's body—an automobile, too many court suits,[5] an overdose of widely-advertised sleep-producing agents. The moment he conceives it to be no longer functional in any way, he backs out. Usually a total occlusion does not occur at this point.

It is not true that a thetan gets some distance from the body and then doesn't care about it any more or forgets all about it. In support of this, incidents have been recorded of times when a thetan backed out of his head and was as mad as the dickens and just kicked the stuffings out of[6] the fellow who had killed him. This made the whole theory of spirits very unpopular. People tried to forget this, so that when they ran around killing people they would get no immediate kickback. Some people would *want* to forget about it, thinking that in this way they could commit a crime without having to suffer for it.

Man has capitalized[7] on the phenomena surrounding death enormously. Look around in any neighborhood—you will find

---

5. **suits:** actions to secure justice in a court of law; attempts to recover a right or claim through legal action.

6. **kicked the stuffings out of:** gave a bad beating to.

7. **capitalized:** took advantage of; turned something to one's advantage.

that if there is any building which is well kept, it is normally an undertaking[8] parlor. Why is it easy to capitalize on death?

Because when people think of death they think of loss and grab something. This explains the behavior of relatives after one of their family has died. Everybody gets in there and tears apart all of the person's clothes and they fight with each other over the possessions. They are still alive, but they have experienced a loss of havingness[9] and they pore over this particular person's effects. They are really to some degree trying to get the person back. They think if they can grab enough possessions, they will get the person back. It actually is not quite as greedy as it looks, it is just obsessive.

I have seen relatives, for instance, pick up some of the weirdest things. I once saw an old lady just screaming over the fact that someone wouldn't let her have a fellow's meerschaum[10] pipe. I pointed out to her that she didn't smoke a meerschaum pipe, and she looked at me sort of dazedly and came out of it and said, "So I don't," and handed it to somebody else. It was a token, a symbol of the person who had just left.

The exact behavior at death could vary from person to person. A person who had to "have" tremendously would get just so far from a body and be liable to say, "I don't care, I don't want to live anyway, I was very unhappy during that whole life and I'm awfully glad I don't care."

Somebody else is just as liable to not even think about it. But

8. **undertaking:** having to do with the profession of supervising or conducting the preparation of the dead for burial, and directing or arranging funerals.

9. **havingness:** the concept of owning, possessing, being capable of commanding, taking charge of objects, energies and spaces.

10. **meerschaum:** a tobacco pipe with a bowl made from a white, claylike substance. The word "meerschaum" comes from German meaning "sea foam."

that person was so little alive, when he was alive, that his aliveness after he has died is also negligible.

With a person who is fairly strong and capable there is an interesting reaction to body death: "I'll show them they can't put me out of the game." It makes him mad and upsets him, and he does a dive halfway across the country, sees a maternity hospital and grabs a baby body.

The exteriorization which occurs at death is very fascinating because the person is totally cognizant of it. He knows who he is; he usually has pretty good perception; he knows where his friends are. Pointing out as a fantastic spiritual phenomenon the occurrence of somebody appearing to a friend after he had died several thousand miles away, is something like being very surprised because a waitress came to the table in a restaurant.

People also sometimes wake up during the night and realize that somebody has died a death of violence. This is usually because of the amount of confusion which is thrown into a being when his body is killed. If a person is killed with sudden violence and is very surprised about it, he can be sufficiently upset and unphilosophical about the whole thing that he is liable to go around and see his next of kin and the rest of his friends in an awful frenzied hurry, trying to reassure himself that he hasn't gone to purgatory[11] or some place.

He has suffered a loss of mass. If you had an automobile sitting out on the street and you went out totally expecting to find the automobile there and it was gone, you would be upset.

11. **purgatory:** the state after death in which, per the teaching of the Roman Catholic Church, the soul destined for heaven is purified. Per this religion, only the perfect can go to heaven, and some believers die who have still unpunished or unrepented minor sins on their conscience, so these go to purgatory to be purged of such sins by suffering and repentance.

That is just about the frame of mind a thetan is usually in when he finds his body dead. His main thought is to grasp another body. This he could do by finding a young child that he could bring back to life.

But the ordinary entrance of a thetan into a new body is sometime around what we call the *assumption,* and the assumption occurs within a few minutes after birth in most cases. The baby is born and then a thetan picks up the baby body.

How do thetans behave when they suddenly haven't got a body? They behave like people. They will hang around people. They will see a woman who is pregnant and follow her down the street. Or they will hang around the entrance to an accident ward and find some body that is all banged up and the being that had that body has taken off or is about to. He may even pick up this body and pretend to be somebody's husband.

Thetans do all sorts of odd things. *When* a new body is picked up, *if* a new body is picked up at all, is not standardized beyond saying it usually occurs (unless the thetan got another idea) two or three minutes after the delivery of a child from the mother. A thetan usually picks it up about the time the baby takes its first gasp.

Would the body go on living without a thetan picking it up? That is beside the point. It is a case of how fast the thetan can pick one up before somebody else gets it. There is a certain anxiety connected with this.

Thetans often say very interesting prayers at the moment they pick up a body. They dedicate themselves to its continued growing and to the family and go through all kinds of odd rituals, all because they are so happy to get a new body. But the odd part of it is, they don't shut their memory off until they pick another body up. The shut-off of memory actually occurs with the pick-up of the new body.

Now, there is a phenomenon known as a between-lives area.[12] Some people go through this. It can be verified that they do this. It's not unusual. However, the phenomena connected with it are so questionable and so variable that the places people go makes one think that some thetans belong to one club and some belong to another club.

But it's not that everybody does this and "now, *I'm* supposed to." It's certainly not a constant.

Another phenomenon of death is that a thetan will stay around a body until it is disposed of properly. For example, let's say a thetan's body has been left out on a cliff or nobody even put the lid on the coffin. There it is exposed to the wind and rain. He will stay around there until that body is totally dust. The rate of decay of a body is not really a point in question except that a thetan will try to accelerate it if the body isn't cared for.

A thetan does not much care about the actual disposition of the body as long as it isn't given any more indignity than it suffered in the lifetime. But he is apt to be very upset about indignities rendered to a dead body. He associates the body with his own identity to the extent that every time an indignity is rendered to the body, he thinks it is to some degree being rendered to him. Therefore, he hangs around a body until it is properly disposed of.

---

12. **between-lives area:** the experiences of a thetan during the period of time between the loss of a body and the assumption of another. At death, the thetan leaves the body and goes to a particular location where he "reports in," is given an implant to make him forget everything, and is then sent back to Earth to a new body just before it is born.

When a person makes a will in which he declares a certain disposition of the body, it is a very wise thing to carry out those wishes, if you want the fellow to go on and live a happy life some place else. It is *his* idea of what is proper care.

The Egyptians had the idea of living forever, and they wanted their bodies to live forever. They thought that was very complimentary, so they would wrap bodies up and mummify them. But don't think that a thetan hung around just because his body had been mummified. That thetan would not be particularly upset about his previous body being hauled out of a tomb and left to rot someplace or being put up in the Metropolitan Museum,[13] because he would already be too far away from it to worry about it.

One very worrisome case I encountered was a thetan whose skull was used by a carnival. The carnival had put a motor in the jaws that made the jaws keep operating. The thetan just couldn't take the fact that the jaws were moving. And a speaking tube had been run through the back end of the skull so that all the time the jaws moved, words were coming out of it. I actually had to unwrap a preclear from that particular skull. He still had a finger on that skull even though he had another body.

Another interesting phenomenon having to do with death is that every once in a while some fellow will go into some area and go completely berserk and not know quite what is wrong with him. He thinks or says "I don't feel safe here. I have a terrible feeling like something awful is going to happen." Very possibly he was killed in the area under similar circumstances.

---

13. **Metropolitan Museum:** the chief museum of art in New York City and the largest in the United States, opened in 1880. The Metropolitan Museum contains a department of Egyptian antiquities which includes entire tomb chambers unearthed by the museum's archeological expeditions.

Don't confuse this with prediction. A thetan can actually predict the future. But one predicts rather easily on the subject of death because it is so all-embracing as a concern. Someday something is going to take your body away from you. Because you have lost many bodies without knowing what took them, it is very easy for you to mock up heavens, hells, angels and all sorts of things that are going to grab your body. You can even mock up something like the old man with the scythe.[14] There are many people who utterly believe that there is a fellow named Death who comes along and takes the body away.

There is no such being.

The subject of death is never a very serious one to a Scientologist beyond the fact that he feels kind of sorry for himself sometimes. For example, he had a friend that was someone of terrific élan,[15] someone who made him real happy to be around, and this person was thoughtless enough to dispose of his body and go out of communication. A person sometimes feels pretty unhappy about it and thinks it is a thoughtless thing for a friend to do.

This, by the way, was a very early concept of death. A person didn't regard it very seriously. The Romans never regarded death very seriously. They probably had a very accurate idea of what happened to them, then they went into idolatry[16] and finally hit bottom.

Death is in itself a technical subject. You can, with considerable confidence, reassure some husband whose wife has just

---

14. **old man with the scythe:** referring to the Grim Reaper: death, especially when personified as a man or skeleton with a scythe.

15. **élan:** spirited self-assurance; exuberant enthusiasm.

16. **idolatry:** the worship of idols.

died that she got out all right and she is going some place to take up a new body. If you got there while that person could still communicate with you, in the last moments, you would find that the person usually has something spotted, something planned.

The person doesn't just back out ordinarily and forget all about it. He backs out of it with full identity and hangs around for quite a while. The being is usually there for the funeral, certainly. He will very often hang around his possessions to see that they are not abused, and he can be given upsets if his wishes aren't carried out with regard to certain things.

It used to happen that thetans would punish people for not carrying out their wishes after death. People then said this was superstition, and science was against superstition. Well, it is quite interesting that in finding out what is science and what is superstition, we have found that a being is capable of almost anything providing it is within his ability to execute.

Losing your pocketbook, some treasured possession or your body are all alike. But because of the mechanism of forgetting, a great mystery is made of this.

And that is death, phenomena of.

Appendix

Appendix A

Modern Counseling

What is it like to reexperience a past life in auditing?

The following are excerpts from recent Dianetics auditing sessions in which past lives were contacted.[1]

The first session is with a preclear who has had an automobile accident. In this session, the impact of an injury to his left side is being relieved. Notice that the experiencing of past lives is actually incidental to the relief of the trauma contained in the incidents. This process addresses and erases engrams. The erasure of engrams is, due to their content, capable of returning a marked degree of awareness and life to a person.

In this first session, the preclear had stated that he had a "pain in the left side."

Auditor: Are you interested in running "pain in the left side"?

Preclear: *Yes.*

---

1. *Note:* The auditing techniques themselves are not given here in full. For information on training in these techniques, contact any of the Scientology churches or organizations listed in the back of this book. —Editor

Auditor: Okay. Locate a time when you had a "pain in the left side."

Preclear: *Yes. Got one.*

Auditor: Good. When was it?

Preclear: *It was my accident two months ago.*

Auditor: Good. Move to that incident.

Preclear: *Okay.*

Auditor: What is the duration of that incident?

Preclear: *Well, less than a minute.*

Auditor: Okay. Move to the beginning of that incident and tell me when you are there.

Preclear: *Uh-huh.*

Auditor: What do you see?

Preclear: *A street and the inside of my car.*

Auditor: All right. Move through that incident to a point "less than a minute" later.

Preclear: *Okay.*

Auditor: What happened?

Preclear: *I started up when the light turned green then suddenly I heard brakes and it was like a big bump—but really* *hard—as the other car crashed into the side of my car. I smacked into the car door just as it buckled, then my car slid off to the right and came to a stop against a street lamp.*

Auditor: Okay. Move to the beginning of that incident and tell me when you are there.

Preclear: *All right.*

Auditor: Okay. Move through to the end of that incident.

Preclear: (silent) *Okay.*

Auditor: Good. Tell me what happened.

Preclear: *I was starting into the intersection and I heard the screech of brakes. And then a smash as his car plowed into mine. The car door buckled just as I was slammed against it. Then my car skidded to the right and into a street lamppost. I was startled. I felt my side and it was all bloody. Then it started to hurt. I held my hand there to stop the bleeding. I thought I'd die.*

Auditor: All right. Is there an earlier incident when you had a "pain in the left side"?

Preclear: *Yes, there is.*

Auditor: Good. When was it?

Preclear: *1962—spring.*

Auditor: All right. Move to that incident.

Preclear: *Uh-huh.*

Auditor: What is the duration of that incident?

Preclear: *About a week.*

Auditor: Okay. Move to the beginning of that incident and tell me when you are there.

Preclear: *Okay.*

Auditor: What do you see?

Preclear: *The football field and stadium at my high school.*

Auditor: All right. Move through that incident to a point "about a week" later.

Preclear: (silently does this, then looks up)

Auditor: Thank you. What happened?

Preclear: *I went out for the track team and after school we jogged around and around the field—to get into shape. I got an excruciating pain in my side almost every day for two weeks.*

Auditor: Okay. Move to the beginning of that incident and tell me when you are there.

Preclear: *I'm there.*

Auditor: Good. Move through to the end of that incident.

Preclear: (silently does this) *Okay.*

Auditor: Good. Tell me what happened.

Peclear: *We ran around and around the field and the coach pushed us a little harder each day and each day the pain would turn on in my side. It hurt terribly.*

Auditor: All right. Is there an earlier incident when you had a "pain in the left side"?

Preclear: *Ummm . . . (long pause) yes, I guess so.*

Auditor: Good. When was it?

Preclear: *World War I, I think. It was 1917.*

Auditor: All right. Move to that incident.

Preclear: *Okay. I did it.*

Auditor: Good. What is the duration of that incident?

Preclear: *Two or three minutes—it's pretty short.*

Auditor: Okay. Move to the beginning of that incident and tell me when you are there.

Preclear: *Okay.*

Auditor: Fine. What do you see?

Preclear: *Well, I can see no man's land in the flashes of explosions and a soldier coming at me with a bayonet.[2]*

---

2. **bayonet:** a knife that can be attached to the end of a rifle and used in hand-to-hand fighting.

Auditor: Good. Move through that incident to a point "two or three minutes" later.

Preclear: *Okay.*

Auditor: Good. What happened?

Preclear: *I was up over the embankment out in front of the trenches and suddenly I saw a soldier coming at me with his bayonet. He stabbed me in the side with it.*

Auditor: All right. Move to the beginning of that incident and tell me when you are there.

Preclear: *Uh-huh.*

Auditor: Good. Move through to the end of that incident.

Preclear: (does so, silently) *Uh-huh.*

Auditor: Okay. Tell me what happened.

Preclear: *I was out in front of the trenches—we were running forward. There were cannons firing and there were flashes from explosions now and then. I suddenly saw an enemy soldier. I called out to warn the men I was with. The soldier leapt at me with his bayonet and stabbed me in the side. It hurt a lot and I bled a lot. I was taken back to a field hospital behind the lines where I died a few days later.*

Auditor: All right. Is there an earlier incident when you had a "pain in the left side"?

Preclear: *Let me see . . . yes, there is.*

Auditor: Good. When was it?

Preclear: *Oh, it had to be . . . it* was, 1823.

Auditor: All right. Move to that incident.

Preclear: *Okay.*

Auditor: Good. What is the duration of that incident?

Preclear: *Five minutes.*

Auditor: All right. Move to the beginning of that incident and tell me when you are there.

Preclear: *All right.*

Auditor: What do you see?

Preclear: *A gatehouse,[3] two horses, trees, a road.*

Auditor: Okay. Move through that incident to a point "five minutes" later.

Preclear: *All right.*

Auditor: Good. What happened?

Preclear: *I had ridden up the road towards a big estate. I'd stopped at the gatehouse and was just getting back onto my horse when he shied and threw me against another rider next to me. I hurt my side against his boot and stirrup. It was*

---

3. **gatehouse:** a house beside or over a gateway; used as a porter's lodge, etc.

very painful and I had to be helped back onto my horse
and I rode slowly on up the road.

Auditor: All right. Move to the beginning of that incident and
tell me when you are there.

Preclear: *Yes.*

Auditor: Move through to the end of that incident.

Preclear: (silent) *Okay.*

Auditor: Tell me what happened.

Preclear: *I had been riding fast to give my neighbor some news—I
was very upset—I don't know what about, though it
seems like someone had died or was dying. I stopped to
tell the gateman what had happened. I ran out to get on
my horse and as I was mounting, the horse shied and
threw me to the left. I landed against the boot and stirrup
of a rider next to me, then fell to the ground. It knocked
the wind out of me and hurt like the dickens.[4] I was
helped up onto my horse.* (preclear laughs)

*Well that's a relief—I mean the pain's gone—that's all
there was to it—I scared my horse. Oh! and that's why I
hurt so much when I was running in school—it was like
riding the horse that day—pushing him faster and faster.
And then the pain would start. It was the same pain. No
wonder. Well, that's the end of that.* (preclear grinning)

---

4. **dickens:** devil; used with *the* in mild oaths.

In the second session the effects of drugs taken during an operation are being addressed. This excerpt deals with a feeling of drowning.

Auditor: Were there any sensations connected with taking the anesthetic?

Preclear: *Yes, a feeling of drowning.*

Auditor: Okay. Were there any other sensations?

Preclear: *No, that's it, pretty much.*

Auditor: All right. Are you interested in running "a feeling of drowning"?

Preclear: *Sure.*

Auditor: Okay. Let's run this.

Preclear: (nods)

Auditor: Locate a time when you had "a feeling of drowning."

Preclear: *Uh . . . Ummm . . . There was a time when I was a kid and some other kids were piled on top of me . . . no . . . that's not the same thing—I've got one. Okay.*

Auditor: All right. When was it?

Preclear: *Well, it wasn't this lifetime. . . .*

Auditor: Okay.

Preclear: *It was . . . it must have been 1943. Yes, it was 1943 and*

I think it was about . . . May—sometime in May.

Auditor: Good. Move to that incident.

Preclear: *Okay, I'm there.*

Auditor: Good. What is the duration of that incident?

Preclear: *Let's see, oh, about forty-five minutes, I guess.*

Auditor: Okay. Move to the beginning of that incident and tell me when you are there.

Preclear: *Uh-huh.*

Auditor: Okay. What do you see?

Preclear: *Looks like some rocks and sand and—there's a soldier lying on the ground, wounded.*

Auditor: Okay. Move through that incident to a point "about forty-five minutes" later.

Preclear: (silently doing this) *Oh, heavens, I can feel it . . . what a shock!*

Auditor: *(quietly)* Okay, continue.

Preclear: (finally looks up)

Auditor: Good. What happened?

Preclear: *Well, you see, I was in Africa and there was this battle going on. I was a medic and this soldier got wounded. I was kneeling over him giving him first aid behind some* *rocks. He was hurt pretty badly. Then we were sprayed by some machine-gun fire and I got hit with three bullets in the chest. Ouch . . . I can still feel them. I was wondering why this had to happen to me. I had a wounded man to help. Then I was looking at the battle from up in the air. That's the end of it.*

Auditor: Okay. Move to the beginning of that incident and tell me when you are there.

Preclear: *Okay.*

Auditor: Move through to the end of that incident.

Preclear: (silently does this) *Okay, I did it.*

Auditor: Okay. Tell me what happened.

Preclear: *Well, I was a medic and I was helping a German soldier (I can tell by the uniform). I thought to myself, "I've been through lots of battles and they haven't shot me yet." I didn't think I would die that day—I was sure I wasn't going to. I was fixing wounds on guys I found on the battlefield. I was working on this one who had his leg all torn up—we were behind some rocks—I was giving him some water from my canteen when a plane buzzed⁵ us with machine guns firing. I took one bullet in my left side and two more in my lungs. At first it was shocking and then it hurt and I felt like I was drowning in my own blood. I left the body and could see much of the battlefield. It was late afternoon or early morning—the sun's rays were at an angle. The next thing I remember seeing is a pool of water and some palm trees and a white*

---

5. **buzzed:** flew very low over an area.

mosque[6]-looking building. It was very still and peaceful. That's the end of the incident.

Auditor: Is there an earlier incident when you had "a feeling of drowning"?

Preclear: *Yes, I think so.*

Auditor: All right. When was it?

Preclear: *1600s . . . 1684.*

Auditor: Good. Move to that incident.

Preclear: *Okay.*

Auditor: Good. What is the duration of that incident?

Preclear: *About fifteen or twenty minutes.*

Auditor: All right. Move to the beginning of that incident and tell me when you are there.

Preclear: *Uh-huh.*

Auditor: Okay. What do you see?

Preclear: *It's kind of dark and—there's only moonlight. There's a full moon and I can see water and some boats.*

Auditor: Good. Move through that incident to a point "about fifteen or twenty minutes" later.

---

6. **mosque:** Muslim temple or place of worship.

Preclear: *Okay.*

Auditor: Good. What happened?

Preclear: *I was in a gondola[7]—in Venice—I was a gondolier[8] and I was pulling in to tie up for the night. I heard a voice call to me in the dark just ahead. I called back. Suddenly I heard the splash of water and was hit in the chest with a pole. It knocked the wind out of me and I fell off the gondola into the water. I drew in a breath to catch my wind while submerged and drowned. That's all.*

Auditor: All right. Move to the beginning of that incident and tell me when you are there.

Preclear: *Got it.*

Auditor: Move through to the end of that incident.

Preclear: (does so silently) *Okay.*

Auditor: Good. Tell me what happened.

Preclear: *Well, I was pulling in to tie up my gondola for the night when another gondolier (a fellow I knew) called to me—to see if it was me. I answered back. Then as I was almost to the sea wall he jammed a long pole (a striped one) into my chest. I fell and just as I hit the water I could see some garbage floating in the moonlight. Then I drowned. I thought to myself, "I really deserve this." I had been*

---

7. **gondola:** a long, narrow boat with high, pointed ends, used on the canals of Venice in Italy.

8. **gondolier:** a person who rows or poles a gondola.

trying to have an affair with his wife and she must have told him. (preclear laughs)

I really deserved it. (laughs again) *You know, when I was a kid I was deathly afraid of striped barber poles.[9] I remember kicking up a terrible fuss about getting a haircut once—I actually felt like I was going to drown. This is where it came from. The feeling of drowning is totally gone.* (preclear is grinning)

As you can see these modern techniques are very simple and direct.

The engram, no matter how gruesome it was, is, when relieved in all its aspects, a subject of great mirth.[10]

9. **barber poles:** poles with spiral stripes of red and white, used as a symbol of the barber's trade.

10. **mirth:** amusement or laughter.

Appendix B

A Historical Sketch of Reincarnation and Past Lives

The belief in reincarnation predates history itself. It is impossible to trace the subject to a single early beginning but traces of it are to be found in all religions, and in the myths of nearly all primitive people.

Cro-Magnon[1] man (60,000–10,000 B.C.) painted the figures of hunted animals in caves, then danced ceremoniously to apologize to the spirits of the hunted animals for having killed them. They believed that the paintings held the souls of the animals, and placed gifts before them during their ritual dances hoping they themselves would take on the strength of the animal spirit.

Roman writers said the belief in reincarnation was prevalent amongst the Gauls[2] and Druids.[3] Traces can also be found

---

1. **Cro-Magnon:** of or belonging to a group of prehistoric people who lived in southwestern Europe and North Africa, characterized by large, long heads and tall stature.

2. **Gauls:** inhabitants of an ancient region in western Europe including the modern areas of northern Italy, France, Belgium and the southern Netherlands.

3. **Druids:** members of a priesthood in ancient Gaul, Britain and Ireland who are said to have studied nature and the physical world, predicted the future, engaged in priestly sacrifices and acted as teachers and judges.

in Celtic[4] peasantry.

The American Indian tribes: the Dakota, Huron, Mohave, Sioux and Natovez all had their versions of "The Happy Hunting Ground"—a paradise of hunting and feasting for warriors and hunters after death.

The Eskimos of Greenland still believe that man is made up of his body, his soul and his name. After death, the soul finds a new body in the sea or the sky and the name returns from the grave when it is given to a newborn babe.

The concept of a future life after death was not unknown to many early tribes around the world, including the Zunis, Incas, Okinawans, Papuans, Melanesians, Fijians, the Dyaks of Borneo and the Arunta and Warramunga tribes.

The Druses[5] of Lebanon and millions in Bengal and Burma believed in rebirth, and in Africa the Mandingo tribe as well as the Yoruba, Zulus, Bantus and Barotse all believed strongly in the spirituality of their tribes and future lives.

The early inhabitants of ancient Egypt laid their dead in graves uniformly facing a single direction. They dismembered their dead believing it would prevent the spirit from returning to his old village.

From 3500 B.C. to 640 A.D., the Egyptians practiced funeral rituals on the dead to ensure their well-being in the afterlife. They maintained that the dead return in other forms.

---

4. **Celtic:** of a group of tribes who dominated central Europe in the 6th and 5th century B.C. They came originally from southwest Germany and spread to the British Isles, France, Spain, Italy and parts of Asia.

5. **Druses:** members of an independent religious sect living chiefly in Syria, Lebanon and Israel in the 16th century. They believed in reincarnation and in the ultimate perfection of humankind.

They believed in all-powerful guides along the road conceived to pass through death and the grave—a road which led into the realm of light and life and into the presence of the divine being Osiris, the conqueror of death, believed to cause men and women "to be born again."

The Aryans[6] settled in India around 1500 B.C. and Hinduism began. The caste system[7] developed—the system of social divisions into which Hindu society is traditionally divided—including the belief that a person was reborn into higher and lower castes as humans or animals based upon his conduct in his previous life.

In the 6th century B.C., Gautama Siddhartha Buddha[8] founded Buddhism, which spread from India to China, Burma, Japan, Tibet and parts of Southeast Asia.

He taught that there was no escaping the result of one's actions; and that without the cycle of rebirth, life would be meaningless and without purpose. Rebirth was said to occur lifetime after lifetime and the individual was regarded as everlasting. The rebirth cycle was believed to continue until the state of *nirvana* was reached. *Nirvana* is defined in Buddhism as the state of liberation from the craving for existence through or from within bodies.

Buddhism, one of the world's oldest surviving religions, civilized two thirds of the world.

6. **Aryans:** an ancient, light-skinned people that invaded India in the period 2000–1500 B.C. and gave Hinduism its current form.

7. **caste system:** a system of social divisions into which Hindu society is traditionally divided, each caste having its own privileges and limitations, transferred by inheritance from one generation to the next. Each distinct class traditionally, but no longer officially, were excluded from social dealings with the others.

8. **Gautama Siddhartha Buddha:** (ca. 563–483 B.C.) Indian philosopher, founder of Buddhism. *See also* **Buddhism** in the glossary.

Jainism arose in India at around the same time as Buddhism (ca. 600–500 B.C.), founded by a Hindu reformer in revolt against the caste system. Jainism is similar to Buddhism in some aspects, notably the doctrine of rebirth and the absence of a belief in a supreme god.

The belief in the human spirit and its immortality was also supported by Plato (427–347 B.C.), one of the classic Greek philosophers. His philosophy dealt with ideal forms and the belief that physical objects are an impermanent representation of unchanging ideas and that ideas alone give true knowledge.

In his classic work, *Phaedo*,[9] Plato stated, "If it were not for it [reincarnation] life would soon disappear from the universe." He wrote about how Socrates,[10] when being put to death, considered himself nothing less than a spiritual being.

Plato acknowledged reincarnation fully in the last part of his work, *Republic*.[11]

Several Greek schools of thought, notably the Orphics[12] and Pythagoreans,[13] subscribed to the philosophy of reincarnation.

---

9. *Phaedo:* a written work authored by Plato which describes the death of Socrates and deals with the immortality of the soul.

10. **Socrates:** (470?–399 B.C.) Greek philosopher. He left no writings of his own; his philosophy was made known through the writings of his disciple Plato. His doctrines are the basis of idealistic philosophy, and have profoundly influenced philosophic thought through succeeding centuries.

11. *Republic:* a written work authored by Plato in which the ingredients of an ideal state are discussed from both a political and spiritual point of view.

12. **Orphics:** those who followed a religion based on writings attributed to Orpheus, a poet and musician of Greek myth. The Orphics believed in the purification of the soul through a cycle of reincarnation.

13. **Pythagoreans:** those who followed the teachings of Pythagoras, the main tenets of which were the transmigration of souls (reincarnation) and the belief that all relationships in the universe could be expressed numerically. *See also* **Pythagoras** in the glossary.

The Neoplatonists[14] and Gnostics[15] also held this belief.

Aristotle (384–322 B.C.), a Greek philosopher and the pupil of Plato, had his own philosophy. Aristotle made the soul little more than a faculty or attribute of the body, comparing it to the axness[16] of an ax.

The birth of Jesus Christ signaled to the people of the times that Jesus was the reincarnation of earlier prophets. The Gospels tell us that Jesus asked his disciples, "Whom say the people that I am?" His disciples offered the answers popular at the time that he was one of the early prophets—Elijah or Jeremiah. The rumor was current that in the person of Jesus, "One of the old prophets is risen again." Thereafter, faith in the resurrection[17] and immortality became a natural belief.

In the early centuries A.D. faith in reincarnation also emerged in Judaism,[18] in three marked stages. The first was a shadowy idea of the persistence of men after death in the Sheol —a place in the depths of the Earth conceived as the dwelling of the dead. The second was the increasing influence of studies about the resurrection and judgment. The third demonstrated the wedding of immortality to the idea of resurrection. From there it formed part of the theology of medieval Jewry.

---

14. **Neoplatonists:** members of a school of philosophy who believed that there was a single source from which all forms of existence emanated and with which the soul sought mystical union.

15. **Gnostics:** members of any of certain sects of early Christians who claimed to have superior knowledge of spiritual matters, and whose unifying principle was that salvation was to be sought through knowledge rather than faith, ritual or good works.

16. **axness:** the state or quality of being an ax.

17. **resurrection:** arising again from death to life. Comes from Latin, meaning "rising again."

18. **Judaism:** the Jewish religion, based on a belief in one God and on the laws and teachings of the Bible and the writings which form the Jewish civil and religious law.

The Christian philosopher and teacher Origen (186–253 A.D.), thought that only in the light of reincarnation could certain scriptural passages be explained.

Saint Jerome[19] (340–420 A.D.) said that reincarnation in a special sense was taught among the early Christians and was given an esoteric[20] interpretation which was communicated only to a select few.

Reincarnation was a fundamental belief in the Roman Catholic Church until 553 A.D., when the second Synod of Constantinople[21] was convened by the Roman emperor, Justinian. The council met, unattended by the Pope from Rome, and condemned the teaching of reincarnation. "If anyone assert the fabulous preexistence of souls," they decreed, "and shall submit to the monstrous doctrine that follows it, let him be anathema."[22] Thus there was a formal curse upon believers and all references to the subject were expunged[23] from the Bible. The belief in the preexistence of souls was declared heresy.[24]

Nonetheless, Saint Augustine, the Roman monk, held a firm belief in the subject. In 597 A.D., he headed a group of missionaries who landed in England and began conversions to Christianity and indeed to the belief in reincarnation. He became the

19. **Saint Jerome:** (ca. 340–420) Christian scholar, responsible for the Latin translation of the Scriptures.

20. **esoteric:** intended or understood by only a chosen few, as an inner group of disciples or initiates, said of ideas, doctrines, literature, etc.

21. **Synod of Constantinople:** one of a series of meetings held at Constantinople, ancient capital of the Roman Empire, where Christian church officials met together for discussion and decision of church matters.

22. **anathema:** a person or thing accursed or damned. Used here specifically in reference to a formal curse or condemnation excommunicating a person from a church.

23. **expunged:** struck or blotted out; erased; obliterated.

24. **heresy:** (Roman Catholic) a willful and persistent rejection of any of the articles of faith by a baptized member of the church.

first Archbishop of Canterbury[25] in 601 A.D.

Saint Thomas Aquinas (1225–1274 A.D.), an Italian philosopher and major theologian of the Catholic church, followed Aristotle's theory regarding the soul as a "form" of the body, and declared a division between the soul and the body as "unnatural." For full existence after death the soul must be reunited with the body. His reasoning was that those saints who pass to heaven or death await the full consummation of blessedness at the "end" of history with the general resurrection. This is interpreted as involving the creation in the next life of renewed bodies.

In the Middle Ages to follow, the belief in reincarnation, though less dominant, was yet evident. Among those who maintained and propagated this belief were Saint Francis of Assisi,[26] founder of the Franciscan Order, Johannes Scotus Erigena[27] the Irish monk, and Thomas Campanella[28] the Dominican[29] monk.

Sikhism began around 1500 A.D., originating from Hinduism, based on worship of one god, rejection of the caste system and idolatry, and with the belief that the soul is reborn into many bodies before it becomes good enough to be joined to the infinite.

---

25. **Archbishop of Canterbury:** the highest-ranking bishop in England. Canterbury is a city located in Kent, England, and has long been the spiritual center of England.

26. **St. Francis of Assisi:** (1182–1286 A.D.) Italian monk and teacher, born in Assisi, a town in central Italy. Saint Francis founded the Franciscan Order of monks, and traveled through Italy, southern France and Spain spreading Christianity.

27. **Johannes Scotus Erigena:** (ca. 810–880) religious philosopher and teacher, apparently born in Ireland. He has been called perhaps the most learned man of his time.

28. **Thomas Campanella:** (1568–1639) Italian philosopher, poet and monk. Known especially for his written work *City of the Sun,* a description of a utopian state similar to that of Plato's *Republic.*

29. **Dominican:** having to do with the religious order founded in 1215 by Saint Dominic, a Spanish priest.

In 1721, the famous "Infant of Lübeck" was born in Lübeck, a seaport in northwest Germany, and talked within the first few hours of his birth. He knew the chief events of the early parts of the Bible at the age of one, of the whole Bible at the age of two, and of world history at the age of three. At the same time he acquired knowledge of both Latin and French. The King of Denmark, hearing of this marvelous child and disbelieving the rumors, called for the child and was astounded. The child predicted his own death, which occurred when he was four.

Near the same time, a child named Jean Cardiac knew the alphabet when he was three months old and could converse in his mother tongue, French, when a year old. He conversed in Latin when he was three years old, in English when four, and in Greek and Hebrew at six, apart from various other languages. He also picked up a number of other arts and skills before dying at the age of seven in 1726.

Other such child "prodigies"[30] helped rekindle the belief in reincarnation.

François Marie Voltaire, the satirical French philosopher, observed that "It is not more surprising to be born twice than once."

Benjamin Franklin,[31] Ralph Waldo Emerson,[32] Henry Ford[33]

---

30. **prodigies:** people, things or acts so extraordinary as to inspire wonder; specifically, a child of highly unusual talent or genius.

31. **Benjamin Franklin:** (1706–90) famous American statesman, scientist and philosopher.

32. **Ralph Waldo Emerson:** (1803–82) one of American's most influential authors and thinkers, also a minister and noted lecturer.

33. **Henry Ford:** (1863–1947) American industrialist, pioneer automobile manufacturer, organizer and president of the Ford Motor Company, one of the largest automobile companies in the world.

and Thomas Edison[34] all espoused the belief.

In the late 1800s and early 1900s, several prominent Christian church leaders made statements supporting reincarnation. Cardinal Mercier of the Belgian Catholics stated that the doctrine in no way conflicts with Catholic dogma.[35] Dean Inge of Saint Paul's Cathedral in London declared, "I find the doctrine [of reincarnation] both credible and attractive."

Sigmund Freud[36] and Carl Gustav Jung[37] found early on that man held a firm belief in his own immortality. This apparently was contrary evidence to already existing theories and the basic "principles" of psychology as laid down by Wilhem Wundt of Leipzig University, who stated that man was an animal without a soul and only lived one life. Man's belief in reincarnation and the immortality of the soul was attributed by the psychologist to fantasy or imagination. Thus the spiritual nature of man was lost to psychology, and from there theories went awry[38] and down the avenue of medicine.

Theories on man's longing to continue his rebirth cycle are many. Some scientists believe they are demonstrated through man's attempts to synthesize the experience through drugs and a feeling of enforced exteriorization from the body. Some consider that the motivation for suicide is really an effort to depart from a failing existence and to begin anew. Much has been said through history to explain away the child genius and the phenomenon of

---

34. **Thomas Edison:** (1847–1931) American inventor. Among his inventions, of which he patented over a thousand, are the phonograph, the microphone and the light bulb.

35. **dogma:** a doctrine or body of doctrines of religion formally stated and authoratively proclaimed by a church.

36. **Sigmund Freud:** (1856–1939), Austrian neurologist, founder of psychoanalysis.

37. **Carl Gustav Jung:** (1875–1961), Swiss psychologist and psychiatrist.

38. **awry:** away from the proper direction; amiss; wrong.

déjà vu (from French, literally meaning "already seen"), the feeling that one has been in a place or had a specific experience before, perhaps in a former existence.

The questions of why people have unaccountable fears, fetishes[39] or sudden deep friendships, or why lovers sometimes feel they "have known each other for ages," are all now answered.

L. Ron Hubbard unlocked the secrets of all these phenomena in 1950 when he wrote his best-selling book *Dianetics: The Modern Science of Mental Health.* The techniques of Dianetics opened the door to past lives.

People everywhere began to apply Dianetics procedures to one another to alleviate psychosomatic illnesses and improve ability. Using the Dianetics technique of *returning*[40] to earlier times and incidents, past lives soon presented themselves.

With this discovery, L. Ron Hubbard's research progressed into the realm of the spirit. Scientology was developed, and the phenomena of past life experiences were encountered and handled routinely in Scientology along with all other phenomena in the course of helping people to live happier, better lives.

In 1968, L. Ron Hubbard, accompanied by a group of Scientologists, set out to verify past existences on an expedition to areas in the Mediterranean which he had not seen in his current life. Ron made maps and miniature models of the locations of

---

39. **fetishes:** any object, idea, etc., eliciting unquestioning reverence, respect or devotion.

40. **returning:** "sending" a portion of one's mind to a past period on either a mental or combined mental and physical basis and reexerpiencing incidents which have taken place in one's past in the same fashion and with the same sensations as before.

---

certain graves and structures prior to the search, all through past life recall. Teams were sent out to various areas who found and verified the exact locations and artifacts of several different lifetimes and events.

One of the discoveries made by Ron through this research is that history as given in textbooks is sometimes faulty both as to date and content. Voltaire was known to have called history "a Mississippi[41] of lies." In some cases more accurate and positive accounts of history have been made through past life accounts.

L. Ron Hubbard's discoveries fully validate man's belief in past lives, which has continued down through the ages.

Today in Scientology the existence of past lives is proven fact, borne out as truth through the results of tens of thousands of people just like yourself.

—The Editors

---

41. **Mississippi:** the principal river of the United States which flows a distance of 2,330 miles from northern Minnesota to the Gulf of Mexico. Used figuratively in this sense.

Bibliography for
"A Historical Sketch on
Reincarnation and Past Lives"

Bernstein, Morey. *The Search for Bridey Murphy, with New Material*. New York: Doubleday and Company, 1965.

Budge, Sir E.A. Wallis. *The Book of the Dead*. New York: McGraw-Hill Book Company, 1969.

Catholic University of America, Washington, DC. *The New Catholic Encyclopedia*. New York: McGraw-Hill Book Company, 1967.

Cavendish, Richard (Editor) and J.B. Rhine (Special Consultant on Parapsychology). *The Encyclopedia of the Unexplained: Magic, Occultism and Parapsychology*. New York: McGraw-Hill Book Company, 1967.

Choron, Jacques. *Modern Man and Mortality*. New York: Macmillan, 1964.

Cooper, Irving Steiger. *Reincarnation, The Hope of the World*. Wheaton, Illinois: Theosophical Press, 1972.

Ducasse, Curt John. *A Critical Examination of the Belief in Life After Death*. Springfield, Illinois: Thomas, 1961.

Guillaumont, A. *Les "Kephalaia Gnostica" D'Evagre le Pontique (The Kephalaia Gnostica of Evagrius Ponticus)*. Paris: 1963.

Harden S.J., John A. *The Catholic Catechism: A Contemporary Catechism of the Teachings of the Catholic Church*. Garden City, New York: Doubleday and Company, Inc., 1975.

Harrington, Alan. *The Immortalist; An Approach to the Engineering of Man's Divinity*. New York: Random House, 1969.

Hendin, Dr. Herbert. *Suicide and Scandinavia, A Psychoanalytic Study of Culture and Character.* New York: Grune, 1964.

Hess, Hamilton; Adams, A.; Altendorf, H.D. *Canons of the Council of Sardica, AD 343.* Oxford Theological Monographs, Volume 1, Oxford: Oxford University Press, 1958.

Julian Press. *Reincarnation, An East-West Anthology; Including Quotations from the World's Religions and from over 400 Western Thinkers.* New York: Julian Press, 1961.

Langone, John. *Death is a Noun; A View of the End of Life.* Boston: Little, 1972.

Leek, Sybil. *Reincarnation the Second Chance.* New York: Stein and Day, 1974.

Lutoslawski, Wincenty. *Pre-existence and Reincarnation.* London: G. Allen and Unwin Ltd., 1928.

Marshall Cavendish Corporation, New York. *Man, Myth and Magic: An Illustrated Encyclopedia of the Supernatural.* Italy: BPC Publishing Ltd., 1970.

Montgomery, Ruth. *Here and the Hereafter.* New York: Coward–McCann, Inc. New York, Fifth Impression, 1968.

Origen. *On First Principles.* Translation by G.W. Butterworth. London: Society for Promoting Christian Knowledge, 1936.

Oxford University Press, Cambridge University Press. *The New English Bible: Old and New Testaments.*

Random House New York. *The Random House Dictionary of the English Language: The Unabridged Edition.* New York: Random House, Inc., First Printing, 1966.

Thödol, Bardo. *The Tibetan Book of the Dead.* Translation by Láma

Kazi Dawa-Samdup. Edited by W.Y. Evans-Wentz. London: Oxford University Press, Milford, 1927.

Toynbee, Arnold; Koestler, Arthur; and Others. *Life After Death.* New York: McGraw-Hill Book Company, 1976.

——; and Others. *Man's Concern with Death.* New York: McGraw-Hill Book Company, First United States Edition, 1969.

Origen. *Prayer, Exhortation to Martyrdom.* Translation by John Joseph O'Meara. Periodical: Ancient Christian Writers, Number 19. Westminster, Maryland: Newman Press, 1954.

About the Author

L. Ron Hubbard is one of the most acclaimed and widely read authors of all time, primarily because his works express a firsthand knowledge of the nature of man as a spiritual being—a knowledge gained not from a lofty study of ancient "mysteries," but by ceaseless work and research in direct contact with mankind in all walks of life.

As Ron said, "One doesn't learn about life by sitting in an ivory tower, thinking about it. One learns about life by being part of it." And that is how he lived.

He began his quest for knowledge on the nature of man at a very early age. When he was eight years old he was already well on his way to being a seasoned traveler, covering a quarter of a million miles by the age of nineteen. His adventures included voyages to China, Japan and other points in the Orient and South Pacific. During this time he became closely acquainted with twenty-one different races in areas all over the world.

After returning to the United States, Ron pursued his formal studies of mathematics and engineering at George Washington University, where he was also a member of one of the first classes on nuclear physics. He realized that neither the East nor the West contained the full answer to the problems of existence. Despite all of mankind's advances in the physical sciences, a *workable* technology of the mind and life had never been developed. The mental "technologies" which did exist, psychology and psychiatry, were actually barbaric, false subjects—no more workable than the methods of jungle witch doctors. Ron shouldered the responsibility of filling this gap in the knowledge of mankind.

He financed his early research through fiction writing. He became one of the most highly demanded authors in the golden age of popular adventure and science fiction writing during the 1930s and 1940s, interrupted only by his service in the US Navy during World War II.

Partially disabled at the war's end, Ron applied what he had learned from his research. He made breakthroughs and developed techniques which made it possible for him to recover from his injuries and help others regain their health. It was during this time that the basic tenets of Dianetics technology were codified.

In 1947, he wrote the first manuscript detailing his discoveries. Ron did not have it published at that time, but gave copies to some friends who copied it and passed it among their friends who then passed it on to others. (This book was formally published in 1951 as *Dianetics: The Original Thesis* and later republished as *The Dynamics of Life*.) The interest generated by this manuscript prompted a flood of requests for more information on the subject.

Ron attempted to make all his discoveries available to the American Psychiatric Association and the American Medical Association. Despite the fact that his work would have benefited them and thereby society immensely, his offers were refused. These same vested interests decided that Dianetics could harm their profits (which were and still are based on the amount of illness and insanity in our culture) and began to attack Ron and his work. He therefore decided to write a comprehensive text on the subject and take it directly to the public.

With the publication of *Dianetics: The Modern Science of Mental Health* on May 9, 1950, a complete handbook for the application of his new technology was broadly available for the first time. *Dianetics* created a wildfire of public interest. The book immediately shot to the top of the *New York Times* best-seller list and stayed there week after week. More than 750 Dianetics study groups sprang up within a few short months of its publication.

Ron's research did not stop with the success of *Dianetics*. As his work advanced, he found that people could recall events that occurred prior to their current lives, incidents that had to be handled to resolve a person's difficulties. A small number of individuals in 1951 protested about his raising the subject of past lives, but Ron persevered. He wrote "A true scientist boldly and fearlessly reports that which he finds," and went on to announce that it is actually *harmful* to a preclear's case to *not* run a past-life incident which presented itself in an auditing session.

Further research along this line opened up a whole new realm of information. Ron discovered that man's time track stretched a previously unimagined distance into the past. He undertook an exploration of this realm of time and developed methods by which others could also contact earlier existences and overcome situations in those lives which *still affected* them in present-day life. As he said, "It *is* true that man never dies, he only forgets, but my how he blinks when he realizes it."

Before Ron began this exploration, mankind's knowledge of his past had been suppressed for decades by the false doctrines of psychology and psychiatry, which allege that man is merely an animal possessed of no soul; and with these false theories came active suppression of religion and of education in the spiritual nature of man. Ron's discoveries have made it possible to overcome the tragic pattern of mankind toward wars, insanity, crime and death brought about by these subjects.

L. Ron Hubbard's confirmation of man's true immortality formed the foundation for many further discoveries and the development of precise methods for returning to man his full potential as a spiritual being.

The number of Ron's books and taped lectures continued to grow as he ceaselessly continued his work. Today these works— including instructional films, demonstrations and briefings—are studied and applied daily in hundreds of Scientology churches, missions and organizations on every continent.

With his research fully completed and codified, L. Ron Hubbard departed his body on January 24, 1986.

Ron's work opened a new door for mankind, out of the trap of ignorance of his own past and his true nature. Through his efforts, there now exists a totally workable technology by which the native abilities of beings can be restored.

Millions of people all over the world consider they have no truer friend.

Glossary

Abased: reduced or lowered, as in rank, office, reputation or estimation; humbled, degraded.

aberration: a departure from rational thought or behavior. It means basically to err, to make mistakes, or more specifically to have fixed ideas which are not true. The word is also used in its scientific sense. It means departure from a straight line. If a line should go from A to B, then if it is *aberrated* it would go from A to some other point, to some other point, to some other point, to some other point, to some other point, and finally arrive at B. Taken in its scientific sense, it would also mean the lack of straightness or to see crookedly as, for example, a man sees a horse but thinks he sees an elephant. Aberrated conduct would be wrong conduct, or conduct not supported by reason. Aberration is opposed to sanity, which would be its opposite. From the Latin, *aberrare,* to wander from; Latin, *ab,* away, *errare,* to wander.

Advanced Clinical Course: one of a number of theory and research courses delivered by L. Ron Hubbard during the years 1953 to 1961, which gave a deep insight into the phenomena of the mind and the rationale of research and investigation. Abbreviation *ACC.*

affronting: insulting openly or purposefully.

Alamo: a fortified mission in San Antonio, Texas. In 1836, during the Texas rebellion (against Mexico—as Texas was originally Spanish territory), a force of Texans was besieged at the Alamo by a much larger Mexican army. After 13 days of fighting, the Mexicans were able to break into the Alamo and every remaining defender was killed in hand-to-hand combat.

ally: a person who associates or cooperates with another; supporter. As used in Scientology, *ally* means someone who protects a person who is in a weak state and becomes a very strong influence over the person. The weaker person, such as a child, even partakes of the characteristics of the ally, so that one may find that a person who has, for instance, a bad leg, has it because a protector or ally in his youth had a bad leg. The word is from French and Latin and means *to bind together.*

amour-propre: (*French*) self-esteem; self-respect. Literally, self-love.

anathema: a person or thing accursed or damned. Used here specifically in reference to a formal curse or condemnation excommunicating a person from a church.

Anatolia: ancient name for the part of modern Turkey that is in Asia.

antipathy: a strong dislike.

aquiline: (of the nose) curving; hooked; prominent, like the beak of an eagle.

Archbishop of Canterbury: the highest-ranking bishop in England. Canterbury is a city located in Kent, England, and has long been the spiritual center of England.

Arunta: (also Aranda) members of an aboriginal people living in the Northern Territory of Australia.

Aryans: an ancient, light-skinned people that invaded India in the period 2000–1500 B.C. and gave Hinduism its current form.

astral: of or relating to the stars.

at odds: in conflict or disagreement, opposed.

attain to: to succeed in reaching or coming to.

auditing: the application of Dianetics or Scientology processes and procedures to someone by a trained auditor. The exact definition of auditing is: The action of asking a person a question (which he can understand and answer), getting an answer to that question and acknowledging him for that answer.

auditor: a person trained and qualified in applying Dianetics and/or Scientology processes and procedures to individuals for their betterment; called an auditor because *auditor* means "one who listens."

automatons: mechanical figures constructed to act as if by their own power; robots.

AWOL: away from military duty without permission. The word comes from "*a*bsent *w*ith*o*ut *l*eave."

awry: away from the proper direction, amiss, wrong.

axness: the state or quality of being an ax.

Babylon: the capital of an ancient empire called Babylonia which was located in southwest Asia and flourished from 2100–538 B.C.

bamboo, under the: beaten or caned with bamboo.

bank: the mental image picture collection of the pc—the reactive mind. It comes from computer terminology where all data is in a "bank." *See also* **reactive mind** in this glossary.

Bantus: members of a large group of Negroid tribes found in equatorial Africa and southern Africa.

barber poles: poles with spiral stripes of red and white, used as a symbol of the barber's trade.

Barotse: a tribe of South Central Africa who worship the sun and the spirits of ancestors.

bay: a reddish brown color.

bayonet: a knife that can be attached to the end of a rifle and used in hand-to-hand fighting.

Beethoven: Ludwig Van Beethoven (1770–1827); famous German composer of symphonies.

beetroot: (same as beet) a reddish colored root vegetable.

beingness: the assumption or choosing of a category of identity. Beingness is assumed by oneself or given to oneself or is attained. Examples of beingness would be one's own name, one's profession, one's physical characteristics, one's role in a game—each and all of these could be called one's beingness.

belligerent: showing readiness to fight or quarrel.

bemoaned: grieved over.

bends, the: a condition caused by the formation of nitrogen bubbles in the blood or body tissues as the result of a sudden lowering of atmospheric pressure, as in deep-sea divers returning to the surface too quickly: it is characterized by tightness in the chest, by pains in the joints, and by convulsions and collapse in severe cases.

Bengal: a region in the northeast Indian peninsula.

between-lives area: the experiences of a thetan during the period of time between the loss of a body and the assumption of another. At death, the theta being leaves the body and goes to a particular location where he "reports in," is given an implant to make him forget everything, and is then sent back to Earth to a new body just before it is born.

biff: a blow; a hit.

boie: an executioner.

Borneo: a large island southwest of the Phillipines.

bosun: a ship's petty officer in charge of rigging, boats, anchors, etc.

brand: a metal rod heated and used for branding.

bric-a-brac: literally means miscellaneous small articles collected because they are antique or for their sentimental, decorative or other interest. Used figuratively in this sense.

brothels: houses of prostitution.

buckboard: an open, flat-bottomed, four-wheeled carriage.

Buddha, Gautama Siddhartha: (ca. 563–483 B.C.) Indian philosopher, founder of Buddhism. *See also* **Buddhism** in this glossary.

Buddhism: the religion founded by Gautama Buddha (563–483 B.C.). The term *Buddha* derives from *Bodhi*, or "one who has attained intellectual and ethical perfection by human means." The hope of Buddhism was, by various practices, to break the endless chain of births and deaths and to reach salvation in one lifetime.

Buddhist: one who follows the doctrines of Buddhism. *See also* **Buddhism** in this glossary.

Burma: a country in southeast Asia, to the south of India.

butter lamp: a lamp which uses butter for fuel instead of oil.

buzzed: flew very low over an area.

camp: a group of people who support some cause, opinion, etc., together.

Campanella, Thomas: (1568–1639) Italian philosopher, poet and monk. Known especially for his written work *City of the Sun,* a description of a utopian state similar to that of Plato's *Republic.*

cangued: placed in a *cangue* (in China, a large, wooden yoke formerly fastened around the neck as a punishment for petty crime).

cans: electrodes used with the E-Meter. They resemble ordinary cans and are tin plated. Electrical leads from the E-Meter are connected to the cans with clips, and the cans are held in the preclear's hands.

capitalized: took advantage of; turned something to one's advantage.

Carthusian: a monk or nun of a very strict order founded at Chartreuse, France, in 1084.

case: a general term for a person being treated or helped. It also refers to his condition, which is monitored by the content of his reactive mind. A person's case is the way he responds to the world around him by reason of his aberration.

caste system: a system of social divisions into which Hindu society is traditionally divided, each caste having its own privileges and limitations, transferred by inheritance from one generation to the next. Each distinct class traditionally, but no longer officially, was excluded from social dealings with the others.

Catherine the Great: (1729–96) Catherine II, Empress of Russia (1762–96); married to Peter III (Russian Emperor) whom she deposed in order to take over the throne.

cause point: the originator of something; the point from which something was begun or dreamed up.

cautery: the operation of cauterizing. *Cauterize* means to burn with a hot iron, electric current, fire or a caustic substance (one that is capable of burning, corroding or destroying living tissue), especially for curative purposes. An example of the use of cautery would be pressing a hot iron against a wart to burn it off; another would be to sear an open wound in order to form a scar and stop it from bleeding.

Celtic: of a group of tribes who dominated central Europe in the 6th and 5th century B.C. They came originally from southwest Germany and spread to the British Isles, France, Spain, Italy and parts of Asia.

charge: harmful energy or force accumulated and stored within the reactive mind, resulting from the conflicts and unpleasant experiences that a person has had. Auditing discharges this charge so that it is no longer there to affect the individual. *See also* **reactive mind** in this glossary.

chiropractic: a therapeutic system based primarily upon the interactions of the spine and nervous system, the method of treatment usually being to adjust the segments of the spinal column.

Clear: the name of a state achieved through auditing or an individual who has achieved this state. A Clear is a being who no longer has his own reactive mind. A Clear is an unaberrated person and is rational in that he forms the best possible solutions he can on the data he has and from his viewpoint. The Clear has no engrams which can be restimulated to throw out the correctness of computation by entering hidden and false data.

clearing: the actions involved with bringing a person to the state of Clear. The word Clear can be used to describe the state itself or an individual who has achieved this state. A Clear is a being who no longer has his own *reactive mind*—that portion of a person's mind which works on a totally stimulus-response basis, which is not under his volitional control and which exerts force and the power of command over his awareness, purposes, thoughts, body and actions. *See also* **Clear** in this glossary.

cobbled: paved with rounded stones (cobblestones), formerly used for paving streets.

cognited: had a realization about life. *See also* **cognitions** in this glossary.

cognitions: new realizations of life. They result in higher degrees of awareness and consequently greater abilities to succeed with one's endeavors in life. A cognition is a "What do you know, I . . ." statement.

coitus: sexual intercourse.

command: in auditing, the exact question an auditor asks a preclear which is to be answered by the preclear.

complicity: partnership in wrongdoing; the fact or state of being an accomplice.

concentrically: arranged so as to have a common center, such as circles one within another.

confront: to face without flinching or avoiding. Confront is actually the ability to be there comfortably and perceive.

congealing: changing from a soft or fluid state to a rigid or solid state, as by cooling or freezing.

consideration: a thought or belief about something.

coolie: an unskilled native laborer, especially formerly in India and China.

cornelian: a red or reddish type of translucent quartz used in making jewelry.

cornice: the ornamental molding that projects along the top of a pillar.

cortège: solemn procession, as at a funeral.

counter-effort: effort is divided into the effort of the individual himself and the efforts of the environment (physical) against the individual. The individual's own effort is simply called effort. The efforts of the environment are called counter-efforts.

counter-intention: an intention that is in opposition to one's own intention. For example, Joe wants to join the army (intention); his wife does not want him to join the army (counter-intention).

cour: (*French*) courtyard.

Cro-Magnon: of or belonging to a group of prehistoric people who lived in southwestern Europe and North Africa, characterized by large, long heads and tall stature.

Cromwellian: of or having to do with Oliver Cromwell (1599–1658), English revolutionary leader who overthrew the king and ruled England from 1653–58.

cycle of action: the sequence that an action goes through, wherein the action is started, is continued for as long as is required and then is completed as planned. The cycle of action of the physical universe is create, survive (which is persist), destroy. For more information on the cycle of action, see the book *Scientology: Fundamentals of Thought* by L. Ron Hubbard.

debasing: making lower in value, character, dignity, etc.

decked out: dressed up or specially decorated for some purpose.

déjà vu: (*French*) (literally meaning "already seen") a feeling that one has been in a place or had a specific experience before.

Dianetics: Dianetics spiritual healing technology. It addresses and handles the effects of the spirit on the body and can alleviate such things as unwanted sensations and emotions, accidents, injuries and psychosomatic illnesses (ones that are caused or aggravated by mental stress). *Dianetics* means "through the soul" (from Greek *dia*, through, and *nous*, soul). It is further defined as "what the soul is doing to the body."

dickens: devil; used with *the* in mild oaths.

diffuse: spread out or dispersed; not concentrated.

diphtheria: an acute infectious disease that causes a sore throat, high fever, and the formation in the air passages of a membrane that can block breathing.

disposition: a getting rid (of something).

dissentients: people who disagree with the methods, goals, etc., of a political party or government.

dive: a disreputable resort for drinking or entertainment.

dogma: a doctrine or body of doctrines of religion formally stated and authoritatively proclaimed by a church.

Dominican: having to do with the religious order founded in 1215 by Saint Dominic, a Spanish priest.

Don Juan: a man who seduces women (from the Spanish legendary character Don Juan, an immoral nobleman and seducer of women).

doped: drugged.

doped off: got tired, sleepy, foggy (as though doped).

Doric: a classic order of architecture characterized by simplicity of form.

dropped: fell to the right. When an E-Meter needle drops, it is an indication that an area of charge has been located.

Druids: members of a priesthood in ancient Gaul, Britain and Ireland who are said to have studied nature and the physical world, predicted the future, engaged in priestly sacrifices and acted as teachers and judges.

Druses: members of an independent religious sect living chiefly in Syria, Lebanon and Israel in the 16th century. They believed in reincarnation and in the ultimate perfection of humankind.

dubbed in: created unknowingly a mental picture that appears to have been a record of the physical universe but is in fact only an altered copy of the past. (It is a phrase taken from the motion picture industry, meaning to record dialogue and various sounds and then integrate them into the film after it has been shot. This is done for scenes where the original recording is faulty, for scenes where it is simply more convenient to add dialogue and other sound later, and for films playing abroad which require new dialogue in the native language of the host country.)

Dyaks: members of an aboriginal people living in the interior of Borneo.

easy meat: those who are easily victimized or defeated.

Edison, Thomas: (1847–1931) American inventor. Among his inventions, of which he patented over a thousand, are the phonograph, the microphone and the light bulb.

effect: the receipt point of a flow (thought, energy or action). For example: If one considers a river flowing to the sea, the place where it began would be the source-point or cause, and the place where it went into the sea would be the effect-point, and the sea would be the effect of the river. A man firing a gun is cause; a man receiving a bullet is effect.

efforts: motions with definite direction and purpose. Effort is different from motion. Motion could be anything, but effort has to be specific: it is at a known point in time, it has a known direction and it is known whether it is inhibited or compelled.

élan: spirited self-assurance; exuberant enthusiasm.

Elijah: a Hebrew prophet of the ninth century B.C.

emanator: a large, glowing body of radioactive material which hangs magically in thin air, a sort of a god, an all-knower. Its outpulse puts one into a trance.

Emerson, Ralph Waldo: (1803–82) one of America's most influential authors and thinkers, also a minister and noted lecturer.

E-Meter: short for *electrometer*; an electronic device for measuring the mental state or change of state of *Homo sapiens*. It is *not* a lie detector. It does not diagnose or cure anything. It is used by auditors to assist the preclear in locating areas of spiritual distress or travail.

emote: to show or pretend emotion.

engram: a mental image picture which is a recording of an experience containing pain, unconsciousness and a real or fancied threat to survival. It is a recording in the reactive mind of something which actually happened to an individual in the past and which contained pain and unconsciousness, both of which are recorded in the mental image picture called an engram. It must, by definition, have impact or injury as part of its content. These engrams are a complete recording, down to the last accurate detail, of every perception present in a moment of partial or full unconsciousness.

entheta: enturbulated theta (thought or life); especially referring to communications, which, based on lies and confusions, are slanderous, choppy or destructive in an attempt to overwhelm or suppress a person or group.

erase: to cause an engram to "vanish" entirely by recounting, at which time it is filed as memory and experience and ceases to be part of the reactive mind. *See also* **reactive mind** in this glossary.

Erigena, Johannes Scotus: (ca.810–880) religious philosopher and teacher, apparently born in Ireland. He has been called perhaps the most learned man of his time.

esoteric: intended or understood by only a chosen few, as an inner group of disciples or initiates, said of ideas, doctrines, literature, etc.

ether: a drug used to produce anesthesia, as before surgery.

expostulating: earnestly reasoning with a person, objecting to his actions or intentions.

expunged: struck or blotted out; erased; obliterated.

exteriorization: the act of moving out of the body with or without full perception.

exteriorized: went exterior to the body. The spirit has moved out of the body and is able to view the body or control the body from a distance.

facsimile: a three-dimensional color picture with sound and smell and all other perceptions, plus the conclusions or speculations of the individual. *See also* **mental image picture** in this glossary.

faction: a group of people in a political party, church, club, neighborhood or other body or organization who stand up for their side or act together for some common purpose against the rest of a larger group.

fenced: sold something which was stolen to a person or place which deals in buying and selling stolen goods.

fetish: any object, idea, etc., eliciting unquestioning reverence, respect or devotion.

fifth invador force?

fifth column: any group of people who aid the enemy from within their own country.

Fijians: natives of the Fiji Islands, an independent chain of some 800 islands in the South Pacific Ocean, north of New Zealand.

fissure: a long, narrow, deep opening or crack.

flash answers: instantaneous replies, the first things that flash into the preclear's mind at the snap of the auditor's fingers upon asking a question.

flexes: flexible insulated electric cords.

flogged: beaten, or punished by being beaten, with a strap, stick, whip, etc.

Ford, Henry: (1863–1947) American industrialist, pioneer automobile manufacturer, organizer and president of the Ford Motor Company, one of the largest automobile companies in the world.

forestall: to act in advance of; get ahead of; anticipate.

for want of: because of the lack or absence of.

Franklin, Benjamin: (1706–90) famous American statesman, scientist and philosopher.

Freud, Sigmund: (1856–1939) Austrian neurologist, founder of psychoanalysis.

furtive: done by stealth; secret.

gamboling: playing; frolicking.

gangrenous: decay of tissue in a part of the body when the blood supply is blocked by injury, disease, etc.

gatehouse: a house beside or over a gateway; used as a porter's lodge, etc.

Gauls: inhabitants of an ancient region in western Europe including the modern areas of northern Italy, France, Belgium and the southern Netherlands.

glaive: a broadsword.

glib: done or spoken in an easy manner, too easy and smooth to be convincing.

Gnostics: members of any of certain sects of early Christians who claimed to have superior knowledge of spiritual matters, and whose unifying principle was that salvation was to be sought through knowledge rather than faith, ritual or good works.

gondola: a long, narrow boat with high, pointed ends, used on the canals of Venice in Italy.

gondolier: a person who rows or poles a gondola. *See also* **gondola** in this glossary.

got on: got or made what one needed; managed.

grief charge: an outburst of tears that may continue for a considerable time, in a session, after which the preclear feels greatly relieved. This is occasioned by the discharge of grief or painful emotion.

habit: garb of a particular rank, profession, religious order, etc.

hand, held in: caused to stay in control.

havingness: the concept of owning, possessing, being capable of commanding, taking charge of objects, energies and spaces.

helling around: going around in a noisy and often immoral way; carousing.

hemorrhage: heavy bleeding, as from a broken blood vessel.

heresy: (Roman Catholic) a willful and persistent rejection of any of the articles of faith by a baptized member of the church.

high-tide mark: literally, the mark left after high water has receded. Used figuratively in this sense.

Hinduism: a religious and social system, especially in India, with belief in reincarnation, worship of several gods, and the caste system as a basis of society. *See also* **caste system** in this glossary.

Hittite: any of an ancient people of Asia Minor and Syria (1700–700 B.C.).

hobbled: tied the feet together to hamper the movement of (a person, horse, etc.).

Hubbard Dianetics Auditor Course: a course which, in the middle and late 1950s trained an auditor in the handling of Dianetics techniques and procedures. Today it is a basic course which trains one to deliver auditing as described in *Dianetics: The Modern Science of Mental Health* by L. Ron Hubbard. The course is available at all Churches of Scientology.

hunt horn: a signal horn used in the chase while hunting.

hypnotism: the act of putting a person into a trance for the purpose of planting suggestions. Hypnotism reduces self-determinism by entering the commands of another below the awareness level of an individual's mind.

idolatry: the worship of idols.

implant: an enforced command or series of commands installed in the reactive mind below the awareness level of the individual to cause him to react or behave in a prearranged way without his "knowing it."

implant station: a place or installation in which implants were administered. *See also* **implant** in this glossary.

imploded: burst inward.

incarceration: imprisonment; confinement.

Incas: members of any of the dominant groups of South American Indian peoples who established an empire in Peru prior to the Spanish conquest.

incognito: with true identity unrevealed or disguised; under an assumed name, rank, etc.

incredulity: unwillingness or inability to believe; doubt.

inculcating: impressing upon the mind by frequent repetition or persistent urging.

in-session: the condition necessary for successful auditing, defined as preclear "willing to talk to the auditor and is interested in his own case."

interiorized: went into something too fixedly, and became part of it too fixedly.

interpolations: insertions of statements, remarks, etc., between or among others.

invalidated: made to feel worthless as a result of someone refuting, degrading, discrediting or denying something one considers to be fact.

iron maiden: a medieval torture instrument, fashioned as a box in the shape of a woman, large enough to hold a human being, and studded with sharp spikes on the inside.

irradiation: exposure to radiation such as X-rays, ultraviolet rays, etc.

Italian Somaliland: a former Italian colony and territory located on the coast of East Africa.

Jainism: a Hindu religion founded in the 6th century B.C.; it teaches that all life is sacred and that one can gain salvation by knowledge, faith and right living.

Jeremiah: a prophet who preached (ca. 628–586 B.C.) in Jerusalem.

Judaism: the Jewish religion, based on a belief in one God and on the laws and teachings of the Bible and the writings which form the Jewish civil and religious law.

Jung, Carl Gustav: (1875–1961), Swiss psychologist and psychiatrist.

Justinian: (483–565 A.D.) Roman emperor from 527 until his death. His greatest accomplishment was the codification of Roman law.

kicked the stuffings out of: gave a bad beating to.

knowingness: awareness not depending upon perception. One doesn't have to look to find out. For example, you do not have to get a perception or picture of where you are living to know where you live.

lackeys: male servants of low rank.

Lebanon: a country in southwest Asia, at the east end of the Mediterranean.

Lord Nelson: Horatio Nelson (1758–1805), English admiral. Nelson was most famous for his naval victory over a combined French and Spanish fleet at Cape Trafalgar, off the southwest coast of Spain.

mace-men: soldiers carrying a mace, a heavy medieval war club, often with a spiked, metal head.

machinations: sly or secret plots or schemes, especially evil ones.

Magna Graecia: ancient Greek colonies in southern Italy.

Mandingo: a Negroid people in west Africa.

man-of-war: an armed naval vessel; warship.

manta rays: large fish having a broad flat body with both eyes on top, wide fins which are horn-like when rolled up and a slender or whiplike tail.

marine: member of a military force at sea.

Marquis of Queensberry: John Sholto Douglas (1844–1900), patron of boxing who supervised the formulation of Marquis of Queensberry Rules in 1867. The Marquis of Queensberry Rules are the basic rules of modern boxing, providing for the use of gloves and the division of a match into rounds, etc.

masonry: brickwork or stonework.

meat wagon: a wagon used to carry the dead.

meerschaum: a tobacco pipe with a bowl made from a white, claylike substance. The word "meerschaum" comes from German meaning "sea foam."

Melanesians: members of a dark-skinned native people of Melanesia—a group of islands in the Pacific south of the equator and east of Australia and New Guinea.

mental image picture: a copy of the physical universe as it goes by; we call a mental image picture a facsimile when it is a "photograph" of the physical universe sometime in the past. We call a mental image picture a mock-up when it is created by the thetan or for the thetan and does not consist of photographs of the physical universe. We call a mental image picture a hallucination, or more properly an automaticity (something uncontrolled), when it is created by another and seen by self. *See also* **facsimile** in this glossary.

mercenary: a professional soldier hired to serve in a foreign army.

meter: short for **E-Meter**. *See* **E-Meter** in this glossary.

Metropolitan Museum: the chief museum of art in New York City and the largest in the United States, opened in 1880. The Metropolitan Museum contains a department of Egyptian antiquities which includes entire tomb chambers unearthed by the museum's archeological expeditions.

milk: short for *milk fever*, a slight fever sometimes occurring in women about the beginning of lactation, originally believed to be caused by a great accumulation of milk in the breasts, now thought to be caused by infection.

mirth: amusement or laughter.

misemotion: a coined word used in Dianetics and Scientology to mean an emotion or emotional reaction that is inappropriate to the present time situation. It is taken from *mis-* (wrong) + *emotion*. To say that a person was *misemotional* would indicate that the person did not display the emotion called for by the actual circumstances of the situation. Being misemotional would be synonymous with being irrational. One can fairly judge the rationality of any individual by the correctness of the emotion he displays in a given set of circumstances. To be joyful and happy when circumstances call for joy and happiness would be rational. To display grief without sufficient present time cause would be irrational.

Mississippi: the principal river of the United States which flows a distance of 2,330 miles from northern Minnesota to the Gulf of Mexico. Used figuratively in this sense.

mocked up: as used here, it simply means "created." In Scientology, the word *mock-up* is used to mean, in essence, something which a person makes up himself. A *mock-up* is more than a mental picture; it is a self-created object which exists as itself or symbolizes some object in the physical universe. The term was derived from the World War II phrase for miniature models that were constructed to symbolize weapons (airplanes, ships, artillery, etc.) or areas of attack (hills, rivers, buildings, etc.) for use in planning a battle.

mosque: Muslim temple or place of worship.

mucking around: wasting time, puttering, going about aimlessly.

Murphy, Bridey: a widely published account of a woman who was regressed back to the 1800s through the use of hypnosis during which a full and detailed life in Ireland was contacted. Her name in that life was Bridey Murphy. Dianetics discoveries inspired and were the impetus behind this 1952 episode.

Napoleon: Napoleon Bonaparte (1769–1821); French military leader and emperor of France (1804–15).

naturopathy: a system or method of treating disease that employs no surgery or synthethic drugs but uses special diets, herbs, massage, etc., to assist the natural healing processes.

''necessary to resolve the case'': a phrase used in Dianetics techniques. If an auditor asks a person for the *engram necessary to resolve the case*, he will always get the engram that is next available to be *reduced* or *erased*. To *reduce* an engram means to take all the charge or pain out of it and render it free of aberrative material as far as possible to make the case progress. To *erase* an engram means to cause it to "vanish" entirely by recountings, at which time it is filed as memory and experience.

needle: a slender rod with a pointed end which is used as the indicator on an E-Meter dial, such as the type of indicator often seen on the dial of an electronic instrument. *See also* **E-Meter** in this glossary.

nefarious: very wicked; evil.

Neoplatonists: members of a school of philosophy who believed that there was a single source from which all forms of existence emanated and with which the soul sought mystical union.

nil: nothing.

nonsequitur: something that has no bearing on what previously occurred or does not follow logically from what comes before it. From Latin, meaning "it does not follow."

nucleus: a central part around which other parts are grouped or gathered; core.

obstetricians: medical doctors who specialize in the branch of medicine dealing with the care and treatment of women during pregnancy, childbirth and the period immediately following.

occlusion: the state of something being hidden or forgotten and not available for conscious recall.

occult: secret; disclosed or communicated only to the initiated.

Okinawans: occupants of Okinawa, an island in the North Pacific

Ocean, located 350 miles south of Kyushu, the southernmost island of Japan.

olfactory: of or relating to the sense of smell.

order of magnitude: how large or how small something is in relation to other things.

Origen: (185?–245? A.D.) Christian theologian and teacher born in Egypt. His teaching had a strong ethical quality which carried much influence.

Orphics: those who followed a religion based on writings attributed to Orpheus, a poet and musician of Greek myth. The Orphics believed in the purification of the soul through a cycle of reincarnation.

orthodox: conforming to the usual beliefs or established doctrines; approved or conventional.

out for the count: knocked unconscious. Comes from boxing, where when one of the opponents is knocked down during a match, the referee counts aloud the seconds from 1 to 10. If the boxer stays down for the count of 10, he is declared defeated.

Oxford Capacity Analysis: a test which consists of 200 questions which measure personality traits. These tests are used to evaluate preclear gains.

Papuans: members of any of the native peoples of New Guinea and nearby islands.

pat: smooth and clever but superficial, as in a *pat* solution to a complex problem.

pc: abbreviation for **preclear.** *See* **preclear** in this glossary.

period: of or like that of an earlier time or age.

perturbation: being worried or upset; being disturbed or troubled greatly.

Phaedo: a written work authored by Plato which describes the death of Socrates and deals with the immortality of the soul.

placenta: an organ within the uterus via which the fetus receives nourishment as it is developing and which is discharged shortly after birth.

Plato: (ca. 427–347 B.C.) Greek philosopher and educator, born in Athens. In 387 B.C., founded a school of philosophy known as the Academy which became the first university known in history.

plot thickens, the: the story becomes more complex or involved.

plotting: marking the position or course of (a ship, etc.) on a map.

Pompeii: an ancient city in southwest Italy, which in A.D. 79 was destroyed (completely covered in lava) by the eruption of the nearby volcano called Mount Vesuvius.

Pope: head of the Roman Catholic Church.

porter: a person who carries things.

postulate: a conclusion, decision or resolution made by the individual himself; to conclude, decide or resolve a problem or set a pattern for the future or to nullify a pattern of the past.

Potala: an eleven-story, gilt-roofed palace in Lhasa, the capital of Tibet. The Potala is so large that it can be seen from miles away. It was built in the 7th century as the residence of the priest king of Tibet and its name means "Palace of the Gods."

powerhouse: a building where electric power is generated.

precipice: a vertical, almost vertical or overhanging rock face; steep cliff.

preclear: a spiritual being who is now on the road to becoming Clear, hence pre-Clear.

present time: the time which is now and which becomes the past almost as rapidly as it is observed. It is a term loosely applied to the environment existing in now, as in "The preclear came up to present time," meaning the preclear became aware of the present environment.

Pretender: James Francis Edward Stuart (1688–1766), English prince of Wales who claimed the English throne and led an unsuccessful revolt to obtain it.

proboscis: a long flexible snout, as an elephant's trunk.

processing: the application of Dianetics or Scientology processes to someone by a trained auditor. The exact definition of processing is: The action of asking a preclear a question (which he can understand and answer), getting an answer to that question and acknowledging him for that answer. Also called **auditing.**

prodigies: people, things or acts so extraordinary as to inspire wonder; specifically, a child of highly unusual talent or genius.

psychosomatic: *psycho* refers to mind and *somatic* refers to body; the term *psychosomatic* means the mind making the body ill or illnesses which have been created physically within the body by derangement of the mind.

purgatory: the state after death in which, per the teaching of the Roman Catholic Church, the soul destined for heaven is purified. Per this religion, only the perfect can go to heaven, and some believers die who have still unpunished or unrepented minor sins on their conscience, so these go to purgatory to be purged of such sins by suffering and repentance.

put the cap on it: finished it; left nothing more to be said or done on it.

Pythagoras: (ca. 582–500 B.C.) Greek philosopher, mathematician and religious reformer.

Pythagoreans: those who followed the teachings of Pythagoras, the main tenets of which were the transmigration of souls (reincarnation) and the belief that all relationships in the universe could be expressed numerically.

quartz: a brilliant crystalline mineral which occurs most often in a colorless, transparent form, but also sometimes in colored varieties used as semiprecious stones.

Why not for transistors as well ?

quay: a wharf, usually of concrete or stone, for use in loading and unloading ships.

rack: an instrument of torture having a frame on which the victim is bound and stretched until his limbs are pulled out of place.

ramping: standing upright on the hind legs.

ramproad: a sloping, sometimes curved, road joining different levels.

rapier: a small sword with a narrow blade, especially from the 18th century.

ravish: to rape.

razed: cut or shaved off.

reactive mind: that portion of a person's mind which works on a totally stimulus-response basis, which is not under his volitional control and which exerts force and the power of command over his awareness, purposes, thoughts, body and actions. The reactive mind is where engrams are stored.

reality: the agreed-upon apparency of existence. A reality is any data that agrees with the person's perceptions, computations and education. Reality is one of the components of understanding.

rebuffed: refused bluntly; snubbed.

recalcitrant: refusing to follow direction, etc.; stubborn and defiant.

remonstrate: to present and urge reasons in opposition or complaint, protest.

reincarnation: the occupation by the soul of a new body after the death of the former body. The word comes from Latin, meaning literally "taking on flesh again." This definition has been distorted and complicated over time, but the original and *correct* meaning of the word is simply "to take on a new body."

repetitive process: an auditing process which is run over and over again, with the same question of the preclear. The preclear answers the question and the auditor acknowledges him. The process is run until it no longer produces change or a reaction in the preclear.

reproached: accused of and blamed for a fault so as to make feel ashamed.

Republic: a written work authored by Plato in which the ingredients of an ideal state are discussed from both a political and spiritual point of view.

restimulation: reactivation of a past memory due to similar circumstances in the present approximating circumstances of the past.

resurrection: arising again from death to life. Comes from Latin, meaning "rising again."

returning: "sending" a portion of one's mind to a past period on either a mental or combined mental and physical basis and reexperiencing incidents which have taken place in one's past in the same fashion and with the same sensations as before.

rheumatism: a popular term for any of the various painful conditions of the joints and muscles, characterized by inflammation, stiffness, etc.

ridge: a solid accumulation of old, inactive energy suspended in space and time. A ridge is generated by opposing energy flows which hit one another, and continues to exist long after the energy flows have ceased.

roll out: arise from bed; get up.

run: to undergo processing on.

run out: erased. *See also* **erase** in this glossary.

Saint Elmo's fire: a visible electric discharge from charged, especially pointed, objects, as the tips of masts, spires, trees, etc.: seen sometimes during electrical storms. After Saint Elmo, patron saint of sailors.

Saint Francis of Assisi: (1182–1286 A.D.) Italian monk and teacher, born in Assisi, a town in central Italy. Saint Francis founded the Franciscan Order of monks, and traveled through Italy, southern France and Spain spreading Christianity.

Saint Jerome: (ca. 340–420 A.D.) Christian scholar, responsible for the Latin translation of the Scriptures.

scarified: scratched or cut superficially.

Scientology: Scientology philosophy. It is the study and handling of the spirit in relationship to itself, universes and other life. Scientology means *scio,* knowing in the fullest sense of the word and *logos,* study. In itself the word means literally *knowing how to know.* Scientology is a "route," a way, rather than a dissertation or an assertive body of knowledge. Through its drills and studies one may find the truth for himself. The technology is therefore not expounded as something to believe, but something to *do.*

scouted: sought, searched for. In doing a meter scout, the E-Meter is used to search out areas of charge.

scythe, old man with the: referring to the Grim Reaper: death, especially when personified as a man or skeleton with a scythe.

seared: scorched or burned on the surface.

self-determinism: a condition of determining the actions of self; the ability to direct oneself.

session: a precise period of time during which an auditor audits a preclear.

Sheol: a place in the depths of the earth conceived as the dwelling of the dead.

shrewish: like a nagging, bad-tempered woman.

shy: to react negatively; be or become cautious or unwilling; draw back.

Sikhism: the religion and practices of a Hindu religious sect founded in northern India about 1500 and based on belief in one God and on rejection of the caste system and idolatry.

sitting duck: an easy target. Because in hunting a sitting duck is an easy target, as compared to one flying.

Socrates: (470?–399 B.C.) Greek philosopher. He left no writings of his own; his philosophy was made known through the writings of his disciple Plato. His doctrines are the basis of idealistic philosophy, and have profoundly influenced philosophic thought through succeeding centuries.

solar plexus: a network of nerves situated at the upper part of the abdomen, behind the stomach and in front of the aorta. *Plexus* means "a network, as of nerves or blood vessels" and it is called *solar* because of the raylike pattern of the nerve fibers.

somatics: physical pains or discomforts of any kind, especially painful or uncomfortable physical perceptions stemming from the reactive mind. Somatic means, actually, "bodily" or "physical." Because the word *pain* is restimulative, and because the word *pain* has in the past led to a confusion between physical pain and mental pain, the word *somatic* is used in Dianetics and Scientology to denote physical pain or discomfort of any kind.

sounding: trying to find out the opinions or feelings of a person, as by roundabout questioning.

squire: a country gentleman in Great Britain, especially the chief landowner in a village or district.

stove in: broken or crushed inward.

street piano: a large music box that is made to play tunes by turning a crank.

subjectively: in a manner which proceeds from or takes place in an individual's mind.

subverted: made weaker or corrupted, as in morals.

sucker: a person easily cheated or taken in.

suits: actions to secure justice in a court of law; attempts to recover a right or claim through legal action.

sulfur: a natural substance that exists in several forms. Most common form is a yellow crystal-like solid that has a suffocating odor when it burns.

Sussex: a maritime county in southeast England.

Synod of Constantinople: one of a series of meetings held at Constantinople, ancient capital of the Roman Empire, where Christian church officials met together for discussion and decision of church matters.

TB: abbreviation for tuberculosis, an infectious disease that may affect almost any tissue of the body, especially the lungs.

teddy-boys: uncouth, rough, idle, usually low-class young toughs (about fifteen to twenty-five years old), often violent; juvenile delinquents.

telepathy: a communication between minds other than by speaking, seeing, etc.

thermonuclear: of nuclear reactions that occur at very high temperatures.

theta: energy peculiar to life or a thetan which acts upon material in the physical universe and animates it, mobilizes it and changes it; natural creative energy of a thetan which he has free to direct toward survival goals, especially when it manifests itself as high tone, constructive communications. *See also* **thetan** in this glossary.

thetan: the person himself—not his body or his name, the physical universe, his mind, or anything else; that which is aware of being aware; the identity which is the individual. The term was coined to eliminate any possible confusion with older, invalid concepts. It comes from the Greek letter Theta (θ), which the Greeks used to represent *thought* or perhaps *spirit*, to which an *n* is added to make a noun in the modern style used to create words in engineering. It is also θ^n, or "theta to the nth degree," meaning unlimited or vast.

theta trap: a means used to trap a thetan. All theta traps have one thing in common: They use electronic force to knock the thetan into forgetting, into unknowingness, into effect. *See also* **thetan** in this glossary.

thumbscrew: an old instrument of torture by which one or both thumbs were compressed.

time track: the consecutive record of mental image pictures which accumulate through a person's life or lives. It is very exactly dated. The time track is the entire sequence of "now" incidents, complete with all sense messages, picked up by a person during his whole existence.

tine: a slender, projecting part that is pointed at the end; prong.

totem: a representation of a natural object or an animate being, as an animal or bird, serving as the distinctive mark of a clan or group.

train, in: in proper order, arrangement or sequence; in process.

transfixed: unable to move.

twinkling of an eye, in the: the time required for a wink; an instant.

two-way communication: a two-way cycle of communication would work as follows: Joe, having originated a communication, and having completed it, may then wait for Bill to originate a communication to Joe, thus completing the remainder of the two-way cycle of communication. Thus we get the normal cycle of a communication between two people.

underdogs: persons who are expected to lose in a contest or conflict; victims of social or political injustice.

undertaking: having to do with the profession of supervising or conducting the preparation of the dead for burial, and directing or arranging funerals.

universes: whole systems of created things. The universes are three in number. The first of these is one's own universe. The second would be the material universe, which is the universe of matter, energy, space and time, which is the common meeting ground of all of us. The third is actually a class of universes—the universe of every other person.

vacillated: wavered in one's mind; showed indecision.

valence: personality. The term is used to denote the borrowing of the personality of another. A valence is a substitute for self taken on after the fact of lost confidence in self. A preclear "in his father's valence" is acting as though he were his father.

verminous: infested with small, objectionable parasites such as fleas, lice, etc.

vertigo: a dizzying sensation of tilting within stable surroundings or of being in tilting or spinning surroundings.

Vesuvius: an active volcano in the south of Italy.

vetted: appraised, verified or checked for accuracy, authenticity, validity, etc.

Voltaire: (François Marie Arouet) (1694–1778) French philosopher, historian and writer.

Warramunga: an aboriginal tribe living in central Australia.

waster: a person who wastes money; spendthrift.

Wundt, Wilhelm: (1832–1920) German physiologist and psychologist.

Yoruba: a member of numerous West African coastal people.

Zulus: members of a cattle-owning people living mainly in Natal province, South Africa.

Zunis: members of a North American Indian people of western New Mexico.

Index

baby, when thetan picks up the baby body, 224

Beethoven, famous person fixation and, 14

behavior, at death could vary from person to person, 222

between-lives area, 225

body,
    fact that a person is not his body but can be detached from his body is too well known for much discussion, 19
    how thetans behave when they suddenly haven't got a, 224
    man is composed of body, mind and thetan, 217
    ordinary entrance of thetan into new body, 224
    picking up a new body, 218
    question of whether body would go on living if not picked up by thetan, 224
    shut-off of memory actually occurs with pick-up of new body, 225
    thetan associates body with his own identity, result, 225
    thetans often say very interesting prayers at moment they pick up a body, 224
    thetan will stay around body until it is disposed of properly, 225

Catherine the Great, famous person fixation and, 14

child,
    newborn child has just died as an adult, 15
    revising our estimations of causes of child behavior, 15

death,
    backing out of body at moment of death with full memory, 221
    dying and coming back to life, 220
    exact behavior at death could vary from person to person, 222
    exteriorization which occurs at death is very fascinating because person is totally cognizant of it, 223
    is not anything of which to be very frightened, 219
    moment thetan conceives body to be no longer functional in any way, he backs out, 221
    phenomena of, 217

Dianetics, definition of, 3

Egyptians, had idea of living forever and wanted their bodies to live forever, 226

experiment, conditions of the past lives experiment, 3

exteriorization, which occurs at death is very fascinating because person is totally cognizant of it, 223

famous person fixation, 14

future, thetan can actually predict the, 227

Hinduism, past lives are not the same as the theory which has been called "reincarnation" in, 13

Homo sapiens, is a spirit and his usual residence is in his head; he looks at his mental image pictures and his body carries him around, 218

identity, thetan associates body with his own identity, result, 225

life,
consequences of having lived before can be reflected in present life, 19
taking it easy for a life or two, 15
man, is composed of body, mind and thetan, 217
memory,
contained in mental image pictures, 11
painfulness of, 11
restoration of memory, importance of, 12, 219
shut-off of, actually occurs with pick-up of new body, 225
thetan backs out at moment of death with full memory, 221
mental image pictures,
memory is contained in, 11
mind maintains and preserves mental image pictures of earlier existences, 219
mind,
maintains and preserves mental image pictures of earlier existences, 219
man is composed of body, mind and thetan, 217
Napoleon, famous person fixation and, 14
past lives,
amusing sidelight on past lives is "famous person" fixation, 14
note on, 11
not the same as theory which has been called "reincarnation" in Hinduism, 13

past lives, *(cont.)*
suppressed because of painfulness of the memory of former existences, 11
person, *see* **thetan**
prayers, thetans often say very interesting prayers at moment they pick up a body, 224
psychosomatic illnesses, 12
reincarnation, past lives are not the same as theory called "reincarnation" in Hinduism, 13
Scientology, definition of, 3
thetan(s), person(s), individual(s),
associates body with his own identity, result, 225
baby is born and then a thetan picks up the baby body, 224
can actually predict future, 227
definition of, 217
fact that a person is not his body but can be detached from his body is too well known for much discussion, 19
how they behave when they suddenly haven't got a body, 224
man is composed of body, mind and thetan, 217
often say very interesting prayers at moment they pick up a body, 224
ordinary entrance of thetan into new body, 224
question of whether body would go on living if not picked up by thetan, 224
will stay around body until it is disposed of properly, 225

Books and Tapes
by L. Ron Hubbard

Basic Scientology Books

The Basic Scientology Books Package contains the knowledge you need to be able to improve conditions in life. These books are available individually or as a set, complete with an attractive slipcase.

Scientology: The Fundamentals of Thought • Improve life *and* make a better world with this easy-to-read book that lays out the fundamental truths about life and thought. No such knowledge has ever before existed, and no such results have ever before been attainable as those which can be reached by the use of this knowledge. Equipped with this book alone, one could perform seeming miracles in changing the states of health, ability and intelligence of people. This *is* how life works. This *is* how you change men, women and children for the better, and attain greater personal freedom.

A New Slant on Life • Have you ever asked yourself, Who am I? What am I? This book of articles by L. Ron Hubbard answers these all-too-common questions. This is knowledge one can use every day—for a new, more confident and happier slant on life!

The Problems of Work • Work plays a big part in the game of life. Do you really enjoy your work? Are you certain of your job security? Would you like the increased personal satisfaction of doing your work well? This is the book that shows exactly how to achieve these things and more. The game of life—and within it, the game of work—can be enjoyable and rewarding.

Scientology 0-8: The Book of Basics • What is life? Did you know an individual can create space, energy and time? Here are the basics of life itself, and the secrets of becoming cause over any area of your life. Discover how you can use the data in this book to achieve your goals.

Basic Dictionary of Dianetics and Scientology • Compiled from the works of L. Ron Hubbard, this convenient dictionary contains the terms and expressions needed by anyone learning Dianetics and Scientology technology. And a *special bonus*—an easy-to-read Scientology organizing board chart that shows you who to contact for services and information at your nearest Scientology organization.

Basic Dianetics Books

The Basic Dianetics Books Package is your complete guide to the inner workings of the mind. You can get all of these books individually or in a set, complete with an attractive slipcase.

Dianetics: The Modern Science of Mental Health • Acclaimed as the most effective self-help book ever published. Dianetics technology has helped millions reach new heights of freedom and ability. Millions of copies are sold every year! Discover the source of mental barriers that prevent you from achieving your goals—and how to handle them!

The Dynamics of Life • Break through the barriers to your happiness. This is the first book Ron wrote detailing the startling principles behind Dianetics—facts so powerful they can change forever the way you look at yourself and your potentials. Discover how you can use the powerful basic principles in this book to blast through the barriers of your mind and gain full control over your success, future and happiness.

Self Analysis • The complete do-it-yourself handbook for anyone who wants to improve their abilities and success potential. Use the simple, easy-to-learn techniques in *Self Analysis* to build self-confidence and reduce stress.

Dianetics: The Evolution of a Science • It is estimated that we use less than ten percent of our mind's potential. What stops us from developing and using the full potential of our minds? *Dianetics: The Evolution of a Science* is L. Ron Hubbard's incredible story of how he discovered the reactive mind and how he developed the keys to unlock its secrets. Get this firsthand account of what the mind really is, and how you can release its hidden potential.

Dianetics Graduate Books

These books by L. Ron Hubbard give you detailed knowledge of how the mind works—data you can use to help yourself and others break out of the traps of life. While you can get these books individually, the Dianetics Graduate Books Package can also be purchased as a set, complete with an attractive slipcase.

Science of Survival • If you ever wondered why people act the way they do, you'll find this book a wealth of information. It's vital to anyone who wants to understand others and improve personal relationships. *Science of Survival* is built around a re-markable chart—The Hubbard Chart of Human Evaluation. With it you can understand and predict other people's behavior and reactions and greatly increase your control over your own life. This is a valuable handbook that can make a difference between success and failure on the job and in life.

Dianetics 55! • Your success in life depends on your ability to communicate. Do you know a formula exists for communication? Learn the rules of better communication that can help you live a more fulfilling life. Here, L. Ron Hubbard deals with the fun-damental principles of communication and how you can master these to achieve your goals.

Advanced Procedure and Axioms • For the *first* time the basics of thought and the physical universe have been codified into a set of fundamental laws, signaling an entirely new way to view and approach the subjects of man, the physical universe and even life itself.

Handbook for Preclears • Written as an advanced personal workbook, *Handbook for Preclears* contains easily done processes to help you overcome the effect of times you were not in control of your life, times that your emotions were a barrier to your success and much more. Completing all the fifteen auditing steps contained in this book sets you up for really being in *control* of your environment and life.

Child Dianetics • Here is a revolutionary new approach to rearing children with Dianetics auditing techniques. Find out how you can help your child achieve greater confidence, more self-reliance, improved learning rate and a happier, more loving relationship with you.

Notes on the Lectures of L. Ron Hubbard • Compiled from his fascinating lectures given shortly after the publication of *Dianetics: The Modern Science of Mental Health*, this book contains some of the first material Ron ever released on the ARC triangle and the Tone Scale, and how these discoveries relate to auditing.

OT[1] Library Package

All the following books contain the knowledge of a spiritual being's relationship to this universe and how his abilities to operate successfully in it can be restored. You can get all of these books individually or in a set, complete with an attractive slipcase.

Scientology 8-80 • What are the laws of life? We are all familiar with physical laws such as the law of gravity, but what laws govern life and thought? L. Ron Hubbard answers the riddles of life and its goals in the physical universe.

Scientology 8-8008 • Get the basic truths about your nature as a spiritual being and your relationship to the physical universe around you. Here, L. Ron Hubbard describes procedures designed to increase your abilities to heights previously only dreamed of.

Scientology: A History of Man • A fascinating look at the evolutionary background and history of the human race. This was Ron's first book on the vast time track of man. As Ron said, "This is a cold-blooded and factual account of your last sixty trillion years."

---

1. **OT:** abbreviation for *Operating Thetan*, a state of beingness. It is a being "at cause over matter, energy, space, time, form and life." *Operating* comes from "able to operate without dependency on things," and *Thetan* is the Greek letter *theta* (θ), which the Greeks used to represent *thought* or perhaps *spirit*, to which an *n* is added to make a noun in the modern style used to create words in engineering. It is also θ^n or "theta to the nth degree," meaning unlimited or vast.

The Creation of Human Ability • This book contains processes designed to restore the power of a thetan over his own postulates, to understand the nature of his beingness, to free his self-determinism and much, much more.

Basic Executive Books

The Basic Executive Books Package consists of the book *The Problems of Work* and the two books listed below. They are available individually or as a set, complete with an attractive slipcase.

How to Live Though an Executive • What are the factors in business and commerce which, if lacking, can keep a person overworked and worried, keep labor and management at each other's throats, and make an unsafe working atmosphere? L. Ron Hubbard reveals principles based on years of research into many different types of organizations.

Introduction to Scientology Ethics • A complete knowledge of ethics is vital to anyone's success in life. Without knowing and applying the information in this book, success is only a matter of luck or chance. That is not much to look forward to. This book contains the answers to questions like, "How do I know when a decision is right or wrong?" "How can I predictably improve things around me?" The powerful ethics technology of L. Ron Hubbard is your way to ever-increasing survival.

Purification Book Package

The books in the Purification Book Package contain data on the only effective way of handling drug and toxic residuals in the body, clearing the way for real mental and spiritual improvement—the Purification program. These books are available individually and as a specially boxed set.

Clear Body, Clear Mind: The Effective Purification Program • This book contains all the information on L. Ron Hubbard's Purification program. This is the only program of its kind in existence that has been found to clean the residues of drugs, toxins and elements harmful to human bodies out of them! Drugs and chemicals can stop a person's ability to improve himself or just to live life. This book describes the program which can make it possible to start living again.

Purification: An Illustrated Answer to Drugs • Presented in a concise, fully illustrated format, this book provides you with an overview of the Purification program. Our society is ridden by abuse of drugs, alcohol and medicine that reduce one's ability to think clearly. This book lays out what can be done about it, in a form which is easy for anyone to read and understand.

Purification Rundown Delivery Manual • This book is a manual which guides a person through the Purification Rundown step by step. It includes all of the needed reports as well as spaces for the person to write his successes and to attest to program completion. This manual makes administering the Purification Rundown simple and *standard*.

All About Radiation • Can the effects of radiation exposure be avoided or reduced? What exactly would happen in the event of an atomic explosion? Get the answers to these and many other questions in this illuminating book. *All About Radiation* describes observations and discoveries concerning the physical and mental effects of radiation and the possibilities for handling them. Get the real facts on the subject of radiation and its effects.

Other Scientology Books

What Is Scientology? • Scientology works. It covers every aspect of life and livingness. But how do you communicate it to someone who has not yet experienced it for himself?

The answer is simple—the all-new edition of *What Is Scientology?* The most comprehensive text ever assembled on the Scientology religion, this book covers its religious heritage, basic principles and practices, organizational structure, worldwide use and expansion, social betterment programs and much, much more.

What Is Scientology? is *the* definitive reference for anyone who wants *all* the facts on the world's fastest growing religion.

Understanding: The Universal Solvent • L. Ron Hubbard's works contain a wisdom which is extraordinary in its perception and power. *Understanding: The Universal Solvent* is a collection of quotations from those works containing over 450 quotes, fully categorized and indexed for ease of reading. This book covers, in concise, strikingly beautiful and often poetic form, some of the most basic truths in this universe.

Knowingness • This collection of quotations has been designed especially for the Scientologist. It contains passages assembled from a broad selection of L. Ron Hubbard's writings and recorded lectures, imparting powerful and poetic truths about ability, mankind and life.

Art • The full collection of L. Ron Hubbard's writings on art, this book cuts through the fog of conflicting opinions on the subject and establishes fundamentals that are vital to any artistic endeavor. Beginning with a simple, workable definition of what art really is and including an analysis of what makes a work of art *good* as opposed to mediocre or poor, the chapters of this book contain basic principles that you can apply—in your art, in your profession and in life itself.

Dianetics and Scientology Technical Dictionary • This dictionary is your indispensable guide to the words and ideas of

Scientology and Dianetics technologies—technologies which can help you increase your know-how and effectiveness in life. Over three thousand words are defined—including a new understanding of vital words like *life, love* and *happiness* as well as Scientology terms.

Modern Management Technology Defined: Hubbard Dictionary of Administration and Management • Here's a real breakthrough in the subject of administration and management! Eighty-six hundred words are defined for greater understanding of any business situation. Clear, precise Scientology definitions describe many previously baffling phenomena and bring truth, sanity and understanding to the often murky field of business management.

Organization Executive Course • The *Organization Executive Course* volumes contain organizational technology never before known to man. This is not just how a Scientology organization works; this is how the operation of *any* organization, *any* activity, can be improved. A person knowing the data in these volumes fully, and applying it, could completely reverse any downtrend in a company—or even a country!

Management Series Volumes 1, 2 and 3 • These books contain technology that anyone who works with management in any way must know completely to be a true success. Contained in these books are such subjects as data evaluation, the technology of how to organize any area for maximum production and expansion, how to handle personnel, the actual technology of public relations and much more.

Ceremonies of the Church of Scientology • Discover the beautiful and inspiring ceremonies of the Church of Scientology. This book contains the illuminating Creed of the Church, church services, sermons and ceremonies.

Introductory and Demonstration Processes Handbook • What's the best way to give someone reality on Scientology and what it can do? *Audit* him! This extensive, easy-to-use handbook equips you with a complete array of introductory and demonstration processes that you can use anywhere—on a bus, in a cafe, at the shopping mall or at home with family and friends.

Assists Processing Handbook • Have you ever wished you could really help a person who was ill, injured or in pain? This book shows you how. A full collection of assist processes used in Dianetics and Scientology, this handbook includes assists developed by L. Ron Hubbard to help ease arthritis, make a person sober, bring down someone's temperature, aid a pregnant woman or a child, and even to help relieve the common cold.

Group Auditor's Handbook • Is it possible to improve the alertness, awareness and communication of a whole group of people, all at one time? Yes—using Group Processing. The *Group Auditor's Handbook* contains the fundamentals of this powerful technology, all the details of how to set up and run a Group Processing session, *and* the auditing commands for thirty-two different Group Auditing sessions. Group Processing is a skill any Scientologist can learn and apply to improve society on a broad scale.

Volunteer Minister's Handbook • This is a big, practical how-to-do-it book to give a person the basic knowledge on how to help self and others through the rough spots in life. It consists of many individual sections—each one covering important situations in life, such as drug and alcohol problems, study difficulties, broken marriages, accidents and illnesses, a failing business, difficult children, and much more. This is the basic tool you need to help someone out of troubles, and bring about a happier life.

The Book of Case Remedies • *The Book of Case Remedies* gives you the exact and precise ways of getting bugged preclears and students really moving up the Bridge again. Ron developed, codified and released a formidable array of technical repair tools that auditors, Case Supervisors, Supervisors and even field staff members can apply on stalled preclears, students and even new public to get them winning. This book is a *must* for all Scientologists.

Research and Discovery Series • These volumes contain the only existing day-to-day, week-to-week record of the progress of L. Ron Hubbard's research in Dianetics and Scientology. Through the pages of these beautiful volumes you follow L. Ron Hubbard's fantastic research adventure, beginning in the depths of man's degradation and obsession with the material universe and soaring to the realms of the spirit, freed from the bondage of the past.

Technical Bulletins • These volumes contain all of L. Ron Hubbard's technical bulletins and issues from the earliest to the latest. Almost any technical question can be answered from the pages of these volumes, which also include an extremely extensive master subject index.

The Personal Achievement Series

The Personal Achievement Series cassettes are some of the all-time favorites among Ron's lectures. Beautifully packaged along with transcript and glossary, these lectures contain discoveries about the mind and life that you will want to always have on hand for your own use, and are also a perfect introduction to Dianetics and Scientology for friends and family.

The Story of Dianetics and Scientology • In this lecture, L. Ron Hubbard shares with you his earliest insights into human nature and gives a compelling and often humorous account of his experiences. Spend an unforgettable time with Ron as he talks about the start of Dianetics and Scientology!

The Road to Truth • The road to truth has eluded man since the beginning of time. In this classic lecture, L. Ron Hubbard explains what this road actually is and why it is the only road one MUST travel all the way once begun. This lecture reveals the only road to higher levels of living.

Scientology and Effective Knowledge • Voyage to new horizons of awareness! *Scientology and Effective Knowledge* by L. Ron Hubbard can help you understand more about yourself and others. A fascinating tale of the beginnings of Dianetics and Scientology.

The Deterioration of Liberty • What do governments fear so much in a population that they amass weapons to defend themselves from people? Find out from Ron in this classic lecture.

Power of Choice and Self-Determinism • Man's ability to determine the course of his life depends on his ability to exercise his power of choice. Find how you can increase your power of choice and self-determinism in life from Ron in this lecture.

Scientology and Ability • Ron points out that this universe is here because we perceive it and agree to it. Applying Scientology principles to life can bring new adventure to life and put you on the road to discovering better beingness.

The Hope of Man • Various men in history brought forth the idea that there was hope of improvement. But L. Ron Hubbard's discoveries in Dianetics and Scientology have made that hope a reality. Find out by listening to this lecture how Scientology has become man's one, true hope for his final freedom.

The Dynamics • In this lecture Ron gives incredible data on the dynamics: how man creates on them; what happens when a person gets stuck in just one; how wars relate to the third dynamic and much more.

Money • Ron talks in this classic lecture about that subject which makes or breaks men with the greatest of ease—money. Find out what money really is and gain greater control over your own finances.

Formulas for Success—*The Five Conditions* • How does one achieve real success? It sometimes appears that luck is the primary factor, but the truth of the matter is that natural laws exist which govern the conditions of life. These laws have been discovered by Ron, and in this lecture he gives you the exact steps to take in order to improve conditions in any aspect of your life.

Health and Certainty • You need certainty of yourself in order to achieve the success you want in life. In *Health and Certainty*, L. Ron Hubbard tells how you can achieve certainty and really be free to think for yourself. Get this tape now and start achieving your full potential!

Operation Manual for the Mind • Everybody has a mind— but who has an operation manual for it? This lecture reveals why man went on for thousands of years without understanding how his mind is supposed to work. The problem has been solved. Find out how with this tape.

Miracles • Why is it that man often loses to those forces he resists or opposes? Why can't an individual simply overcome obstacles in life and win? In the tape lecture *Miracles*, L. Ron Hubbard describes why one suffers losses in life. He also describes how a person can experience the miracles of happiness, self-fulfillment and winning at life. Get a copy today.

The Road to Perfection—*The Goodness of Man* • Unlike earlier practices that sought to "improve" man because he was "bad," Scientology assumes that you have *good* qualities that simply need to be *increased*. In *The Road to Perfection*, L. Ron Hubbard shows how workable this assumption really is—and how you can begin to use your mind, talents and abilities to the fullest. Get this lecture and increase your ability to handle life.

The Dynamic Principles of Existence • What does it take to survive in today's world? It's not something you learn much about in school. You have probably gotten a lot of advice about how to "get along." *Your survival right now is limited by the data you were given.* This lecture describes the dynamic principles of existence, and tells how you can use these principles to increase your success in all areas of life. Happiness and self-esteem *can* be yours. Don't settle for anything less.

Man: Good or Evil? • In this lecture, L. Ron Hubbard explores the greatest mystery that has confronted modern science and philosophy—the true nature of man's livingness and beingness. Is man simply a sort of wind-up doll or clock—or worse, an evil beast with no control of his cravings? Or is he capable of reaching higher levels of ability, awareness and happiness? Get this tape and find out the *real* answers.

Differences between Scientology and Other Studies • The most important questions in life are the ones you started asking as a child: What happens to a person when he dies? Is man basically good, or is he evil? What are the intentions of the world toward me? Did my mother and father really love me? What is love? Unlike other studies, which try to *force* you to think a certain way, Scientology enables you to find your own answers. Listen to this important lecture. It will put you on the road to true understanding and belief in yourself.

The Machinery of the Mind • We do a lot of things "automatically"—such as driving a car. But what happens when a person's mental machinery takes over and starts running him? In this fascinating lecture, L. Ron Hubbard gives you an understanding of what mental machinery really is, and how it can cause a person to lose control. You *can* regain your power of decision and be in full control of your life. Listen to this lecture and find out how.

The Affinity-Reality-Communication Triangle • Have you ever tried to talk to an angry man? Have you ever tried to get something across to someone who was really in fear? Have you ever known someone who was impossible to cheer up? Listen to this fascinating lecture by L. Ron Hubbard and learn how you can use the affinity-reality-communication triangle to resolve personal relationships. By using the data in this lecture, you can better understand others and live a happier life.

Increasing Efficiency • Inefficiency is a major barrier to success. How can you increase your efficiency? Is it a matter of changing your diet, or adjusting your working environment? These approaches have uniformly failed, because they overlook the most important element: *you*. L. Ron Hubbard has found those factors that *can* increase your efficiency, and he reveals it in this timely lecture. Get *Increasing Efficiency* now, and start achieving *your* full potential.

Man's Relentless Search • For countless centuries, man has been trying to find himself. Why does this quest repeatedly end in frustration and disappointment? What is he *really* looking for, and why can't he find it? For the real truth about man and life, listen to this taped lecture by L. Ron Hubbard, *Man's Relentless Search*. Restore your belief in yourself!

More advanced books and lectures are available. Contact your nearest organization or write directly to the publisher for a full catalog.

Get Your Free Catalog
of Knowledge on
How to Improve Life

L. Ron Hubbard's books and tapes increase your ability to understand yourself and others. His works give you the practical know-how you need to improve your life and the lives of your family and friends.

Many more materials by L. Ron Hubbard are available than have been covered in the pages of this book. A free catalog of these materials is available on request.

Write for your free catalog today!

Bridge Publications, Inc.
4751 Fountain Avenue
Los Angeles, California 90029

NEW ERA Publications International ApS
Store Kongensgade 55
1264 Copenhagen K, Denmark

Improve Your Life
with Scientology
Extension Courses

Scientology books by L. Ron Hubbard give you the knowledge to achieve a happier, more successful life. Now learn to take and *use* that knowledge to gain greater control of *your* life. Enroll on a Scientology Extension Course.

Each extension course package includes a lesson booklet with easy to understand instructions and all the lessons you will need to complete it. Each course can be done in the comfort and convenience of your own home. Simply mail the completed lessons once a week to the Extension Course Supervisor at your Church of Scientology, who will review it and mail the results back to you. When you complete the course you will be sent a beautiful certificate suitable for framing.

The Fundamentals of Thought
Extension Course

Here is *practical, workable* knowledge that can improve your life in today's troubled world. The *Fundamentals of Thought Extension Course* contains lessons to ensure that you fully understand the data and can use it. Under the guidance of a professional Extension Course Supervisor, you can gain far greater understanding of life as you complete each lesson by mail. Order the *Fundamentals of Thought Extension Course* today!

A New Slant on Life
Extension Course

Life does not have to remain the same. You *can* reach higher levels of knowledge, ability and freedom. Discover the two rules for happy living, the secret of success, how to avoid being a "cog in a machine," how to reach your goals and more. Do the *New Slant on Life Extension Course* and gain a refreshing new outlook on life!

The Problems of Work
Extension Course

Trying to handle a job and keep it can get to be a deadlier struggle with each working day. What are the secrets to increasing your enjoyment of work? How can you gain the personal satisfaction of doing your work well? Find the answers and apply them easily. Do *The Problems of Work Extension Course!*

Enroll on a
Scientology Home Study
Extension Course Today!

For information and enrollment and prices for these extension courses and the books they accompany, contact the Public Registrar at your nearest Church of Scientology. (A complete list of Scientology churches and organizations is provided at the back of this book.)

"I am always happy to hear from my readers."

L. Ron Hubbard

These were the words of L. Ron Hubbard, who was always very interested in hearing from his friends and readers. He made a point of staying in communication with everyone he came in contact with over his fifty-year career as a professional writer, and he had thousands of fans and friends that he corresponded with all over the world.

The publishers of L. Ron Hubbard's works wish to continue this tradition and welcome letters and comments from you, his readers, both old and new.

Additionally, the publishers will be happy to send you information on anything you would like to know about Ron, his extraordinary life and accomplishments and the vast number of books he has written.

Any message addressed to the Author's Affairs Director at NEW ERA Publications will be given prompt and full attention.

NEW ERA Publications International ApS
Store Kongensgade 55
1264 Copenhagen K, Denmark

Church and Organization Address List

United States of America

Albuquerque
Church of Scientology
8106 Menaul Blvd. N.E.
Albuquerque, New Mexico 87110

Ann Arbor
Church of Scientology
2355 West Stadium Blvd.
Ann Arbor, Michigan 48103

Atlanta
Church of Scientology
2632 Piedmont Road, N.E.
Atlanta, Georgia 30324

Austin
Church of Scientology
2200 Guadalupe
Austin, Texas 78705

Boston
Church of Scientology
448 Beacon Street
Boston, Massachusetts 02115

Buffalo
Church of Scientology
47 West Huron Street
Buffalo, New York 14202

Chicago
Church of Scientology
3011 North Lincoln Avenue
Chicago, Illinois 60657

Cincinnati
Church of Scientology
215 West 4th Street, 5th Floor
Cincinnati, Ohio 45202

Clearwater
Church of Scientology
Flag® Service Organization
210 South Fort Harrison Avenue
Clearwater, Florida 34616

Columbus
Church of Scientology
30 North High Street
Columbus, Ohio 43215

Dallas
Church of Scientology
Celebrity Centre® Dallas
10500 Steppington Drive, Suite 100
Dallas, Texas 75230

Denver
Church of Scientology
375 South Navajo Street
Denver, Colorado 80223

Detroit
Church of Scientology
321 Williams Street
Royal Oak, Michigan 48067

Honolulu
Church of Scientology
1146 Bethel Street
Honolulu, Hawaii 96813

Kansas City
Church of Scientology
3619 Broadway
Kansas City, Missouri 64111

Las Vegas
Church of Scientology
846 East Sahara Avenue
Las Vegas, Nevada 89104

Church of Scientology
Celebrity Centre Las Vegas
1100 South 10th Street
Las Vegas, Nevada 89104

Long Island
Church of Scientology
99 Railroad Station Plaza
Hicksville, New York 11801

Los Angeles and vicinity
Church of Scientology
4810 Sunset Boulevard
Los Angeles, California 90027

Church of Scientology
1451 Irvine Boulevard
Tustin, California 92680

Church of Scientology
263 East Colorado Boulevard
Pasadena, California 91101

Church of Scientology
3619 West Magnolia Boulevard
Burbank, California 91506

Church of Scientology
American Saint Hill Organization
1413 North Berendo Street
Los Angeles, California 90027

Church of Scientology
American Saint Hill Foundation
1413 North Berendo Street
Los Angeles, California 90027

Church of Scientology
Advanced Organization of
   Los Angeles
1306 North Berendo Street
Los Angeles, California 90027

Church of Scientology
Celebrity Centre International
5930 Franklin Avenue
Hollywood, California 90028

Miami
Church of Scientology
120 Giralda Avenue
Coral Gables, Florida 33134

Minneapolis
Church of Scientology
1011 Nicollet Mall
Minneapolis, Minnesota 55403

Mountain View
Church of Scientology
2483 Old Middlefield Way
Mountain View, California 96043

New Haven
Church of Scientology
909 Whalley Avenue
New Haven, Connecticut 06515

New York City
Church of Scientology
227 West 46th Street
New York City, New York 10036

Church of Scientology
Celebrity Centre New York
65 East 82nd Street
New York City, New York 10036

Orlando
Church of Scientology
1830 East Colonial Drive
Orlando, Florida 32803

Philadelphia
Church of Scientology
1315 Race Street
Philadelphia, Pennsylvania 19107

Phoenix
Church of Scientology
2111 W. University Dr.
Mesa, Arizona 85201

Portland
Church of Scientology
323 S.W. Washington
Portland, Oregon 97204

Church of Scientology
Celebrity Centre Portland
709 Southwest Salmon Street
Portland, Oregon 97205

Sacramento
Church of Scientology
825 15th Street
Sacramento, California 95814

Salt Lake City
Church of Scientology
1931 S. 1100 East
Salt Lake City, Utah 84106

San Diego
Church of Scientology
635 "C" Street, Suite 200
San Diego, California 92101

San Francisco
Church of Scientology
83 McAllister Street
San Francisco, California 94102

San Jose
Church of Scientology
80 E. Rosemary
San Jose, California 95112

Santa Barbara
Church of Scientology
524 State Street
Santa Barbara
California 93101

Seattle
Church of Scientology
2226 3rd Avenue
Seattle, Washington 98121

St. Louis
Church of Scientology
9510 Page Boulevard
St. Louis, Missouri 63132

Tampa
Church of Scientology
3617 Henderson Blvd.
Tampa, Florida 33609

Washington, DC
Founding Church of Scientology
of Washington, DC
2125 "S" Street N.W.
Washington, DC 20008

Church of Scientology
Celebrity Centre
Washington, DC
4214 16th Street N.W.
Washington, DC 20011

Puerto Rico

Hato Rey
Church of Scientology
272 JT Piniero Avenue
Hyde Park, Hato Rey
Puerto Rico 00918

Canada

Edmonton
Church of Scientology
10187 112th St.
Edmonton, Alberta
Canada T5K 1M1

Kitchener
Church of Scientology
104 King St. West
Kitchener, Ontario
Canada N2G 2K6

Montreal
Church of Scientology
4489 Papineau Street
Montréal, Québec
Canada H2H 1T7

Ottawa
Church of Scientology
150 Rideau Street, 2nd Floor
Ottawa, Ontario
Canada K1N 5X6

Quebec
Church of Scientology
350 Bd Chareste Est
Québec, Québec
Canada G1K 3H5

Toronto
Church of Scientology
696 Yonge Street, 2nd Floor
Toronto, Ontario
Canada M4Y 2A7

Vancouver
Church of Scientology
401 West Hasting Street
Vancouver, British Columbia
Canada V6B 1L5

Winnipeg
Church of Scientology
388 Donald Street, Suite 125
Winnipeg, Manitoba
Canada R3B 2J4

United Kingdom

Birmingham
Church of Scientology
Albert House, 3rd Floor
24 Albert Street
Birmingham
England B4 7UD

Brighton
Church of Scientology
5 St. Georges Place
London Road
Brighton, Sussex
England BN1 4GA

East Grinstead
Church of Scientology
Saint Hill Foundation
Saint Hill Manor
East Grinstead, West Sussex
England RH19 4JY

Advanced Organization Saint Hill
Saint Hill Manor
East Grinstead, West Sussex
England RH19 4JY

Edinburgh
Hubbard Academy of
    Personal Independence
20 Southbridge
Edinburgh, Scotland
EH1 1LL

London
Church of Scientology
68 Tottenham Court Road
London, England W1P 0BB

Manchester
Church of Scientology
258 Deansgate
Manchester, England
M3 4BG

Plymouth
Church of Scientology
41 Ebrington Street
Plymouth, Devon
England PL4 9AA

Sunderland
Church of Scientology
51 Fawcett Street
Sunderland, Tyne and Wear
England SR1 1RS

Austria

Vienna
Church of Scientology
Schottenfeldgasse 13/15
1070 Wien, Austria

Church of Scientology
Celebrity Centre Vienna
Senefeldergasse 11/5
1100 Wien, Austria

Belgium

Brussels
Church of Scientology
61, rue du Prince Royal
1050 Bruxelles, Belgium

Denmark

Aarhus
Church of Scientology
Guldsmedegade 17, 2
8000 Aarhus C, Denmark

Copenhagen
Church of Scientology
Store Kongensgade 55
1264 Copenhagen K, Denmark

Church of Scientology
Gammel Kongevej 3–5, 1
1610 Copenhagen V, Denmark

Church of Scientology
Advanced Organization
    Saint Hill for Europe and Africa
Jernbanegade 6
1608 Copenhagen V, Denmark

France

Angers
Church of Scientology
10–12, rue Max Richard
49100 Angers, France

Clermont-Ferrand
Church of Scientology
1, rue Ballainvilliers
63000 Clermont-Ferrand
France

Lyon
Church of Scientology
3, place des Capucins
69001 Lyon, France

Paris
Church of Scientology
65, rue de Dunkerque
75009 Paris, France

Church of Scientology
Celebrity Centre Paris
69, rue Legendre
75017 Paris, France

Saint-Étienne
Church of Scientology
24, rue Marengo
42000 Saint-Étienne, France

Germany

Berlin
Church of Scientology
Sponholzstraße 51–52
12159 Berlin, Germany

Düsseldorf
Church of Scientology
Friedrichstraße 28
40217 Düsseldorf, Germany

Church of Scientology
Celebrity Centre Düsseldorf
Grupellostraße 28
40210 Düsseldorf, Germany

Frankfurt
Church of Scientology
Darmstädter Landstraße 213
60598 Frankfurt, Germany

Hamburg
Church of Scientology
Steindamm 63
20099 Hamburg, Germany

Church of Scientology
Celebrity Centre Hamburg
Eppendorfer Landstraße 35
20249 Hamburg, Germany

Hanover
Church of Scientology
Hubertusstraße 2
30163 Hannover, Germany

Munich
Church of Scientology
Beichstraße 12
80802 München, Germany

Stuttgart
Church of Scientology
Urbanstraße 70
70182 Stuttgart, Germany

Israel

Tel Aviv
Dianetics and Scientology College
42 Gorden Street, 2nd Floor
Tel Aviv 66023, Israel

Italy

Brescia
Church of Scientology
Via Fratelli Bronzetti, 20
25125 Brescia, Italy

Catania
Church of Scientology
Via Garibaldi, 9
95121 Catania, Italy

Milan
Church of Scientology
Via Abetone, 10
20137 Milano, Italy

Monza
Church of Scientology
Via Cavour, 5
20052 Monza, Italy

Novara
Church of Scientology
Corso Cavallotti, 7
28100 Novara, Italy

Nuoro
Church of Scientology
Via Lamarmora N. 115
08100 Nuoro, Italy

Padua
Church of Scientology
Via Mameli, 1/5
35131 Padova, Italy

Pordenone
Church of Scientology
Via Montereale, 10/C
33170 Pordenone, Italy

Rome
Church of Scientology
Via Della Pineta
 Sacchetti, 201
00185 Roma, Italy

Turin
Church of Scientology
Via Bersezio, 7
10152 Torino, Italy

Verona
Church of Scientology
Via Vicolo Chiodo, 4/A
37121 Verona, Italy

Netherlands

Amsterdam
Church of Scientology
Nieuwe Zijds Voorburgwal 271
1012 RL Amsterdam
Netherlands

Norway

Oslo
Church of Scientology
Storgata 9
0155 Oslo 1, Norway

Portugal

Lisbon
Instituto de Dianética
Rua Actor Taborda 39–5°
1000 Lisboa, Portugal

Russia

Moscow
Hubbard Humanitarian Center
103064 Moscow
Homutovskiy Tupik 7, Russia

Spain

Barcelona
Asociación Civil de Dianética
Calle Pau Clarís 85,
    Principal dcha.
08010 Barcelona, Spain

Madrid
Asociación Civil de Dianética
Montera 20, Piso 1° dcha.
28013 Madrid, Spain

Sweden

Göteborg
Church of Scientology
Odinsgatan 8, 2 tr.
411 03 Göteborg, Sweden

Malmö
Church of Scientology
Lantmannagatan 62 C
214 48 Malmö, Sweden

Stockholm
Church of Scientology
St. Eriksgatan 56
112 34 Stockholm, Sweden

Switzerland

Basel
Church of Scientology
Herrengrabenweg 56
4054 Basel, Switzerland

Bern
Church of Scientology
Dammweg 29, Postfach 352
3000 Bern 11, Switzerland

Geneva
Church of Scientology
Route de Saint-Julien 7–9
C.P. 823
1227 Carouge
Geneva, Switzerland

Lausanne
Church of Scientology
10, rue de la Madeleine
1003 Lausanne, Switzerland

Zurich
Church of Scientology
Badenerstrasse 141
8004 Zürich, Switzerland

Australia

Adelaide
Church of Scientology
24–28 Waymouth Street
Adelaide, South Australia 5000
Australia

Brisbane
Church of Scientology
106 Edward Street
Brisbane, Queensland 4000
Australia

Canberra
Church of Scientology
108 Bunda Street, Suite 16
Civic Canberra
A.C.T. 2601, Australia

Melbourne
Church of Scientology
42–44 Russell Street
Melbourne, Victoria 3000
Australia

Perth
Church of Scientology
39–41 King Street
Perth, Western Australia 6000
Australia

Sydney
Church of Scientology
201 Castlereagh Street
Sydney, New South Wales 2000
Australia

Church of Scientology
Advanced Organization Saint Hill
  Australia, New Zealand and
  Oceania
19–37 Greek Street
Glebe, New South Wales 2037
Australia

Japan

Tokyo
Scientology Organization
1-23-1 Higashi Gotanda
Shinagawa-ku
Tokyo, Japan 141

New Zealand

Auckland
Church of Scientology
32 Lorne Street
Auckland 1, New Zealand

Africa

Bulawayo
Church of Scientology
Southampton House,
  Suite 202
Main Street and 9th Ave.
Bulawayo, Zimbabwe

Cape Town
Church of Scientology
St. Georges Centre, 2nd Floor
13 Hout Street
Cape Town 8001
Republic of South Africa

Durban
Church of Scientology
57 College Lane
Durban 4001
Republic of South Africa

Harare
Church of Scientology
PO Box 3524
87 Livingston Road
Harare, Zimbabwe

Johannesburg
Church of Scientology
Security Building, 2nd Floor
95 Commissioner Street
Johannesburg 2001
Republic of South Africa

Church of Scientology
1st Floor Bordeaux Centre
Gordon and Jan Smuts Ave.
Bordeaux, Randburg 2125
Republic of South Africa

Port Elizabeth
Church of Scientology
2 St. Christopher Place
27 Westbourne Road Central
Port Elizabeth 6001
Republic of South Africa

Pretoria
Church of Scientology
306 Ancore Building
Jeppe & Esselen Streets
Pretoria 0002
Republic of South Africa

Colombia

Bogotá
Centro Cultural de Dianética
Calle 95 No. 19-A-28
Barrio Chicó
Bogotá, Colombia

Mexico

Guadalajara
Organización Cultural de
  Dianética, A.C.
Pedro Moreno #1078 Int 3
Sector Juárez
Guadalajara, Jalisco, México

Mexico City
Asociación Cultural de
  Dianética, A.C.
Naranjo 71-B Colonia Florida
Delegación Álvaro Obregón
C.P. 01030
México, D.F.

Instituto de Filosofía
  Aplicada, A.C.
Juan de Dios Arias No. 83
Colonia Vista Alegre
México, D.F.

Centro Cultural
  Latinoamericano, A.C.
Durango 105
Colonia Roma
C.P. 03100
México, D.F.

Instituto Tecnológico de
  Dianética, A.C.
Avenida Juan Escutia #29
Colonia Condesa
C.P. 06140
Delegación Cuauhtemoc
México, D.F.

Organización de Desarrollo
  de Dianética, A.C.
Heriberto Friás #420
Colonia Narvarte
C.P. 03020 México, D.F.

Organización Cultural de
  Dianética, A.C.
Nicolás San Juan #1734
Colonia Del Valle
C.P. 03100 México, D.F.

Venezuela

Caracas

Organización Cultural de
  Dianética, A.C.
Avenida Principal de las Palmas,
  Cruce Con Calle Carapano
Quinta Suha, Las Palmas
Caracas, Venezuela

Valencia

Asociación Cultural de
  Dianética, A.C.
Avenida 101 No. 150-23
Urbanización La Alegría
Apartado Postal 833
Valencia, Venezuela

To obtain any books by L. Ron Hubbard which are not available at your local organization, contact any of the following publishers:

Bridge Publications, Inc.
4751 Fountain Avenue
Los Angeles, California 90029

Continental Publications
  Liaison Office
696 Yonge Street
Toronto, Ontario
Canada M4Y 2A7

NEW ERA Publications
  International ApS
Store Kongensgade 55
1264 Copenhagen K
Denmark

ERA DINÁMICA EDITORES,
  S.A. de C.V.
Nicolás San Juan No. 208
Colonia Narvarte
C.P. 03020 México, D.F.

NEW ERA Publications UK, Ltd.
Saint Hill Manor
East Grinstead, West Sussex
England RH19 4JY

NEW ERA Publications
  Australia Pty Ltd.
Level 3 Ballarat House
68–72 Wentworth Ave.
Surry Hills, New South Wales 2000
Australia

Continental Publications Pty Ltd.
Security Building, 6th Floor
95 Commissioner Street
Johannesburg 2001
Republic of South Africa

NEW ERA Publications
  Italia Srl
Via L.G. Columella, 12
20128 Milano, Italy

NEW ERA Publications
  Deutschland GmbH
Bahnhofstraße 40
21629 Neu Wulmstorf
Germany

NEW ERA Publications
  France E.U.R.L.
111, boulevard de Magenta
75010 Paris
France

NUEVA ERA DINÁMICA, S.A.
C/De la Paz, 4, entpta dcha.
28012 Madrid, Spain

NEW ERA Publications Japan, Inc.
5-4-5-803 Nishi Gotanda
Shinagawa-ku
Tokyo, Japan 141

NEW ERA Publications Russia
B. Pereyaslavskaya 50, Suite 511
Moscow 129041

To obtain any cassettes by L. Ron Hubbard which are not available at your
local organization, contact:

Golden Era Productions
6331 Hollywood Boulevard, Suite 1305
Los Angeles, California 90028-6313